IRON
butterflies

Birute Regine

IRON
butterflies

WOMEN TRANSFORMING
THEMSELVES
AND THE WORLD

Prometheus Books

59 John Glenn Drive
Amherst, New York 14228–2119

Published 2010 by Prometheus Books

Inquiries should be addressed to
Prometheus Books
59 John Glenn Drive
Amherst, New York 14228–2119
VOICE: 716–691–0133
FAX: 716–691–0137
WWW.PROMETHEUSBOOKS.COM

14 13 12 11 10   5 4 3 2 1

Library of Congress Cataloging-in-Publication Data

Regine, Birute.
    Iron butterflies : women transforming themselves and the world / by Birute Regine.
         p. cm.
    Includes bibliographical references.
    ISBN 978–1–61614–169–1 (pbk. : alk. paper)
    1. Leadership in women. 2. Feminist theory. I. Title.
HQ1233 .R444 2010
305.4209—dc22

2009050899

Printed in the United States of America on acid-free paper

For Lina and the next generation

CONTENTS

Acknowledgments   7

Chapter 1:   Webs: Earning My Wings   11

Chapter 2:   Remember: Tracing Herstory   33

Chapter 3:   Caterpillars: Close the Gender Gap   57

Chapter 4:   Choices: Pursue Your Passion   77

Chapter 5:   Gladiators: Dealing with Mucho Macho   103

Chapter 6:   Tears: Heal the Hidden Wound   125

Chapter 7:   Split Vision: Dispelling Gender Distortion   141

Chapter 8:   Chrysalis: Shedding Self-Imposed Limitations   163

Chapter 9:   Bodies: Listen to Inner Wisdom   179

Chapter 10:   Divinities: Following the Spiritual Light   197

Chapter 11:   Tilt: Accepting the Gift of Injustice   219

Chapter 12:   Relationships: Letting the Heart Fall Open   235

Chapter 13:   Leadership: Cultivating Feminine Presence   255

Epilogue   281

References   283

Appendix: The Women Participants and   293
             Some Web Sites/Books by Iron Butterflies

ACKNOWLEDGMENTS

During this project I was privileged to hear the stories of struggles and triumphs of over fifty wonderful women. They were generous with their time, and they opened their hearts to me. Although not every woman's story is included, all their thoughts and ideas have nevertheless influenced the insights in this book. I thank them all most sincerely.

I thank the women who took the time to read this manuscript at various stages of development and offered their feedback for improving it: Linda Barker, Lynn Bikofsky, Kathy Bollerud, Linda Brimm, Lisa Kimball, Jane Margolis, and Mary McCann.

Dear friends Susan Saraca, and Victor and Jeanne Babel, thank you for being there.

Many thanks for substantial financial support from the Hana Foundation, and additional support from the Institute for the Study of Cohesion and Emergence, the Center for Self-Organizing Leadership, and Henri Lipmanowitz, which enabled this project to continue.

My editor at Prometheus Books, Mark Hall, instantly saw clearly the message of the book. Thank you, Mark.

My agent and friend Michael Snell also saw clearly the message of this book. His passion for the work, his insights that guided the writing of this book, his tenacity to find the right publisher, and his delightful wit was outstanding. My deepest gratitude to you, Michael.

I give a special thanks to my daughter Rasa: for being ever alert for relevant material, for contributing her important insights, and for keeping me company on this often challenging journey. A special thanks to my son Romas, who cheered me on and stood with me in thick and thin even while serving in Iraq.

And to Roger, whose belief in this project was unwavering, who made financial sacrifices to keep this project going and did it without a grumble, and whose support of me and my work was steadfast. There are no words than can express my depth of gratitude.

If ever the world sees a time when women shall come together purely for the good of humanity, it will be a power such as the world has never seen.

Matthew Arnold

Chapter 1

WEBS

Earning My Wings

I am iron butterfly . . .
I am she/we
of flesh
and iron
and silk wings,
healing,   flying
into a gentle   blue sky.

Janice Mirikitani, from *Love Works*

As I stood on my deck overlooking the Contoocook River in Hancock, New Hampshire, a gossamer mist, like gauze, shrouded the trees, the river dock, the ferns. The scent of sweet pine and the pungent dampness of river water filled the morning chill of early autumn. Having spent several days immersed in reading the transcripts of the women I had interviewed for this book, I was filled with their many insights, their heartfelt truths, and felt honored that these amazing women had entrusted me with their stories, their legacy to future generations of women.

In the midst of the morning stillness, the power of their stories suddenly hit me, and I felt an unexpected rush of vulnerability. These women's lives had deeply moved me—moved me to tears, tears of love and gratitude. They gave me such valuable gifts: their candidness, their generosity, their firm conviction and clarity of mind, their compassionate presence, their humor, their iron will. Something emerged from their collective voice that embraced me and validated me. Feeling their support also revealed paradoxically how much I had unknowingly isolated myself while writing this book. You know the feeling—like finding yourself navigating through a dense forest alone but determined to tough it out and keep your chin up. You don't even realize you feel lonely until someone places a gentle hand on your shoulder, utters a kind word, or offers you a drink of water. Suddenly a hidden reservoir of vulnerability opens up and you collapse into your own quiet softness.

As I walked down the wooded path toward the river, sunlight split the clouds, splintering the mist. Suddenly, all around me, I saw hundreds of spider webs. Some were draped like hammocks between diminutive princess pines. Others hung like upside-down parachutes suspended from twigs or nestled in ground cover, the mist captured in their delicate weaving. Orb spider webs, beaded with dew, dangled from trees like sparkling gems in an exquisitely strung necklace. Single threads, like silken tightropes, spanned the trees, forcing me to duck my head to avoid breaking them. Though I had walked down this path many times, I had never seen such a spectacle. The dispersing fog caught in emerging morning light had revealed a community of webs, an amazing world hidden in plain sight.

Those webs called to mind the women's stories I had gathered for this book. Their stories had also revealed an amazing, ever present, but often unseen world. With little fanfare, women around the world are weaving a reality filled with compassion, cooperation, and grit that challenges the status quo and transforms the meaning of power, leadership, and success. Their achievements demonstrate how feminine power is changing our businesses, our organizations, and our world into better places to work and live. Like the webs exposed by the sun refracting the mist, these women's stories reveal a social revolution hidden in plain sight whose time has arrived.

BRING BALANCE TO A WORLD OUT OF BALANCE

Since 9/11, the world has seemed tipped off its axis, and not just because our planet has been visited by the attack on the World Trade Center, a devastating tsunami, earthquakes, floods, fires, tornadoes, and hurricanes. Preemptive military strikes, unilateralism, corporate scandals, violation of human rights, murder and assassinations, genocide, wars, torture, world poverty, pedophiles in religious institutions, environmental degradation, violence, sex slave trade, terrorism and roadside bombs, global economic havoc—all have conspired to silence people who would speak out for peace and safety and love. Such acts share one common denominator: the urge to dominate, to exert *power over others*, an urge all too deeply embedded in human society. However, this approach has reached its limits; no longer can we resolve the world's complex problems only by brute force, by imposing our will, or by flexing our muscles and unleashing our weapons. Instead we should strive to find a better way, a more humane, civilized, caring, and loving way, to resolve differences of opinions and conflicts of interest. My travels, my interviews, and my research have convinced me that a better way lies just around the corner. By encouraging strong women to step forward, speak out, and display the power of their inherent feminine skills, we can, I think, bring some much-needed balance to a masculine-infused world and restore humanity and safety back to our torn and ravaged planet.

We can sit around feeling depressed or helpless about the sorry state of the world, or we can do something about it. The women leaders I met and interviewed while writing this book have done something about it, either in their own small, local world or on the broader world stage. Their life stories and their work gripped me because their selective wisdom seemed to be saying, "We can create a better place."

Imagine such a place. Women gathering in vast numbers to create cooperative webs of connection that replace the old and tired domination approach of conquer, control, and coerce; women no longer restricted by sex discrimination; the end of the sex slave trade and other forms of violence against women; women unafraid to walk the streets at night; eliminating the feminization of poverty due to the devaluation of all the caring and care giving that women worldwide provide for free; an equal number of women sitting at the power and peace tables that decide our future; women collaborating with each other rather than competing; families with plenty of resources for childcare and proper training of childcare workers; a greater investment in other professions long associated with the feminine, such as teaching and nursing; quality care for our elderly and educational opportunities for everyone; and women uniting for peace and justice in a world that does not need any more wars and violence. In their gathering and connecting, women are already weaving another way of living and working together that does not rely on hierarchies devoted to exercising *power over* others, but rather evokes a world of working together. Although their efforts have been largely off the radar screen in a world where the sensationalized media preoccupy themselves with celebrities and bad news, it is out there and it's a potent, ever-increasing presence, with sufficient power to shift our world.

I have seen women from all walks of life all around the world mid-wifing, in small and large ways, a different reality, based on cooperation, inclusion, and power *with and for* others, serving the greater good, and bringing out the best in people and the humanity in us all. They are nurturing a higher level of consciousness that transcends greed, self-interest, and survival. They are bound by their caring, in the service of progress. They are igniting a feminine consciousness.

When we engage a feminine consciousness, we think about our children's future for seven generations ahead, as the Native American Mohawks do; we care for Mother Earth as a way of caring for ourselves; we learn from each other and work together globally to find better solutions to common problems; we reject short-term gains in profits driven by ego-interests that harm and limit long-term aims for improving the community; we wage peace through education and healthcare and the eradication of poverty; we heal traumatic wounds inflicted by the violence of domination with compassion and love, and break the seemingly endless cycle of violence and revenge.

Women around the world are engaging in social transformation. And they are doing this one person at a time, one relationship at a time. They showed me a different world I could believe in; they filled me with hope.

SHAPE THE ERA OF WOMEN

A prophecy shared among indigenous Mayan and Mongolian people, despite their geographical separation, predicts that, in 2010, the 5,400-year cycle known as the Era of Man ends and the Era of Woman begins. I would amend that to the Era of Women, because women's unrealized power is a collective power. Unlike the Era of Man that revered such masculine role models as Superman, John Wayne, and the Lone Ranger—powerful, fearless, strong men who epitomized individuality, autonomy, and independence—the Era of Women respects and values feminine models, be they men or women, who embrace the power of a collective effort, community, and interdependence. Unlike the Era of Man that excluded women from circles of power, in the Era of Women, men and women work together as global citizens and pool their resources and skills in service of the greater good, such as redirecting impulses of aggression locally and globally. You'll meet many of these new models in the pages ahead: from Kim Campbell, former prime minister of Canada, and Jody Williams, Nobel Peace Prize laureate, to Australian aboriginal elder Violet and Cynthia Trudell, former CEO of Saturn cars.

The prophecy affirmed what I came to believe after coauthoring my last book with Roger Lewin, *The Soul at Work: Embracing Complexity Science for Business Success*, that women are in a position to lead in the twenty-first century. In a complex environment and an interconnected world, skills associated with women will prove more and more effective and keenly pertinent: their holistic view of the world, their ability to see interconnections among things, their relational intelligence, their tendencies toward collaboration and inclusion, their ability to empathize. Daniel Pink made this prediction in his book *A Whole New Mind*: "The future belongs to a very different kind of person with a very different kind of mind—creators and empathizers, pattern recognizers, and meaning makers. These people—artists, inventors, designers, storytellers, caregivers, consolers, big picture thinkers—will now reap society's richest rewards and share its greatest joys." In other words, the future belongs to people, regardless of gender, who embrace their feminine power, and we need to move in a direction that emboldens women to step forward and speak their mind and truths in a world begging for a different kind of leadership.

The Era of Women ushers in a time for high-touch, right-brain, feminine aspects of our psyche to come fully into play. We associate these qualities with women, but unfortunately, in the past, leaders in the realm of politics, business, and media have disdained, marginalized, or dismissed these qualities as frivolous, ineffectual, and touchy-feely. Seldom were feminine skills ever granted authority. That attitude consigned women to a subordinate position in business and government organizations. Now, however, the very qualities that have kept women out of the mainstream are the very same qualities that empower them to lead in the Era of Women.

The Era of Women calls us to be open and not afraid, to find the courage to take back our power. As Gloria Steinem insists, "Power can be taken, but not given. The process of taking is empowerment in itself." Throughout history, when women took back their power, they created change—the abolitionists freed the slaves, the suffragettes won women's right to vote, the feminists created equal opportunities for women and control over their own bodies. When we take back our power, we place value on the abundant fecundity of feminine power that sustains and nurtures life in all its diversity. When we take back our power, we bring balance to the world. Whether women act or don't act, women will make the difference in shaping this new Era of Women. Women's role is to rescue society from abusiveness, competition, and violence created by men holding unchallenged dominance. But not just for women. For men as well. As philosopher Richard Tarnas urged, it's high time for men "to enter into a fundamentally new relationship of mutuality with the feminine in all its forms. The feminine then becomes not that which must be controlled, denied, and exploited, but rather fully acknowledged, respected, and responded to for itself. It is recognized: not the objectified 'other,' but rather source, goal, and immanent presence." Without the feminine counterbalancing the masculine, the human spirit languishes as a one-winged creature unable to soar.

BECOME AN IRON BUTTERFLY

The women I met during my global journey represented a wide range of ages, races, nationalities, and occupations. In talking to them, I discovered that although many of these women were very public personalities, they often felt alone in their work. I wondered if I should coin a phrase that would convey the qualities they all shared, something memorable that would not only describe them but would also serve to unify and honor them as sisters and kindred spirits.

When I interviewed Janice Mirikitani, poet laureate for San Francisco, she gave me a book of her poetry, *Love Works*. The book fell open to the page with the poem titled "Iron Butterfly," which opens this chapter. My first thought was of the rock group from the seventies of the same name. As I read her poem, the two words conjured up a beautiful feminine image that also captured strength and perseverance, a powerful metaphor for the essence of feminine power these women displayed. For me, the term captured their individual resilience and fragility, their conviction and poignancy, their inner beauty and outer strength.

And of course, the butterfly symbolizes life reinventing itself, an image of transformation. A once crawling creature, enclosed in a cocoon of its own becoming, miraculously emerges as a winged creature, unfolds its wings, and takes flight. The wings of an Iron Butterfly may consist of gossamer threads, but her heart beats like an iron drum, a drum tempered by life's hard lessons and her own deep reflections. Iron Butterflies deploy their natural, even vulnerable, feminine gifts while maintaining an unbreakable will.

The Iron Butterflies in this book come from many parts of the world:

the United States, Canada, England, Italy, Colombia, Australia, Israel, Lebanon, and Iraq. They are married with children, have lost children; are single mothers, single women, divorced, married once, twice, three times; and are straight and gay. They come from all walks of life and include doctors, artists, a federal judge, a novelist, businesswomen, a governor, a wine maker, a priest, CEOs, lawyers, a professor, a housewife, a Nobel Peace Prize laureate, nurses, a congresswoman. As mostly middle-aged American women, they struggled through the civil rights movement, the women's movement, the Vietnam peace movement, and they fought for equal access to education and job opportunities, and for reproductive rights.

These women have achieved a certain status in their communities. We often read about successful women when they have reached the top of the ladder. But we don't often hear about their struggles, their fallibilities, their journey on the rocky road to becoming strong women. The Iron Butterflies in this book have earned their successes. They are also forthright about the obstacles they have overcome. They have been neglected or, sexually, physically, or emotionally abused. Some have been robbed, assaulted by fist or gun or knife, and raped. Others described themselves as having been anorexic, bulimic, alcoholic, drug addicted, neurotic, or depressed. Think of any weakness or victimizing situation, and they have "been there, done that." But no matter how grave the injustices and hardships they have suffered, they have in their brilliance never let it turn them into victims. Rather, they have become kinder, stronger, and wiser.

Despite their many differences and unique journeys, these women share common patterns in terms of how they live in the world and create change. Their qualities range over all human attributes, but eventually I narrowed them all down to five essential ones. Iron Butterflies are (1) radically vulnerable and (2) r*evolution*ary; they are (3) healers while being (4) strong; and they (5) welcome the paradoxical. Do you possess these traits yourself? If you do, you are already an Iron Butterfly and welcome to the club. If you'd like to acquire and develop them, welcome to the journey.

BE RADICALLY VULNERABLE

If someone forced me to pick one quality that distinguishes these women, I wouldn't hesitate to say "vulnerability." Initially meeting these women, "vulnerability" would have been the last word I used to describe them because they all exuded an ease with themselves and a quiet self-assurance. This self-assurance was in part the fruit of their ability to manage and learn from vulnerable moments and times in their lives. Vulnerability also serves as a crucible for generating the other qualities, and allowing it is the most essential step on the path to personal and social transformation.

This finding, vulnerability as the doorway to change, took me by surprise and exposed what I would come to regard as the radical behavior of Iron Butterflies. I call it radical because vulnerability is all but taboo in a domination-based culture that shuns and ridicules vulnerability as a shameful weakness to avoid at all costs. We will see in later chapters coercive, controlling, aggressive leaders who cannot tolerate vulnerability in themselves and exploit it in others and the roots of these behaviors. Iron Butterflies, on the other hand, recognize it as a wellspring of potential strength. But it is, nevertheless, a challenging path. Former administrator of the EPA Christine Todd Whitman told me how she tried to address our vulnerability as a nation after 9/11.

> After 9/11 I had a vulnerability study done, a lessons-learned effort. We were the first agency to do that, and much to my surprise FEMA had never done a lessons-learned after any disaster. The purpose of the study was to find out what we did right so we could strengthen and build on it, and to find out where we could do a better job. If we are afraid to look at vulnerabilities then we lose opportunities to improve and strengthen things.
>
> It wasn't about finding fault or blame. Yet when you publish these things, the press and others tend to look at it only as self-criticism. "Aha, they admitted to doing this wrong; they failed here." They don't see the whole picture, and instead focus exclusively on the criticism. That makes it difficult for people to admit to an area of weakness. I think women are more willing to look at vulnerability, but the problem is that you take a bigger hit for it. You have to be willing to say it's worth looking at those vulnerable places and not be afraid to look and find out.

We will see throughout this book the influence vulnerability has on defining leadership and power and the challenges it presents.

By *vulnerability* I mean a profound experience of openness. Think of the word as a coin. On one side is the openness that exposes you to potentially being harmed and diminished; on the other side is the openness that allows you to be receptive to a depth of connection to others and all their thoughts and emotions, which is otherwise not possible. We are all well aware of the dangers associated with vulnerability, but we don't often acknowledge the benefits that we can also gain.

Often women learn to dissociate from their vulnerabilities as a way of surviving in a culture that derides it, but doing so limits our self-knowledge. When we let ourselves experience vulnerability, we nurture the full range of our reactions and expressions to the world: all our yearnings, our needs, our shyness, our humility, our hope, our fears. This doesn't mean we walk around with our beating hearts in our hands, but it does mean that we discern those moments when opening ourselves to people can transform our lives and the lives of others. When we do so, we transform harming into healing, weakness into strength, isolation into love, ignorance into wisdom.

Here's an example of what I'm talking about. Linda Rusch, whom you will get to know a lot better in later chapters, is the vice president of Patient Care Services at Hunterdon Medical Center in New Jersey. One of the strongest leaders I have ever met, she also exemplifies radical vulnerability. Among her many initiatives, Linda has addressed the hierarchy between nurses and doctors, what she calls the "not-knowing" nurse and the "all-knowing" doctor. Nurses sometimes complain bitterly about the way doctors treat them, as if they were handmaidens compared to omnipotent gods.

Linda dismantled that hierarchy, and not just because it hurt nurses' feelings. The old hierarchy actually threatens lives. For instance, a nurse, fearing a reprimand, intimidation, or worse, abuse, might refrain from calling a doctor at two in the morning to report an emergency with a patient. It wasn't easy to change that pattern of intimidation because confronting abusive doctors was not something nurses learned in school. Linda got the word out that allowing abusive behavior was not part of a nurse's job. As Linda puts it, "What you permit, you promote." In one particular case, a nurse I'll call Jane came to Linda with a typical tale of abuse.

The doctor in question was generally well liked, though he did tend to lose his temper. He had yelled at Jane, derided her in front of patients over a small mistake she'd made with one of his patient's charts. "I'll talk to him," Linda promised. For the next week, however, the doctor appeared to avoid Linda, perhaps because he knew she would not let his misbehavior go unnoticed. Then one day, she found an attempt at a humorous message from him on her answering machine: "Just want to report to you that one of your nurses intimidated me, and so I'm calling you as the hotline number." Was he trying indirectly to apologize for his behavior? Perhaps, but Linda did not feel comfortable letting the matter drop. So she wrote him a handwritten note inviting him to have a cup of coffee with her.

Somewhat surprisingly, he scheduled an appointment and dropped by her office with two steaming cups of coffee. Linda had decided beforehand that she wasn't going to talk about the incident with the nurse. She wanted to talk to him at a totally different level, not from anger or disapproval but, as she told me, from "a place of love."

She never uttered Jane's name. Instead, Linda started their conversation by saying, "I care about you. I don't like the way you are coming across. I know that's not who you are when you act this way." She could see a look of relief spread across his face. Starting with an attitude of care and concern created the context for a very different conversation, and the doctor opened up, confiding that he had grown up in poverty and that his mother had raised him and lifted him out of the ghetto, and shepherded him through college and medical school. And here he was, a successful doctor. He admitted that growing up in the streets made him tough and angry and taught him to intimidate people. He was critical and tended to see a half-empty glass, an attitude that spilled over onto the nurses.

Linda responded to him by saying, "I want you to be successful. I want people to love working with you because I know that's who you are." Any hierarchy that may have existed melted away as two colleagues chatted and formed a stronger relationship. They talked about how stress might be a factor in his edginess, and together they devised a plan for constructively dealing with it. "Speaking to the best in him," Linda recalls, "I could see the shift. Over time, I could see his behavior changing."

Note the dynamic here. By making herself vulnerable, "I care about you," Linda set a nonthreatening context for their conversation and the doctor felt safe enough to permit his own vulnerability to come out. Soon they were playing on a level field. Care had replaced intimidation, openness had replaced defensiveness, and trust had replaced fear. By working together on the problem, Linda modeled a different behavior, a cooperative one that he could replicate with the nurses.

As Linda demonstrates, one person at a time, one relationship at a time, and one opportunity at a time, we can create profound openings between people that can change a workplace and, in the long run, transform an organization, an industry, and the world into a better place.

I love how Linda defined vulnerability during our conversation. "Vulnerability is a power. It's letting yourself feel the love and be in the love." She describes it as an "incredible connectedness" with other human beings, in the moment, where you are heard and validated. "It's about being authentic and having this dance go on between you and the other person, when you can really understand what the other is feeling and thinking."

Opening yourself, as Linda did, takes incredible courage and conviction, but when you see its power to transform your life and the lives of others, it becomes easier to do. The more you enter this space, the more you sharpen your other Iron Butterfly qualities. Remember what I said earlier about radical vulnerability serving as a crucible in which a certain alchemy occurs, in which an almost magical chemistry forges the other key attributes of an Iron Butterfly? In the remainder of this chapter, we will note the role that vulnerability plays in the other Iron Butterfly qualities: becoming r*evolution*ary, vowing to heal, remaining strong, and welcoming the paradoxical within oneself.

BECOME R*EVOLUTION*ARY

When Carol Jamison's eight-year-old daughter, Becky, asked her, "Why does the church hate women? Does God not like women?" Carol could no longer ignore her own growing uneasiness with the church. "Why aren't we hearing about women in the history of our church? If God is male, where does that leave women?" she asked herself. For her own sake as well as her daughter's, she felt compelled to do something about it. When she initiated conversations with the parish priest and other women, she met Paula Slovenkai-Driscoll, whom you will meet later. Paula started a group exploring women's role in the church. This group ultimately evolved into a gathering each month at a different member's home to celebrate the feminine divine. "The whole vision of God being a woman and taking you in her arms changed something within me," recalls Carol. She would leave these meetings rejuvenated, refreshed, and refocused.

While Carol had always enjoyed wonderful relationships with her girlfriends, she experienced a different sort of bond with this group, which she came to value as a revolutionary force. Although the group provided mutual support, it didn't deal exclusively with solving personal problems. Instead the women devoted their time together to awaken the feminine divine in themselves. At a given gathering, the hostess would choose a theme and create an experience that connected the guests to their own spirituality. "It's about spiritual growth of ourselves as human beings and what we are capable of doing in this world," Carol told me.

For instance, Carol loved gardening but never seemed to find time to create a garden for herself. With the support and urging of the women in her group, she finally dug up a garden, placed a hollowed tree trunk resembling a womb in the middle of the space, and filled it with her favorite plants. To celebrate her new garden, she invited the group, accompanied by their daughters, to meet there at dawn. Each woman brought something from her own garden, such as lavender or lemon thyme, to plant in Carol's garden. Carol's daughter painted a bright blue bench adorned with yellow daisies as her offering. Carol handed out some of her favorite quotes and poems about gardens, and each woman read aloud a poem that held a special meaning for her. The daughters, wearing flower wreathes woven for them by one of the women, listened intently. This celebration of Mother Earth represented an important milestone for Carol, her friends, and their daughters. The new garden not only symbolized Carol's own spiritual evolution but also represented the transformative and unifying power of the feminine divine that left no woman untouched.

Paradoxically, this spiritual process prompted Carol to reevaluate her priorities at a mundane level. "I began to look more closely at my own interests, what was really important to me. What do I really want to do with my life and how can I share that with my family? Playing in my garden is really important to me." Before she had built this personal playground, she had always put everyone else in her life first. Now she feels this "new me" could set a better example for her children. As she said, "You have to be a human in your own right and not just live for other people." Feeling more like the master of her own destiny, Carol's self-confidence grew; she felt more capable to take on whatever challenges she met in life.

This new sense of herself spilled over into her work life. A customer service executive in the software industry, Carol works with a lot of women. Having experienced the impact of the group's support on her life, she found herself drawn to supporting the younger women at work. Carol would invite the women into her office, close the door, and encourage the women to talk about their lives, their work, and their personal struggles with striking a work/life balance. Carol would help them think through their priorities, and in this way she extended her personal evolution to revolutionize the workplace. "Before we didn't bring anything personal to the workplace," said Carol. "Now that we do, we're a closer group. That closeness helps us to brainstorm better and more fully explore options for our customers, and we are a more effective group."

Carol's personal evolution and growing confidence also affected her behavior with customers. She spends a lot of time managing relationships and has always been a good listener. But now that she has shed much of her former timidity, she more confidently confronts customers in a positive way, which has made her work a lot less stressful. Customers appreciate the way Carol has evolved. As one customer wrote in an evaluation, "Carol always asks me how I'm doing. She cares about me as a person and as a customer, and that's something that I appreciate."

Iron Butterflies, like Carol, embark on a personal, inner journey that leads them down the road to social transformation. That journey may take each Iron Butterfly beyond herself to family and community and a nation or the world, but as with the caterpillar, there comes a time when she spends time alone wrapped in a cocoon, as Carol did when she created her new garden. As we will see in later chapters, that time of aloneness can be difficult, perhaps even a descent into despair, where all the images about herself are let go, where beliefs she once held come into question, and hard realities, once clouded and out of sight, emerge in full view. Then through a personal transformation, both spiritual and psychological, a journey often taken more than once, Iron Butterflies greet the world with a greater sense of themselves and their mission in life. Like the caterpillar, they reinvent themselves.

Like a stone cast in a pond, personal evolution expands its influence and leads to social revolution. Note the ripple effect of Carol's personal evolution that in turn affected her family, her co-workers, and her customers in a positive way. In fact, the gardening itself had its own ripple effect. Carol's gardening has expanded from her own little plot into her community. The Main Street of West Concord, Massachusetts, now has flowers stretching for a half mile along the beach strip, a result of a collaboration forged between Carol, her neighbors, and the town. She most recently designed and planted a garden for Minuteman ARC for Human Services, an organization that supports people with developmental disabilities. Carol has found many places that can benefit from a garden.

When I spoke with Nobel Peace Prize laureate Jody Williams, she called this "enlightened self-interest," a balance between individual will and community good. Whether you head a fledgling software company or a major corporation, whether you work in business or government, or the arts or activist causes, whether you sit on a board of directors or chair a PTA meeting, you can help evolve the rules of the domination game as Carol did, by simply reordering your priorities. Iron Butterflies show us how our feminine power enables us to attain our goals, to excel at what we do, and to guide others to another way of being successful at work and in the world, and everyone benefits.

VOW TO HEAL

In 1999, Swanee Hunt, former ambassador to Austria and lecturer at Harvard's Kennedy School of Government, founded Women Waging Peace, now known as the Institute for Inclusive Security. The idea for the organization came to Swanee in a very concrete moment. One day, while she was serving as ambassador to Austria during the Clinton administration, a woman named Vjosa Dobruna called on Ambassador Hunt and told her a compelling story. Dr. Dobruna, founder of the Center for Protection of Women and Children and cominister for democratization with the United Nations mission in Kosovo, had crossed several war lines at great personal risk to come to Vienna to meet Swanee and implore her to get the US government to intervene in Kosovo. Swanee recalls their encounter: "Vjosa said, 'We've seen what happened in Croatia. We've seen what happened in Bosnia. It's going to happen in Kosovo.' I said, 'You've come so far. Here, have some coffee, have a pastry.' We talked and then she left. My next appointment was waiting, about genetically engineered soybeans, then the opening of an art exhibit, a political problem, the family tragedy of a staff member, and so on. I thought I should send a cable to the State Department saying I had met an interesting woman from Kosovo. But I didn't."

After Swanee left Vienna and came to Harvard, her mother was diagnosed with terminal cancer. In the fall of 1998, Swanee and her husband, Charles, flew to Dallas to stay with her. One night, sitting on her mother's bed and watching the television news, Swanee saw footage of the exodus of thousands of Kosovo refugees fleeing to Macedonia. Later, when Charles found his wife rocking back and forth on the porch, he asked if she was weeping for her mother.

Swanee replied, "No. My mother has twenty-four-hour nursing care to make sure that she is in no pain. Think about these refugees sitting on the tractors. How many of them are psychotic at this point? How many of them are diabetic and can't get their insulin and are in shock? Babies are being born on the side of the road, camps are being set up in mud. A few years ago, a woman came to me in Vienna because she had heard that there was someone in Austria who cared and could help. She traveled for days for that one-hour appointment. I was the only hope of a certain number of people in Kosovo." That was Swanee's epiphany, the precise moment she vowed to heal. "I had so failed to do what I should have done," she told me, "that I had to reverse myself."

Swanee transformed her vulnerability, her failure to respond, into a healing power by creating Women Waging Peace, a network empowering more than eight hundred women in over forty conflict areas by connecting them to each other and to policymakers. As Carol Jamison did, she began by exploring her own soul, and then she tossed the stone into the still pond, causing ripples to spread to the edges of the world.

Like so many of the Iron Butterflies you will meet in this book, Swanee was shaken into going where she wouldn't go on her own. It took an outside stimulus and an epiphany to ignite her dedication to heal. When Iron Butterflies peer into their bare and vulnerable souls, as Swanee did, they become more empathic to others, more welcoming of the fallibilities of the human spirit and embrace it with their wings. Only when leaders gain such self-knowledge of vulnerability can they transform themselves into healers. When you listen to and empathize with those who suffer, you see the need to rally against the sort of domination culture that causes such suffering. When leaders are healers, their leadership is transformative.

For millennia, the women I call Iron Butterflies have sustained and mended the social fabric of community, developing webs of connection, locally or globally, addressing the needs of the marginalized, the ignored, and the disenfranchised. Studies show that in spite of our accelerated technological access to each other, people today feel more alienated than ever in the United States. Iron Butterflies strive to heal feelings of alienation by fostering a sense of shared needs and beliefs and of being in it together. Paradoxically, it takes an iron spine to usher in this softer era of interdependence.

As healers, they also cultivate a new way of being. Like butterflies that generate life by pollinating flowers, Iron Butterflies regenerate individuals, organizations, and communities by pollinating the soul. As generous and giving women, they find pleasure in bringing out the best in people, in evoking and expecting the highest self. We will see how they actually do this in later chapters.

Like the butterfly effect, where a butterfly flitting its wings in the Amazon jungle can cause a storm thousands of miles away, the small actions of Iron Butterflies that heal and cultivate the best in people hold the potential for a huge effect in their workplaces, their communities, and the world. And like the butterfly effect, we don't know which one of those small acts will be the catalyst to a big change. Iron Butterflies teach us that we do not need to move mountains in order to transform ourselves and the world; a little pollinating will do it.

BE STRONG

After working in the corporate world for many years for companies such as Cable and Westinghouse, Laura Liswood grew restless and began questioning the worth of selling a cable television service to the world. She relished the camaraderie, the results orientation, and, of course, the paycheck, but the work lacked any sense of higher purpose, and that bothered her. Wanting to involve herself in something that might contribute more value to the world, she set out on her own as a consultant. With more free time on her hands, she opened herself to new possibilities and let herself, as she recalls, "ramble in my thought processes." She had been involved in women's issues in Seattle and had even published her own magazine, now defunct, called *Seattle Women*. When she heard about a study that showed women legislators legislating differently from men, that piqued her interest and she decided to investigate that finding for herself. Maybe she could interview one woman leader.

After confiding this idea to her friends, a friend of a friend of a friend finally brought her to a woman leader halfway around the world who granted her an interview—Corazon Aquino, president of the Philippines. Laura would learn there were fifteen living women presidents at the time and in the end interviewed them all. This ultimately expensive undertaking included video crews, which Laura, far from rich, paid for out of her pocket. The personal sacrifice paid off because from that project was born the Council of Women World Leaders, with Laura serving as its secretary general.

Here is how Laura describes her vision:

> I wanted to create institutions, structures, a network for women because I believe one reason women haven't made as great an impact as men on history is that women played second fiddle and helped the wounded while the men built structures. The structures are what last and create the history that you learn. I think there are enough powerful women to create a critical mass of power that can change how we think about leadership. Change happens when you get a few people to do it, get a larger group to go along, and then you get your tipping point.

Like the other women I interviewed for this book, Laura answered a central question, one I actually never asked: What does it mean to be a strong woman? Laura needed tremendous strength to realize her vision, a strength that came from managing her feelings of vulnerability. "The overriding emotion you have in doing something like this," Laura told me, "is fear. Fear you cannot do it, fear you cannot handle it well, and fear you will not be diplomatically correct in doing it."

Laura, however, had learned to master her fear even before this project. In 1992, she had decided to bicycle across central Asia, hoping to prove something to herself while at the same time enjoying an atypical adventure. It certainly wasn't typical. Her constant companion on the trek? Fear. Fear was in fact the right animal instinct. Imagine a woman bicycling across a remote Siberian landscape, bouncing along a rutted, unpaved road, with no medical centers in sight should she injure herself or get sick. One day she encountered a band of escaped prisoners. She could just disappear and never be heard from again. What did she do with this daily companion, fear? "I learned how to *not* conquer my fear," laughed Laura, "but to carry it with me." She told me how the experience made her be honest with herself and admit her fear, and how this paradoxically taught her that she could be strong and vulnerable at the same time. She also learned perseverance, to keep moving forward. What else could she do? She couldn't turn back. "That experience prepared me for this work, to keep going forward one step at a time. It's like climbing a rope, hand over hand until you reach that next ledge where the next thing opens up. And then you start the ascent again."

Iron Butterflies, like Laura, discover inside themselves the strength to persist in the most difficult situations, and like monarchs who fly two thousand miles to their destination, they persevere against all odds. Strong women stand up for themselves and protect themselves because they know they are worth it, and they stand up and protect others for the same reason. When Iron Butterflies challenge the status quo, they are immediately vulnerable. As they learn to deal with fear, to take risks, to handle unpredictability and uncertainty, they become stronger.

Iron Butterflies are also strong because, like butterflies, they are sensitive to shifts in the environment; they both sound the alarm and act when they see unhealthy, unethical changes taking place. They are the whistle-blowers, the troublemakers, the resisters who can take down corrupt institutions as Sharron Watkins did at Enron, Colleen Rowley did at the FBI, and Cynthia Cooper did at WorldCom. When Iron Butterflies see inequities and wrongdoing, they speak for those who cannot or will not speak for themselves.

Iron Butterflies are strong in their openness; they are willing to be influenced by others and invite opposing and different points of view, which we will see prove to be highly effective negotiating skills. Their wings stir fields of resonance and encircle dissonance. They are strong because they take their place but make room for others. They are strong because they are willing to be outrageously honest and will admit if they are wrong. And they are fun. They have a full body, bawdy laugh, and sometimes like to swear. But most of all, Iron Butterflies are paradoxically strong enough to be vulnerable.

WELCOME THE PARADOXICAL

When I set out on this project, I had just one condition, that the women demonstrated both feminine and masculine skills and capabilities. I didn't want "sperms with perms," women who lost their womanhood on the path to success, or the all-sacrificing mother figure who cared for everyone but herself. I wanted women who could hold and balance seemingly opposite realities.

When I looked back at my previous book, *The Soul at Work*, I realized I had interviewed all male leaders who had come to embrace their more feminine side, such as valuing and forming deep relationships in a way that balanced their more masculine goal-driven nature. For this new book, I wanted to know how that manifested in female leaders.

The ability of the women I interviewed to strike a balance between masculine and feminine values and skills provided them, I found, with an enormous range of resources. Their masculine side helped them deal with their domination-oriented environments. They could talk football with the "boys" and push that project over the goal line. But their feminine side enabled them to act as agents of transformation because it infused their environment with more inclusive, emotional, cooperative, intuitive approaches, as we saw Carol do.

Already you have seen many paradoxes in these pages: strong yet vulnerable, tough yet soft, practical yet spiritual. Paradox is a quality that kept emerging among these women. For example, I was struck by how comfortable these women were with themselves, and how they continued to reach, to learn, and to grow. Paradoxically, they were in a constant state of becoming while remaining the same person in all contexts.

Think about the paradoxes in your life. Do you feel insignificant but also dedicate yourself to giving people a sense of their own importance? Do you feel both saddened and outraged, courageous and fearful, detached and empathic, calm and excitable, patient and impatient, private and public, humble and proud? Are you both flexible and orderly, linear and holistic, analytic and intuitive? Iron Butterflies do, which makes them both fascinating and powerful women. List some of your own personal traits and then list their opposites. Are both true? How do you feel about the paradoxes in your life? Holding paradoxes isn't an either/or proposition, but rather a both/and. Welcome the paradoxes that you hold because they create a tension from which new possibilities and creative solutions emerge.

SUSPEND DISBELIEF

Does a woman who possesses all these qualities sound too good to be true? I would have thought so myself before I heard their stories and learned about both their struggles and their triumphs, as you will as you read this book. I ask you to suspend your disbelief. Their stories are true, their voices real. I have myself been troubled from time to time by what Buddhism calls the "monkey mind," that nattering self-critic that fills us with doubts and worries and doesn't like risks or change. It's the little voice that tells us that life's not supposed to be this hard, that in a million years I couldn't possibly do what these Iron Butterflies do. It chatters most loudly when we dare to challenge the status quo. If your pesky monkey mind starts nagging for attention while reading these stories, bonk it on the head and tell it to shut up. Knock that monkey off your back. You need to focus your full energy elsewhere as you do both your valuable feminine work, such as care giving and uniting with your sisters and brothers in the service of transformation, and your masculine work, such as taking the helm to pilot the ship of change through all the troubled waters ahead. Only when we bond the fully feminine with the fully masculine can we evolve to a third possibility where genderless leadership abounds, where the spheres and responsibilities of men and women overlap, dissolving boundaries between what we think of as masculine and what we think of as feminine. When women have more opportunities to lead, and men are relieved of their burden and privilege of decision making, we can discover a new synergy between genders.

Listen to what David Gergen, commentator, educator, and advisor to three presidents, has to say about the matter:

> Yet women are clearly the solution to many of the world's problems. We know, for example, that one of the most productive investments to foreign assistance is in the education of women. We know that microfinancing in places like India and Bangladesh empowers women and lifts the quality of life. We know that empowering women with the vote

deepens the roots of democracy. . . . Back in the early 1990s, we had the Year of the Woman. It wasn't enough. Some writers like Tom Peters called the 1990s the Decade of the Woman, but that wasn't enough either. Now it's critical that we truly show our commitment to justice by making this the Century of the Woman.

But that's not enough either. We need to usher in the Era of Women.

There are many paths to actualizing this goal and, like the threads of a web, these paths come from different directions that all lead to a core truth—the wisdom of vulnerability. The nearer each woman comes to this truth, the closer she is to all women, who are simultaneously approaching it on their own paths.

THE PARADOX OF ONE

I end this chapter where I began, in the woods of New Hampshire. Imagine a pristine early spring day with crystal blue skies and the fresh scent of melted snow lingering in the air. The sun, like a parent warming up a child's hand, absorbs the chill in the air, caressing the still-dormant bare trees with their tiny buds. Silver light dances on tiny river swells, pregnant with the spring runoff. I had just finished writing the last sentence of this book, and with that final period came a sense of emptiness, a feeling akin to sending your child off to school for the first time. I wondered how my words and ideas would find their way into the world, and whether you, dear reader, would welcome them into your life. The confident and proud mother was overwhelmed by feelings of doubt. And humility.

Then as I walked down the path toward the river, the ground moist beneath my feet, I heard the sound of returning birds echoing through the woods. I felt at one with Mother Nature. She, like me, was in transition, moving into a new season and a new age. As I came to the river's edge, I remembered how choreographer Paula Josa-Jones described leadership to me. "Leadership," she said, "is being the banks of a river." I looked in the distance and saw the purple majesty of Mount Monadnock, a three-thousand-foot mountain I have scaled many times, as have countless others. It is, after all, the most climbed mountain in the world. It is a magical mountain, purportedly a place that enfolds a convergence of meridians, the invisible channels where the life force circulates, the *qi* as it is known in traditional Chinese medicine. Locals call this area the vortex.

The word *monadnock* is a geological term meaning an isolated rocky hill rising above a plain as a result of erosion. Once part of a chain of mountains, Mount Monadnock alone has survived the work of rain and river because the rock is erosion resistant. Like Mount Monadnock, Iron Butterflies also resist and are not eroded by the false myth that domination is normative. Like the mountain, the collective power of women stands alone and, at the same time, is connected to and is part of something bigger than itself. I knew then, as I stood at the river's edge gazing at the distant purple summit, that as we press forward for social transformation, Iron Butterflies are always alone and never alone; we are paradoxically one. We remain strong, yet vulnerable.

Chapter 2

REMEMBER

Tracing Herstory

> Stories have to be told, or they die; and when they die,
> we can't remember who we are or why we're here.
>
> Sue Monk Kidd

Violet, an aboriginal elder in her sixties, sat across from me smoking a cigarette. Sitting together in her garden under a crystal blue sky and surrounded by exuberant plants, we could hear bird songs reminiscent of Villa-Lobos's plaintive soprano aria from Bachianas, *Brasileiras* no. 5. I had journeyed to Perth, Australia, on business and, as so often happens when I tell people about my project on women leaders, I had been urged to interview this particular woman.

As she spoke, Violet's belly undulated, her bottom lip intermittently retracted from a lack of bottom teeth, and her eyes shone bright and mischievously in her lined face. She exuded a good-naturedness and an aura of power. Often consulted by local authorities on aboriginal culture and sacred places, she is regarded by her people as the guardian of mysteries, the keeper of the gateway.

Only moments into the interview, she said to me, "You don't need to interview me. You already know what you need to know. Instead, I'll initiate you into our ancient ways." How did she know I already had the knowledge I was seeking? Puzzled and loath to lose an interview with this amazing woman, I went along with her offer. As she began mixing ochre, the blood of the earth, with lavender scented oil, she told me about herself:

I work with cosmic realities. A reconstruction is happening now, tapping into an ancient pattern of destruction and creation. It's a repeated cycle, and we have the opportunity of repatterning the energies of the past. Fire is a creative force, and there has been misuse of the fire stick of technology. We have a psychic imbalance, corrections are needed. However, the planet is being energized and patterns are changing. A lot of us have been sleeping. We're waking up because the fire has been ignited. We are reconnecting to the Earth Mother manifested on different levels of consciousness. We all have the story of Mother deep within us. As we connect with Her, we change within, and we change the patterns around us. She was in quarantine for a long time because She got contaminated. She's out of quarantine now, and we're trying to repair her and ourselves and hope She doesn't shrug Her shoulders and throw us all out.

Although I felt Violet was telling me something vitally important, I did not know exactly what she meant at that moment, but as I traveled further on my journey, Violet's message, uttered by other indigenous people, would become clearer. We are entering the Era of Women.

Although I promised Violet to keep the initiation process a secret, I know she would approve if I reveal just one wonderful moment. In my mind's eye, I imagined a circle of elder women sitting together, looking at me, exuding both a powerful and a playful presence. Violet stood behind them, laughing. Complete in themselves and so welcoming as they invited me to join their circle, their sisterhood brought home to me just how fragmented women's collective power has become. As tears moistened my eyes, I could feel the earth's energy run into my feet, through my body, and out the top of my head, rattling me into alignment with myself, nature, and the Great Black Mother. The experience shook me to the bone.

I opened my eyes to see Violet looking at me. "Women hold the wisdom," she said, "and men hold the love. That's how it should be." I sat there dumbstruck. How could this be? Our culture seems to reflect the exact opposite. If Violet spoke a deeper truth, how in the world did we lose sight of women holding the wisdom and men holding the love? I decided then and there to seek an answer to that question, and, as a result, my initiation that day into the ancient ways marked the first step in my personal journey of remembering, uncovering, and giving voice to the wisdom women hold.

In this chapter I want to bring together some of the pieces of women's fragmented history in a way that might help uncover some of their lost wisdom. You may know many of these pieces of women's history, but I want to review them in the context of power and leadership. I've found it a splintered history, somewhat stifled by a collective amnesia that we resist remembering in our desire to move on and to create a different future. Paradoxically, we cannot truly create a new future and let go of the past until we collectively remember. Remember how history has omitted women's contributions. Remember the biases, embedded in recorded history. Remember how a history of violence against women has served to silence women's wisdom. And finally, remember the Great Mother.

> **Remember:**
> - Women's contributions
> - Biases in written history
> - Violence against women
> - Magna Mater

By recalling that women once held the wisdom, we open the door to validating women's capability to lead. The loss of the collective memory that women hold the wisdom has undermined their authority and the perception that they can, in fact, lead. We'll talk more about this in chapter 7. For now, however, let's concentrate on remembering together, on reviving our common past, and on using our regained wisdom to take back our authority in our own terms and shape our future.

REMEMBER HER CONTRIBUTIONS

French feminist Simone de Beauvoir wrote that because women have no past, no history, no religion of their own, they cannot easily organize themselves as a unit. What did she mean by "no past, no history?" For at least the past 2,500 years, patriarchy, the domination-driven, male hierarchy of power, has kept women subordinate by omitting, denying, and distorting women's contribution to the human story. By excluding her story, patriarchal systems secured women's cooperation by disconnecting women from each other, from their spiritual life, and from their wisdom. Consequently, women's contributions throughout history grew less visible. Most history books simply ignore women's contributions to our culture and civilization. Consequently, his story became our history, and her story, along with her wisdom, was buried or lost.

Iron Butterflies strive to unearth women's unheralded contributions to society and thus restore their wisdom. Some of them are doing this by creating new institutions to fill in the missing gaps in old institutions. For instance, a coalition of professional women campaigned to build the National Women's History Museum in Washington, DC, a first of its kind in the United States. Led by Senator Susan Collins and supported by the fund-raising efforts of Meryl Streep, the idea has passed in the Senate and now awaits approval in the House. The museum would provide a solid understanding of the roles women played in the nation's history and correct oversights such as the contribution of Catherine Littlefield Greene, who invented the revolutionary cotton gin. Even now, history books credit the invention to Eli Whitney because, in 1793, it was considered "inappropriate" for a woman to hold a patent. The exhibit would also remind us that on Lewis and Clark's heroic expedition, a Shoshone woman, Sacagawea, not only helped guide the arduous trek, but did it with an infant at her breast. Few know that silent movie star Mary Pickford, "America's Sweetheart," was more than a pretty face. At the turn of the century, she was the first woman to own her own film company, and in 1919 she cofounded United Artists. Or that Lise Meitner, who developed the theory of nuclear fission, was excluded when the Nobel Prize was given for this work in 1944. Setting the record straight on the "forgotten past" of women's contributions to our nation enriches our history and all our lives.

Another effort to uncover women's wisdom has begun in San Francisco with the funding of the International Museum of Women, an online community dedicated to honoring and valuing the lives of women around the world. Originally founded as Women's Heritage Museum in 1985, it celebrates women's attributes, roles, accomplishments, and spiritual lives.

We now celebrate International Women's Day on March 8. Begun in 1909 in the United States, the event has grown into an international event that celebrates women's contributions and advancement and continues to remind us that only constant vigilance will ensure women's equality. Surprisingly, people in Cameroon celebrate only three holidays—Independence Day, Youth Day, and International Women's Day.

With the rebirth of feminism, in 1978 the local women's commission in Sonoma County, California, dedicated a weeklong celebration to women's history. The idea spread and led to a congressional resolution that established the first National Women's History Week in 1983. Today many universities dedicate an entire month to women's history.

For decades scholars in women's studies have worked to recover and uncover the contributions of women and their unheralded courage. For example, Harriet Tubman, a monumental figure in the pre–Civil War Underground Railroad, has finally won from historians the attention she deserves. Three biographies, all written by women, reveal her work with the antislavery supporters and how she led her family and acquaintances to freedom. In an effort to put women on the historical time line, Cokie Roberts's book *The Founding Mothers: The Women Who Raised Our*

Nation makes the point that the men couldn't have done what they did without women maintaining their homes and families. They tended the farms, took care of everybody, and sustained the fabric of the community, as they have done for millennia. Women have provided the backbone of society, and perhaps, like a backbone, it's easy to take it for granted. By remembering, we resuscitate the half of history that is ours. By remembering, we add both mind and heart to the story.

REMEMBER MAGNA MATER

Why do we need to uncover her story and her wisdom in the first place? How did we develop this collective amnesia? As I said in the first chapter, the Era of Man that favored empowering men over women has ruled the world for at least 5,400 years. Viewed within the context of human evolution, this is but a flashing moment, less than 10 percent of our residence on earth. But it has left an indelible mark. Think of the past 5,000 years as a relentless effort to eradicate feminine wisdom through systematic economic and political subjugation. Throughout this time in history, male dominance marginalized, demonized, or silenced women's wisdom. Religion, for all the good it has done, did little more than reinforce gender inequity by emphasizing and preserving traditional roles that maintain a power differential between men and women.

If we look back 25,000 years further in time, we must invoke our imagination. Reconstructing the past is like writing science fiction in reverse. Conjuring up the truth of the story is found in its resonance as well as in its relics. Scholars have produced a large body of fascinating work on this time period; I would like to look at this time in the context of women's lost authority, leadership, and wisdom.

Before patriarchy stamped its mark on society, evidence points to women and men fulfilling quite different roles. Then men and women enjoyed certain equality in a world where both genders treated the feminine aspects of life and women's wisdom as something sacred. It was the time of the hunter-gatherers when men and women connected more deeply to the earth and the cycles of nature. Their nomadic culture dictated that they moved freely and peacefully, sharing food and the responsibility of childcare, as we can see among the few remaining hunter-gatherer societies that exist today. Work was not gender driven but egalitarian. As anthropologist Olga Soffer put it, "This is not the image we've always had. Instead, it's been Upper Paleolithic macho guys out killing animals up close and personal."

Countering this image of the aggressive, dominant male, Soffer argues that men also cared for offspring, while women also hunted. Hunting with nets, in particular, required a communal effort by men, women, and even children. Soffer has also obtained artifacts from women buried with banner stones used as weights on spear launchers, a finding that lends credence to the notion that some women hunted with just as much skill as men.

Traditionally, archaeology displayed a masculine bias that glorified Man the Hunter while affording little attention to female activity. Anthropologist Adrienne Zihlman and others have corrected this imbalance by noting that for 25,000 years in the preagricultural band societies, 80 percent of their sustenance came from gathering and 20 percent from hunting. Rather than the stereotype of Man the Hunter as provider, Woman the Gatherer put food on the table. With women procuring 80 percent of the sustenance, they must have lived lives of great autonomy, since they largely determined the band's movement and camp locations. According to author Rosalind Miles, men did not command or exploit women's labor, and "they exerted little or no control over women's bodies or those of their children, making no fetish of virginity or chastity, and making no demands of women's sexual exclusivity."

Writing about this period in human history, archaeologist Marija Gimbutis and author Riane Eisler speculated that a goddess culture existed overseen by a divine Mother Earth, a time of Magna Mater. During the time of the Great Mother Goddess, the culture revered feminine attributes and women as creators and protectors of life. Did men at that time comprehend their role in creating life? It's hard to know, but connecting their role in sexual activity to a baby emerging out of a woman's body must have been a great revelation!

Goddess figurines dating back to this time displayed generous breasts and sacred pubic triangles, exuding fertility and sexuality, suggesting the Great Mother Goddess's abiding concern for the sacredness of life. The Venus of Malta figurine, with one hand resting on her belly and the other pointing to the earth, emphasizes the relationship of birth to earth, as both sources of life. The Great Mother Goddess held and encompassed all: life and death, creation and destruction, lightness and darkness. She was both feminine and masculine, but as the figurines show, she was feminine first, as we all are in the womb.

I have seen the ruins of this culture when I visited the ancient temples in Malta, a small island a hundred miles south of Sicily. Oddly, I visited the site when the orbit of Mars (the god of war) brought the planet the closest it's been to Earth in nearly sixty thousand years. Could that have been an omen that the war god had peaked and might now retreat? Given the endless cycle of war waged on our planet, I hoped so. The temples on this rocky island date back more than 5,000 years, to the Neolithic period, and mark the beginning of the end of the goddess culture.

Today the Goddess, although transformed, persists in daily Maltese life. The many Catholic churches and roadside crosses are almost exclusively feminine, honoring Mary and female saints. During festas celebrated by each church, the men carry female statues out of the church on a platform they balance on their shoulders, precariously at times, for a ceremonial parade around the town.

Many myths, called giantess stories, still linger around the ancient temples. The temple Gargantua, for example, on the island Gozo, just off the shore of Malta, consists of enormous slabs of stone. How did ancient people erect such massive objects? The story told insists that a goddess built it with one hand in one day, all the while holding a baby on her hip. Now that's a supermom!

Not only do the myths linger, but Magna Mater's presence looms. In the Tarxien temple, which is located in the middle of the city by the same name, there stands the bottom portion of a colossal statue of an obese, abundant Mother Goddess with a pleated skirt, enormous calves, and tiny feet. The size of this statue and many like it in other temples indicates her importance to the culture. Evidence suggests that this was a peaceful culture, and when you look at friezes, you get a sense of serenity and calm. None of the animals depicted appear speared or bleeding; they remain whole. Likewise, you see no images of killing nor evidence of weapons. Instead, at the National Museum of Archeology you will see displays of tools, many huge bowls and vases, and beautiful beaded jewelry.

My favorite temple was Hagar Qim, perched majestically atop limestone cliffs, overlooking the deep blue expanse of the Mediterranean Sea, where the tiny island of Filfla lies in a gray haze. A lone spreading thorn tree stands near the temple, providing the only shade from the unrelenting sun. The day I stood there, the temperature reached 108° F. My shirt was soaked; even my shins and bare toes glistened with perspiration. But it was not the heat that took my breath away and clutched at my chest; it was the sight of the pale honey structure of Hagar Qim made of huge blocks of soft globigerina limestone. It exuded a feminine energy that revived an ancient memory of a woman's place and power, as priestess, as dancer, as healer, as oracle, as nurturer, as creator of life.

In the entrance to this temple stood two large platforms where statues of the Goddess probably once rested, welcoming her visitors. These platforms, pitted with small circles, looked like a honeycomb. A feminine hive,

I mused. The temple's four apses—round, womblike rooms with implications of now-eroded curved ceilings—exposed the sky. Each entrance to a room featured a stone slab with a curved window carved into it, and behind that room lay another small, round room, and sometimes beyond that yet another smaller room. It seemed like a labyrinth space of feminine curves.

One room contained hollowed out stone tables perhaps used for preparing ointments, herbs, and oils. In another I could see an oracle hole. Outside the temple, facing the oracle hole, stood a pubic triangle of stone, and behind that a huge phallus stone—together displaying masculine and feminine in balance. Weaving and circular images of spirals and vine patterns adorning the structure implied the cycles of life. Everywhere images of snakes and serpents conveyed symbols of the Goddess's wisdom.

How the power of the Mother Goddess diminished and, along with it, women's wisdom and feminine arts, has spawned much speculation. Leonard Shlain makes one especially cogent argument in his provocative book *The Alphabet and the Goddess*. The goddess culture, he argues, was principally informed by a holistic, right-brain mentality. The alphabet and the task of writing, largely a male domain, engaged linear, left-brain thinking, minimizing the right-brain function and upsetting the balance between men and women. He argues that a preference for linear thinking over holistic thinking fostered a patriarchal perspective that diminished a feminine counterpart and, with it, women's power in culture. In other words, writing undercut the value of a right-brain, holistic way of thinking, wholeness, simultaneity, and synthesis, by valuing left-brain reliance on sequence, analysis, and abstraction. The decline of the feminine ushered in the hierarchical world of patriarchy and misogyny

Another version of the downfall of the goddess culture revolves around the rise of city-states and nation-states that began 5,000 years ago. When hunter-gatherers adopted a semisedentary way of life five millennia earlier, land became a valuable resource that demanded fierce protection. That new social imperative to defend land in agricultural societies became ever more acute in the dawning age of civilization: not just crops, but towns, cities, and temples needed protection. Two dramatic social shifts accompanied this accelerating transformation. First, people found themselves in a society in which specialization of everyday and valued tasks (potters, carpenters, masons, as well as bureaucrats and priests) became more and more pronounced, a development that consigned women to the role of child caretakers as never before. Second, humans placed greater and greater premium on the aggression and military prowess needed for survival and defending or capturing land.

What a seismic shift from hitherto small, egalitarian social groups in which women held high status, to large, hierarchical settlements driven by acquisition and defense of resources, with men dominant and women subservient. Patriarchy, in the temples as well as on the field of battle, had arrived in the wake of civilization's materialistic obsession. Men doubly asserted their dominance by subduing nature and subduing women. Women, once partners, became chattel.

Whereas a woman never doubts her maternal relationship to her child, a man could never be certain about his paternity. Given that fact and the need to ascertain inheritance rights and legacy issues, men eventually demanded virginal brides and monogamous wives. If men could control female sexuality, they could restrict her freedom. Anthropologist Gayle Rubin concludes that the "world-historical defeat of women occurred with the origins of culture and is a prerequisite of culture." In other words, the origins of a patriarchal culture were built upon a foundation of subjugation.

As women lost their power, so did the Goddess. When a male god supplanted her, "feminine" came to signify weak and inferior, and by association, so were women. Over time, the Great Goddess was fragmented into many less powerful goddesses. For instance, Isis, worshipped for 25,000 years as a principal goddess, a Great Mother, fragmented into a mother, wife, and consort, until she all but disappeared from view. Sophia, the goddess of wisdom, who appeared in nearly every culture and society, also lost her status to male gods.

Even women's ability to give life was symbolically taken from the Goddess. For instance, Aphrodite, goddess of love, was formed from a mixture of sperm and male blood and sea foam, without needing a womb. Athena, the goddess of wisdom, sprang fully formed from Zeus's head as a tame warrior goddess, girded and helmeted. Preceding this image, however, the Greeks had depicted an older, lesser-known image, of a wild and awesome goddess, her head wreathed in snakes and the head of a serpent, symbol of life, death, and wisdom, gripped firmly in her left hand.

Later, another male birthing would take place in the story of the Garden of Eden, where God created Eve from Adam's rib. The male and female images depicted in this story clearly convey the former's dominance. Eve's transgression in the garden puts the weight of human pain, hardship, and death on a woman's shoulders—she is forever guilty. Women, the givers of life, were now blamed for the death of every mortal. The story brands feminine curiosity as the greatest sin, and casts women as gullible, naive, conniving, and dangerously sexy temptresses, basically incompetent and inferior. The serpent, once a symbol of wisdom and feminine power, becomes the embodiment of temptation and evil.

Other sacred symbols of the Goddess also suffered in the transition to patriarchal culture, often around the theme of fertility and sexuality. The pig, once a symbol of fertility, became dirty and forbidden food. Hair, the symbol of sexuality, was to be shorn on the wedding night. The once beautiful Medusa with her serpent hair would turn anyone who looked at her to stone. Men, fearful of a woman's power, killed her as they would other feminine power.

The rise of Christianity in the first to fifth centuries sealed the Goddess's doom. Celibacy, eternal virginity, and a virgin birth replaced the fertility and pleasure associated with the Goddess. Worshipping the feminine divine, however, was never completely suppressed. The Roman Catholic Church elevated Mary, the Mother of Christ, to goddess status, but they insisted on her virginity, thus robbing her of her sexuality and fecundity. Astonishingly, in earlier scriptures, she was no virgin.

St. Augustine of Hippo, leading the way toward an antierotic stance, not at all consistent with Jesus' teachings and early scriptures, took the sexuality that the Hebrew and early Christian traditions understood as a gift of God, and turned it into something evil, something compulsive that humans must control rather than celebrate, even though Augustine himself violated that policy. Religious scholar Elaine Pagels identifies St. Augustine as a major source of Western society's negative attitudes toward sex.

With the denigration and fragmentation of the Goddess, the holistic view of nature as cyclical, interdependent, communal, and egalitarian broke into dichotomies: division and hierarchy, monotheism and nation-states—all of which favored a domination model and linear thinking. The written word drove the final nail into the Goddess's coffin. As Leonard Schlain observes, "The first commandment 'I am the Lord thy God. Thou shalt not have other gods before me' announces the disappearance of the Goddess." As the wisdom and power of the Goddess declined, women were increasingly demeaned, feminine power marginalized, and female authority denied. Schlain continues, "There is something inherently anti-female in the written word." What does he mean by that bold statement?

REMEMBER GENDER BIASES

Consider three of the most widely known forms of written history: the Bible, the Qur'an, and the Talmud. Scholars like Bernadette Brooten, director of the Feminist Sexual Ethics Project at Brandeis University, see patriarchy deeply embedded in these three religious texts. After all, fallible men with their gender-driven biases, conscious or unconscious, wrote them. Leonard Schlain went so far as to say that the mainstream writers for every major religion were unremitting misogynists who consistently demeaned women.

In the New Testament, for instance, when Paul writes to Timothy (1 Timothy 2:11–120), "Women should listen and learn quietly and submissively. I do not let women teach men or have authority over them," he speaks for himself. American televangelist Pat Robertson, in his book *Bring It On*, used Timothy's verse to justify his statement that God's pattern is for men to be the elders both in the church and in the family. Can anyone deny that this position represents a male bias against women that silences their wisdom and strips them of any authority? Recognizing this bias, suffragette Elizabeth Cady Stanton, who praised Jesus for being the leading radical of his time, also claimed that no book other than the Bible so fully taught "the subjection and degradation of women."

If you find this a little strong, review the story of Mary Magdelene, who was depicted in the Bible as a whore. The characterization of Magdelene as a fallen woman didn't originate in the Bible as the word of God but in a sermon by sixth-century Pope Gregory the Great. In truth, rather than a fallen woman, Magdelene may have been the first and favored apostle of Jesus. Karen King, of Harvard Divinity School, gained access to fragments from the Gospel of Mary that were lost for 1,500 years in which she sees Mary Magdelene's authority in the early church, and women's role in general, as a target of jealousy because Mary Magdelene threatened Peter's status. By transforming her into a reformed whore, the church fathers killed the argument for women's leadership, and in some cases suppressed countervailing views as heresy. Reporter Richard Covington wrote that "the sexy, reformed Mary Magdelene is a symbol that's proven difficult to abandon. But the visionary Mary, full of faith at the foot of the cross and messenger of the Resurrection, a founding disciple entrusted by Jesus with a special mission to spread God's words, carries the greater ring of truth."

On the contemporary front, take a look at the mega-blockbuster bestseller *The Da Vinci Code* by Dan Brown. A modern-day fictional interpretation that addresses the distortion of Magdelene's story, *The Da Vinci Code* has brought this subject of Mary Magdelene's true identity to the masses and understandably generated bitter attacks aimed at discrediting Brown's thesis that Mary and Jesus created a child together. Despite a scathing denunciation by the Catholic Church, an energetic discussion questioning women's role in the church has ensued, bringing into question and challenging a history that denies women authority in the church.

In spite of the Bible's fairly consistent lowering of women's status, a close reading of biblical stories about women unveils a good many Iron Butterflies. As Naomi Harris Rosenblatt, the author of *After the Apple: Women in the Bible*, wrote:

> One is hard put to find in them a hint of alienation, cynicism, or ennui. On the contrary, they convey a can-do approach to life as they prevail, overcome, and refuse to bow in the face of overwhelming odds. They make and execute their imperfect decisions to the best of their abilities, and they are willing to acknowledge and live with the consequences of their actions—the essential meaning of responsibility and accountability that accompanies free will, God's greatest gift to humans.

Having said that, there are also plenty of stories illustrating the opposite, such as the story of Dinah, who was raped, betrothed to the rapist, and widowed by her brothers' murderous rage. Caught in the crossfire between men, Dinah herself remains silent and oddly a minor character.

Women's traditionally limited leadership roles in Christian religions has begun to shift, however, at least in some sects, such as the Episcopalian church, which now ordains women as priests and bishops. In fact, in 2006 Bishop Katharine Jefferts Schori was the first woman ever to head and lead the US Episcopalian Church.

In Judaism, similar questioning has arisen concerning the portrayal of women's authority in the major texts. Barbara Geller, a professor of religion at Wellesley College who studies Jewish history, cites archaeological and written evidence of women serving as synagogue leaders early in a tradition that supposedly limited leadership to men. Although women do not perform official leadership in the Old Testament, they nevertheless demonstrate leadership in their actions. Witness the fighter Deborah, the courageous midwives Puah and Shifrah, who saved male babies in defiance of the pharaoh's edict to drown them, and Rahab, who risked her life to help Joshua's spies escape from Jericho. Although the text recounts their actions, the personal story of their struggles and their decision making remain absent, rendering them less-than-effective role models. Today, however, the reformist movement does accept women rabbis.

Azizah al-Hibri, founder of Karamah: Muslim Women Lawyers for Human Rights and professor of law at the University of Richmond School of Law, Virginia, has been studying the Qur'an and women's role in Islam. "Men, throughout history, used force to exercise power, slowly exiling women from the public square," she told me.

We know that some Islamic scholars studied under women in the past. Where are the books or views of these women? Manuscripts were preserved only when somebody wanted to preserve them, and that meant the men in power chose what is to be preserved. A lot of the women's contributions are not with us today. I am in the midst of studying various interpretations of the same verse, ancient and relatively new ones, and they can vary significantly in some cases. There are examples where patriarchal cultural biases colored the interpretation, and when that happens, the resulting interpretation tends to be patriarchal as well, not feminist.

On another front, male bias that undermines women's authority and leadership crops up in Buddhism. Despite the fact that the Dalai Lama admits there have been great female Bodhisattvas and Bhikkunis, can anyone recite their names and tell their stories? There is, of course, Kuan Yin, the goddess of compassion and liberation, whose legend is found in China and India. Many women must have started temples, but we know little about them because translators and historians have been men who tended to ignore the accomplishments of women.

Buddha may have proclaimed that women can reach enlightenment by the same path as men, but he did refuse to ordain women. Eventually, he agreed to ordain nuns but placed them in a markedly subordinate position to monks, largely because the society at large could not accept women's equality, and might not financially support a monastery that did. Today, Western monastic women must let monks eat first, must sit in the back of the room during religious instruction, and must bow down before all monks, no matter what their level of religious attainment.

Karen Andrews of the Institute of Buddhist Studies at Berkeley, California, writes that in reaction to such biases a number of revolutionary women have split off from the traditional monastic path. "Their way is one of dissolving boundaries," she writes of these revolutionaries, "between lay and monastic life, and between traditional male and female roles. Somehow, all this dissolving of boundaries strikes me as being quite true to the Buddha's original teachings."

Recognizing the biases against women's leadership in religions and their written texts is one thing. Challenging it is another—one that can become a quest of biblical proportions as Katherine Ragsdale discovered. Her story underscores the power of courageous vulnerability, the bravery to be true to our hearts in difficult and unjust situations.

Katherine Ragsdale, the former national board chair of the Religious Coalition for Reproductive Choice, is an Episcopal priest, a pro-choice activist, and a lesbian. As a spokesperson for that organization, she spoke on its behalf on National Public Radio and the Public Broadcasting Service, and she has even testified before the United States Congress. She sits on the board of the White House Project and the national board of directors of NARAL: Pro-Choice America. Today she is director of the Episcopal Divinity School in Arlington, Massachusetts, which trains women and men for the priesthood. The story of her call to the ministry is remarkable. She weathered a storm of systematic retribution that punished her for being a woman and a lesbian. While it challenged her courage and taxed her vulnerability, ultimately it could not thwart the restoration of her spirit and much-deserved justice.

Like most kids, Katherine didn't know what she wanted to be when she grew up. Yet she found herself in almost constant demand for advice and counsel. Not until she went to college, however, did she discover that a priest fulfilled just such a function for parishioners. As she confided to me, "Then I realized that I'd always known what I wanted to be; I just didn't know there was such a job."

At college, she involved herself in the campus ministry, took religion classes, and graduated with a double major in English and religion. After graduation she began the ordination process and joined the Diocese of Southern Virginia, unaware that this diocese refused to ordain women. Her faith soon hit the wall of prejudice.

She recalls her surprise at the time:

> I was too young and religiously naive. You know, God is calling you and God will find a way. Eventually She did, but it wasn't through the Diocese of Southern Virginia. They would never say they were turning me down because they don't do women; instead they told me that they ordained women, but not me. I was twenty, and they told me all these things that were wrong with me. I felt inadequate and it was horrible. I went through the ordination process again and again and was rejected.

Katherine sought help from an unexpected advisor, the college chaplain with whom she did not get along at all. "Because you don't like me," she told him, "and you won't be blinded by affection, I need you to tell me the truth. Is it me or is it the system? He said, 'You would be ordained by now if you were a man.'" The chaplain put Katherine in touch with Pat Merchant, one of the first illegally ordained women, "the Philadelphia 11." Pat herself had been working for the ordination of women for years. When Katherine phoned her, Pat sprang into action, finding her new friend a position in another diocese of Virginia.

In short order, after years of misery and inertia, Katherine entered the seminary. After two years there, she met with the bishop, who gave her a two-page letter that, once again, detailed all her flaws. "He said he was not going to ordain me. So why don't I just leave and not waste my time?" Somewhat ironically, his letter faulted her for being too smart and too independent to serve as a priest. Worse, she lacked any sense of community. "He was groping. He had figured out that I was a lesbian and that's why he wanted to get rid of me. I was just figuring that out for myself!" Katherine refused to withdraw from the seminary, stayed the course, and earned her degree.

Even more walls and hurdles blocked her path, but Katherine stayed the course until five years later, still short of fulfilling her dream of ordination, when she almost quit. She had spent a decade of her life in a seemingly futile struggle. "It was all-consuming emotionally. I get emotional just thinking about it now. I remember saying to myself that I'm called by God to be ordained, but I am *not* called to be in the ordination process for the rest of my life." Normally, once a candidate graduates from the seminary, she is ordained over the summer as a deacon, and then six months later as a full-fledged priest. The diocese of Newark, where she was working, persuaded her to stay, promising it would expedite the process. Eventually, the church, after fourteen grueling years, ordained Katherine. Had she finally made it?

Longing to serve as a parish priest, she feared her dream would remain unrealized. Then she received a call from a parish in Massachusetts saying it needed a priest for six weeks between Advent and Christmas. Imagine her joy when, after six weeks, the parishioners asked her to stay. But even that was tarnished by the lingering emotional bruises of the ordination process.

> When they asked me into their parish, I said they deserved someone who could give them more time and attention—make them more of a priority —than I could. I told them I had all these other involvements, such as speaking engagements related to pro-choice. If a Sunday talk show wanted me to appear, I would have to go. They said, "That's OK. When you are here, you are here; when you come back, you'll have great stories." I told them they were hiring an internationally known abortion-rights activist, out-lesbian priest. I told them it was a violent time, that anti-abortionists might vandalize or blow up their church. They said, "Well, I guess we would just rebuild."

Katherine ultimately realized her calling, to head an organization that trains men and women to be priests. She epitomizes courageous vulnerability; she did not let others dim her light. Her patience and perseverance paid off. Transcending gender bias, justice was restored to Katherine. And Magna Mater smiled.

> Stand up against violence.
> Expose gender biases.
> Speak out at oversights.
> Act on your beliefs.

REMEMBER THE USE OF VIOLENCE TO SILENCE

Deep in our history is the use of violence to silence women. Violence to establish dominance over women and stifle their wisdom occurred most dramatically during the Inquisition, which resulted in the deaths of so many so-called heretics. An untold part of the story of that violent period—the story of hating women, fearing women, and eliminating their wisdom—remains profoundly repressed. It was quite literally a holocaust that consumed, according to some estimates, from two to nine million women. In 1489, Pope Innocent VIII had declared that witchcraft posed a threat to Christendom, an edict that launched a relentless witch hunt. Since 80 percent of the suspected witches were women, the Inquisition amounted to little more than a "woman hunt." Women, once respected healers, herbalists, and counsels, drew fire as consorts of Satan deserving not respect but torture, mutilation, and death. The inquisitors, all male, of course, even killed the daughters of supposed witches for fear that they would continue their mother's practice of dark arts. All the attributes of the Goddess—joyous fertility rites, dancing, the moon, sexuality, procreation—became profanities. The female breast, a source of nourishment, became a witch's tit, an evil appendage.

From the Grand Inquisition rose the perverted image of the witch so prevalent at Halloween: the misshapen green face, stringy scraps of hair, toothless mouth beneath a deformed nose, gnarled fingers, and bent and twisted torso. The image? Evil incarnate? No, despair incarcerated. During the Inquisition, men abducted women in the night, carting them off to dungeons and prisons for "questioning." Violence done to them there prompted not silence but abject confessions. In the light of day, the witch would be paraded through town before suffering an excruciating death of burning, hanging, stoning, and drowning. The jeering crowd witnessed a creature deformed by hours of brutal physical torture, her face twisted in pain from countless blows, her skin mottled with green and purple bruises, her hands and body broken. She would have appeared to be truly a demon. During this reign of terror, an entire culture and generation of women were annihilated, a whole treasury of feminine values vanquished. Ancient female wisdom, accumulated over eons, went up in flames with the witches. Women, robbed of their wisdom, got the message: if you speak up and speak truth, then fear for your very life. This message, I believe, lingers in our cellular memory.

So why bring up this repulsive history now? Haven't we progressed light-years from that era of misguided misogyny? You need only look around the globe to see similar violence against women today. Staggering amounts of violence that harm or kill women and girls are unleashed every day. The news revels in stories about women who come to gruesome ends at the hands of violent men. Fashion ads play off that violence with themes of death and submissiveness. We've become so used to violent treatment of women we hardly notice. Did we notice when in Guatemala a "femicide" occurred? Between 2001 and 2006, authorities registered 2,300 women and girls as kidnapped, raped, tortured, and murdered in this small Central American country. No one may ever know the real number, probably much higher, nor will the true motive likely emerge. Calls for investigations from Amnesty International and other organizations fall on deaf ears. Barely any cases have been solved. In fact, families who attempted to find the murderers often fell victim to intimidation and violence themselves.

The patriarchal bargain dictated that if women would only submit to male authority, they would receive protection. But patriarchal institutions have failed miserably to protect women, as we see in Guatemala and elsewhere around the world. Violence continues to provide an effective tool for silencing women's wisdom, a tool for subjugation and subordination. A 1994 study based on World Bank data found the greatest risk factor for women ages fifteen to forty-four was rape and violence. This is higher than cancer, motor vehicle accidents, malaria, and war. *One in six* women will experience an attempted or completed rape at some time in her life according to US Department of Justice's Sexual Assault Program. According to a 2003 report by the United Nations Development Fund for Women (UNIFEM) one *in every three* women around the world will be raped, beaten, coerced into sex, or otherwise abused in her lifetime, usually by someone she knows. The report called "Not a Minute More: Ending Violence against Women" finds "despite progress at the international, national, and grassroots levels to address gender-based violence, there has not been a dramatic reduction in violence against women." In other words, *abuse is normative for women.* Look at any three women worldwide walking down the street. One of them has suffered at the hands of a contemporary inquisitor. If you as a woman have been abused, know that you are far from alone.

Consider another startling statistic, the number one cause of death for pregnant women in America. Murder. Could anyone imagine a more blatant defiling of feminine fertility and sexuality, and the sacredness of life? The cases of Laci Peterson and Lori Hacking and Maria Lauterback make headlines, but many more get relegated to the back page. The *Journal of Midwifery & Women's Health* found that 38 percent of pregnant women who died in Washington, DC, between 1988 and 1996 were victims of homicide. Their names appear only on tombstones.

Moreover, the US Department of Justice estimates that husbands and lovers kill 1,500 to 2,400 young women each year. Every fifteen seconds, a man who "loves" her physically assaults a girlfriend or wife. Domestic violence ranks as the number one cause of injury to women in America, more than all the rapes, muggings, and automobile accidents combined. Three to four million women are beaten each year. It happens to men as well: men are twice as likely as women to be victims of violence. But rarely at the hands of a woman.

Rape, another form of violence against women, occurs somewhere in America every two minutes according to the Department of Justice. Nine out of ten rape victims are females. In 1995, local child protection agencies identified 126,000 children who were sexually abused, 75 percent of them girls, and nearly 30 percent of them between the ages of four and seven. Rape is about power, not sex, and there is no action that more forcefully exerts dominance over a woman or a girl than the violent insertion, not just of the penis, but at the same time of the traumatic emotions of fear, confusion, and worthlessness. In some places, rape is institutionalized—Pakistani women are gang-raped as punishment; the Burmese government gives the military a "license to rape" women; and women in the Democratic Republic of the Congo are raped by both militia and government troops in a culture of impunity. In Basra, Iraq, women have been killed in the most brutal fashion—in front of their children, strangled to death, tortured, beheaded—because they failed to wear a headscarf.

Violence against women takes many forms. According to the Women and Public Policy Program at Harvard University, human trafficking, comprised of 80 percent females worldwide, forces girls into labor and sexual exploitation, including prostitution, bride trafficking, and pornography. Twelve to fourteen is the average age of entry into prostitution in the United States. Twenty-seven million are held in slavery worldwide and approximately 800,000 are trafficked across national borders annually. Two million girls between five and fifteen are introduced into the commercial sex market each year

In Asia, 163 million girls have gone "missing" as a result of sex-selective abortions, infanticide, or neglect, according to the United Nations Population Fund. That's more than the total number of people killed in all the wars of the twentieth century. The female population is lower than it should be, in China a staggering 6.7 percent of the expected female population and 7.9 percent in India. Honor killings take thousands of women's lives, mainly in Asia, and North and South Africa. If a Nigerian woman has sex out of wedlock, she can legally be stoned to death. Placing no value on women justifies violence and discrimination. For millions of women, violence against them is a way of life.

So why doesn't the existence and increasing rate of rape and violence against women provoke mass movements? Do people actually think sexism and misogyny only happened in the ancient and medieval eras or only occurs in "backward" societies? As columnist Bob Herbert wrote, "The disrespectful, degrading, contemptuous treatment of women is so pervasive and so mainstream that it has just about lost its ability to shock." Degrading women is the rule, not the exception.

And what does it mean when so many people insist they abhor such behavior, yet do little or nothing about it? As Michael Albert, author and founder of *Z Magazine*, observes, "Just as whites need to deal with racism, men need to deal with sexism. We ought to make known our desire to support a reawakened militant feminism. Even more important, we should compel the still male-dominated institutions we operate in to restructure themselves to offer both material and organizational support for national and local women's organizing."

Numbers reveal the extent of violence, but they do not capture the deeply personal and human effects. Janice Mirikitani's story does. Janice, poet laureate of San Francisco in 2000 and 2001, is president of Glide Foundation, a human service program providing services for overcoming poverty and a lack of self-worth. She knows the subject firsthand, and her own experience has driven her dedication to make a difference in people's lives. A Sansei, a third-generation Japanese American, she listens to women's stories of abuse as a healing process for them and for herself. Her story reflects her personal devastation from, and her triumph over, domination through violence and her journey from silence to an outspoken advocate. She encourages other women to shed their reluctance to make their voices heard. When we see and hear successful women like Janice, we often don't imagine that they have suffered great injustices, partly because, in many cases, they feel shame in revealing their painful, personal experiences. However, Janice demonstrates courageous vulnerability.

My stepfather became my main perpetrator of incest. He would do things like sexualize a kitten with his hands, demonstrating to me the kind of power over life and death he had in his hands, showing me he had ultimate control over my life. It wasn't just my stepfather; I was incested by a lot of men in my family—uncles, cousins—starting from the age of five until I left home at the age of seventeen. I would fight, but it didn't make a difference. I would tell my mother, but she would just pretend she didn't hear. I would be furious with her. For years, I was more angry with her than I was with my stepfather, because she didn't protect me, and she did not believe me.

Although an excellent student in college, Janice grew deeply depressed and attempted suicide on a couple of occasions. The pain of sexual violence inflicted is far deeper and more profound than the act itself; it damages personal integrity, devastates lives, stalls development. Janice felt unloved, unlovable, and undeserving of love. She felt little control over her own life. Like many women abused by men, she focused her attention on men, believing they were her ticket out of her misery and could lead her to her power, to a sense, as she told me, of "somebodyness." She felt attracted to what she had experienced, to very domineering and brutal men who gave her less love than violence. "I thought love was brutality," she said. "Abuse is not only an issue of having no self-worth, but also of feeling like everything that I did deserved the punishment of brutality. I discovered that being abused, I internalized brutality as being sexy. I was not turned on by men who were gentle and nice. Blah! But guys that beat the shit out of me, what a turn on! The brutality destroyed me for a long time by crossing my wires about what love was, what sexuality was."

Janice recalled a time when a guy came up to her on the street and asked her for directions. Her boyfriend, who was very volatile and violent, saw her talking to this guy, ran up to Janice, and started slapping her in front of the stranger. The stranger yelled, "What are you doing? I was just asking her for directions!" Her boyfriend told him that she wasn't supposed to be talking to him. He dragged her into the house, berated her, and threatened to leave. How did she react to such behavior? "I, who was so addicted and desperate, grabbed onto his legs as he tried to walk out the door and held on while he kicked me in the mouth. I was screaming for him not to leave me. Talk about self-brutality! I write about it and talk about it because I think it is the only way that women can say to each other, 'You don't deserve this, no matter who you are.'"

As Janice will tell you, violence destroys any shred of "somebodyness." Stripped of her self-worth, a woman becomes easier to control.

With her words, Janice exposes the insidiousness of abuse that undermines feminine power—women internalize the message that they are worthless nobodies. In this situation, it's easy for a woman to become a self-abuser by keeping herself in an abusive relationship because she believes she deserves no better. Unknowingly, she participates in her own oppression and inadvertently perpetuates a system that diminishes women by diminishing herself. And as Janice points out, sexual violence perverts a woman's desire: her torture becomes her delight. Desire, the force that propels a person forward, becomes a misdirected drive that prevents her from becoming a whole person. Abuse blocks her ability to connect with her vulnerability, which can make her whole.

By facing her vulnerability, that feeling of being worthless, Janice has acquired new strengths and the courage to tell her story, not to mention the compassion to listen to others. She leads the way to a place where women together can heal and transform their vulnerability into a collective experience of self-empowerment.

STANDING TOGETHER AGAINST VIOLENCE

For women to reclaim our authority and command a leadership position, we must stand, stand individually and collectively, against violence toward women. We must speak up. We must speak out. We must join and support each woman who does. In October 2005, New York Senator Hillary Clinton cosponsored legislation renewing the Violence Against Women Act (VAWA), originally signed into law by her husband, President Bill Clinton, in 1994. The Senate passed the legislation unanimously. The act provides money to enhance investigations of violent crimes against women and must receive reauthorization in 2010, coincidentally the beginning of the Era of Women.

When José Luis Rodriguez Zapatero became prime minister of Spain in April 2004, he proceeded to appoint women to head eight of the sixteen ministries and crafted the Law against Gender Violence, a sweeping bill designed to increase punishment for perpetrators and provide financial and social aid to victims. Conservatives immediately criticized the bill as unconstitutionally favoring female domestic violence victims. The response from the government? You can't fight for equality without first creating a solution to the urgent problem of violence against women. I believe Zapatero would agree with Segolene Royal, who came close to becoming the prime minister of France, when she said that there is a strong correlation between the status of women and the state of justice or injustice in a country.

Here's my modest proposal. Why don't we do what women in some African nations do? When a woman in the village finds herself in trouble, which includes a beating by any man, she blows a whistle! A real whistle, not a symbolic one. When other women hear it, they rush to their sister's aid. They shame the man, who loses face in the village.

In Namibia, where rapes and degradation of women occurred daily during a long guerrilla war, women sprang into action when a two-year-old was raped. They called together an initiative against sexual violence that led to Namibia's president condemning sexual violence in a new law.

In 1999, the United Nations designated November 25 as International Day for the Elimination of Violence against Women to promote the halt to all gender-based violence. The proclamation is important, but more important is the execution. That's where Eve Ensler steps in.

Eve Ensler, who created the stage presentation *Vagina Monologues*, also created the V-day event that started in 1997, a global alliance and movement among women to stop violence against women and girls. V-day promotes creative events to increase awareness and revitalize the spirit of existing antiviolence organizations. V-day also promotes large-scale benefits, such as the Afghan Women's Summit. In 2008, to celebrate the tenth anniversary of V-day, a coalition of many organizations across the globe participated in a celebrity-studded, two-day event to change the story of woman, to change "herstory."

Herself a survivor of physical and sexual abuse, Eve has courageously transformed her vulnerability into a new strength for all women, imagining a world where there is no violence against women, a world where women can speak their minds freely and walk alone and unafraid at night. In an interview with iVillage she said,

> It dawned on me that nothing was more important than stopping violence toward women—that the desecration of women indicated the failure of human beings to honor and protect life, and that this failing would, if we did not correct it, be the end of us all. I do not think I am being extreme. When you rape, beat, maim, mutilate, burn, bury, and terrorize women, you destroy the essential life energy on the planet. You force what is meant to be open, trusting, nurturing, creative, and alive to be bent, infertile, and broken.

Be courageously vulnerable. Be open and creative as you stand for your beliefs. Speak and act against violence toward women. Participate in events like V-day that seek social change through nonviolent action. Expose gender biases and misogyny when you see them. Shout out when oversights occur. And remember herstory.

By remembering herstory, Iron Butterflies hold the wisdom of their worth and the worth of their wisdom.

Chapter 3

CATERPILLARS

Close the Gender Gap

No one can make you feel inferior without your consent.

Eleanor Roosevelt

Ada Aharoni grew up in Egypt with two grandmothers who held opposing views. While her maternal grandmother, Regina, believed that a girl's value equaled a boy's, her paternal grandmother, Esther, with whom Ada's family lived for a while, saw men as the rulers of the world and women as their servants. Given Esther's view, her astonishment at seeing her seven-year-old granddaughter Ada playing the strategic game of chess with her nine-year old brother surprised no one. Ada's brother, who had taught Ada to play, made his moves swiftly, gliding his pieces across the board, confident that he would decisively beat his little sister. But instead, clever Ada checkmated him. "I thought he was going to kiss me because I won," Ada recalls with a chuckle. "Instead he slapped me across the face. I was so astounded. Instinctively, I slapped him right back." Grandmother Esther watched in shock as this wisp of a girl slapped the future man of the house! "She grabbed my arm, looked me in the eye, and said, 'You have to remember a boy is worth sixty girls, and in your life, don't you dare raise your hand to your brother or any man. You have to understand this if you want to live in peace in this world.'"

When Ada asked her grandmother why sixty girls equaled one boy, her grandmother grappled for an explanation, but nothing convinced little

Ada. "I am not going to live this way," Ada declared as she stomped her foot down. "I am worth one boy!" When Ada's mother and grandmother Regina heard of the incident, they backed up Ada's conviction; she was worth one boy. "So, I became a feminist at the age of seven!" Ada proudly told me.

Today Ada, a professor, author, poet, and founder of the International Forum for the Literature and Culture of Peace, lives in Israel. In her seventies, she is as vibrant and passionate as ever, refusing to let anyone extinguish her fiery desire to be whole or to block her work to help bring peace to the Middle East. Ada has created conditions for peace between Arab and Jewish women by having them come together and gain knowledge of each other's culture by sharing stories of peace.

I love the spirit of little Ada, who stood tall and refused to heed the old adage "little girls should be seen and not heard" and was not mesmerized into thinking of herself as less than her brother. We can learn so much from Ada and all other young girls whose sense of fairness makes them unbending in the face of gender discrimination. Like little Ada, we should all resist monolithic authoritarian beliefs that stereotype males as the leaders, females as their followers. By refusing to walk behind her brother, Ada thwarted indoctrination into a domination culture that wanted nothing more than to silence and subdue her. It's not just men who perpetuate the traditional view. Women, such as Ada's grandmother Esther, collaborate in sending the message of domination and submission to their daughters and granddaughters. By propagating beliefs and behaviors that sabotage women's power, women like grandmother Esther help perpetuate systems that oppress women. Why do they do it? Because, in a misguided way, they believe their view will ensure peace in the household and, by extension, peace in the world. But peace at what cost?

Although Ada's momentous chess game took place more than fifty years ago, the inequality of women continues in as many households throughout the world as it did then. For instance, in Afghanistan today, women have made some progress, albeit fragile, toward equity and have begun to participate in the political arena. And yet we must wonder about the quality of that participation. On one occasion, women delegates protested that no women had been appointed as a chairman's deputy on any of the committees, thus excluding women from any leadership positions. Although the head of the assembly, Mojaddedi, grudgingly picked a female deputy, he also rebuked the female caucus by reminding them that it took the opinion of two women to equal that of one man.

"That may happen in a country like Afghanistan," you may be

thinking, "but surely not in a democracy like the United States where women enjoy equal rights?" The answer begins in the US Constitution, which does not mention equal rights for women. The Equal Rights Amendment, most recently promulgated in the 1970s and 1980s, failed to pass because conservatives opposed changing the Constitution, even though many of them favor amendments to ban gay marriages, abortion, and flag burning. Among the industrialized nations only the United States has refused to ratify the UN Convention on the Elimination of All Forms of Discrimination Against Women (CEDAW), thus aligning itself with such strange bedfellows as Brunei, Somalia, Sudan, and Oman. As Jessica Neuwirth, president of Equality Now, observes, "We've abdicated a leadership role in the single most important ongoing international women's rights process."

In 2005, the World Economic Forum ranked fifty-eight nations according to their "gender gaps," based on job opportunities, pay, political representation, healthcare, and education for females. Sweden, Norway, and Iceland, often and rightly called the "mother countries," topped the list. The United States came in seventeenth; Egypt last.

If you still think one woman equals one man in the United States, look at who holds the reins of power. Who enacts laws and decides on the allocation of resources? Who heads your company or organization? Your local, state, and federal government? Your church? Who heads countries around the world? With few exceptions, you will find men at the helm. They do a spectacular job, don't they? As former prime minister of Canada Kim Campbell put it, "Lest you think that all we aspire to for the world can be accomplished by male-dominated organizations, I have only to say to you: Enron, Taliban, the Roman Catholic Church."

We saw in the last chapter how women's wisdom has so often been discredited, their voices silenced, and their authority undermined, placing them in subordinate positions in society. Here we will look at how inequality persists, how sex discrimination continues to hold women back in spite of all the obvious progress women have made (the subject of the next chapter). We will see women display courageous vulnerability as they strive to overcome these deeply embedded prejudices and stereotypes that still impede women from realizing their full potential as leaders simply because they are women. We will also look at the generation gap that exists between women on these issues.

STAND UP TO SEX DISCRIMINATION

You may be thinking to yourself, "Sex discrimination, equality? Aren't we over that by now?" No, we're not. Unfortunately, sex discrimination and misogyny are alive and well, and still thrive so virulently that I feel compelled to wave a red flag. Remember Don Imus's ill-advised reference to the Rutger's basketball team as "nappy-headed hos?" That was not a joke; it was the tip of a veritable iceberg of gender bias and misogyny. It happens every day. For instance, a police sergeant in Brooklyn called three women officers "hos" when he ordered them to stand up. The women, two black and one Latina, refused to stand, decided to fight back, and hired a lawyer after higher-ups brushed aside their complaint about the sergeant's behavior. "Just words," some might say. But contrary to the old adage, words can wound us, especially when they signal disrespect or, worse, a deep and abiding prejudice.

Even worse than hurtful words and insulting behavior, sex discrimination impedes women from fully exercising the feminine leadership skills the world so desperately needs right now. Author of *Female Advantage* Sally Helgesen made this point clear at the Simmons 2003 Leadership Conference in Boston, a stellar event celebrating women leaders. "When my book was published in 1990, it was apparent to me that the economic, demographic, and technological changes we were living through were going to make women's gifts and strengths even more appropriate. The changes that have occurred have been more rapid than could have been predicted in 1990, more far-reaching, and the skills that women bring are more appropriate than they have ever been. And yet women's progress has not been commensurate with that."

If women have all these skills, why haven't more of us achieved positions of power? We will grapple with the answer to this complex question throughout the book, but here I want to draw attention to one cause: sex discrimination.

Baby boomers like Marsha Firestone know about sex discrimination. President and founder of Women's President Organization, a group that provides supportive and educational environment for business owners, Marsha grew up in a middle-class, entrepreneurial family. Coming up against limitations because she was a girl infuriated her.

> I was eleven years old and every night after dinner, my mother would instruct me to help clear the table and wash and dry the dishes. Meanwhile, my brother would go out and play football. I was just furious about the inequality. I asked "Why?" My mother said, "Because he's a

boy and you're a girl. And boys don't have to take care of a house." Now the irony of that is that my mother was in business with my father and she always worked every day and helped in every way, but she didn't get the credibility or the visibility for what she was contributing. And I decided that was unfair, and one of the things that makes me madder than hell is injustice. That has really stuck with me through my life.

After Marsha graduated with honors from Sophie Newcombe College of Tulane University, she wanted to apply to law school. During an interview, the dean of admissions asked her, "You have a boyfriend, don't you?" She said, "Yes, I do." He said, "Why should I give this spot to you when I can give it to some guy who can support his family? You're just going to get married and have babies anyway." Reflecting on this event, Marsha said, "I was a straight-A student and had been involved in a lot of leadership activities at school. I was rejected, I did not get in."

While Marsha never did make it to law school, she did earn her PhD in communication from Columbia University and went on to help other women fulfill their dreams by creating a supportive environment. But you wonder, what if Marsha hadn't been stopped because of her gender?

Today, sex discrimination exists at all levels of society, and even in the most prestigious institutions. The former president of Harvard University, Lawrence Summers, speaking at a conference on women and minorities in science and engineering in January 2005, attributed women's lack of success in science and math to the fact that they bring less innate ability to these disciplines. Given that stereotype, it's not surprising that, under his leadership, only four out of fifty-four tenured jobs in the Faculty of Arts and Science were offered to women. Nancy Hopkins, a biologist at MIT and a main force behind a study documenting inequalities for women at MIT, walked out of that January conference, upset to see brilliant young women at Harvard being led by a man who viewed them in that way. Although Summers later apologized for his failed "attempt to be provocative," it did little to placate the outrage among women and men alike, although the fiasco prompted a study into the size of the gender gap and did stimulate a more than $50 million commitment over the next decade to increase opportunities for women and minorities in the Harvard faculty and science programs. Ultimately, it also prompted Summers's early departure from his post.

The brouhaha at Harvard also brought out the counterforces who support discrimination against women. Summers's defenders, labeling him a victim of political correctness, argued that he was merely provoking fresh ideas. Fresh idea? How did we come full circle from an old stereotype of women as innately inferior to men in math or science to it being classified as a fresh idea? Scientists may not know about the innate differences between men and women, but women do know all about the attitudes that can hold them back. As Barbara Grosz, chair of the Harvard task force on women in science and engineering, said, "The criticism of Summers's talk was not that the ideas he expressed were politically incorrect, but that they were just plain incorrect."

Grosz's statement proved to be all too true. In 2008, the Center of Work-Life Policy reported the results of a study it conceived in response to Summers's assertion that women lacked what it took to excel in science, engineering, and technology (SET). The problem isn't that women aren't making strides in education in the hard sciences, where, for example, 46 percent of PhDs are awarded to women. And it isn't that women aren't entering the SET in sizable numbers, where 41 percent of the earliest rungs of the career ladder were women. And it isn't due to poor performance. The study found that 75 percent of the performance reviews of women between the ages of twenty-five to twenty-nine described them as "superb," "excellent," or "outstanding," words used for only 61 percent of men in the same age group. In spite of this, an exodus occurred among women between the ages of thirty-five and forty: 52 percent dropped out. The reason, the study concluded, was a macho culture where women were perceived as simply not being as good in math and science as men. The report was filled with tales of sexual harassment, dismissive attitudes, a lack of mentors, and hours that suit men with wives who are not working mothers. "It's almost a time warp," said Sylvia Ann Hewlett, the founder of the center. "All the predatory and demeaning and discriminatory stuff that went on in workplaces twenty, thirty years ago is alive and well in these professions." And then in 2008, the National Science Foundation did a study of math scores of seven million students in ten states and found that girls were on par with boys. Girls, it turns out, do not lack a math gene, nor is there an "intrinsic" difference between the abilities of boys and girls as Summers suggested.

There may not be inequality, but discrimination, unfortunately, is alive and well. Take just one year, 2004, for example.

- An unprecedented sex discrimination suit was filed against Wal-Mart Stores Inc. by 1.6 million former and current female employees, charging that the company paid them lower wages than men and bypassed them on promotions and job training.
- Wall Street Morgan Stanley (now Morgan Stanley Smith Barney),

the world's second-largest security firm, paid $54 million to settle a sex discrimination suit that involved 340 former and current women employees who complained they were denied promotions and were victims of lewd behavior. Just minutes before Allison Schieffelin, who filed the complaint, was to tell her story, Morgan Stanley made a deal in which the company gained ownership of her story and sealed the facts under maximum security, effectively silencing Schieffelin from revealing how the company treated women on the job there. It is striking how unapologetic Morgan Stanley was, a trend among many companies, never admitting wrongdoing, never saying they are sorry, never holding themselves personally accountable for impeding women's growth. It's as if they throw women a bone to shut them up, rather than seriously address the changes the company needs to make in order to bring fairness to the workplace, changes that will ultimately benefit the organization as a whole. Proving my point, three years later, in 2007, Morgan Stanley again settled another class-action suit for $64 million. This settlement would not only increase the wages of women brokers but also would automate the distribution of accounts to avoid gender bias.

Wall Street is one of the most male-dominated bastions in business. It could use an infusion of women and a feminine ethic of care and responsibility, given the financial meltdown that began in 2008. In support of that view, that same year, the *Journal of Evolution and Human Behavior* reported a study that found men are particularly likely to make high-risk bets when under financial pressure and surrounded by males of similar status.

- Costco, a wholesale company with a reputation as the most worker-friendly retailer in the country because it pays higher wages and offers better benefits, is being sued for sex discrimination. Shirley Ellis, who filed the suit, claimed that the warehouse club chain engaged in systematic discrimination because only 17 percent of its top manager positions are held by women, while 50 percent of its employees are women. Frustrated at getting stuck in a number two position, Ellis decided to help women get their fair share of management positions, the most important and highest-paying jobs. In 2007 the Court granted permission for the suit to proceed as a class action suit.

The success of the lawsuits should encourage all women to not be afraid to stand up and speak out when they feel they are being treated differently. Equality will never happen until women receive their fair share of the power and the economic benefits in our society. Otherwise, not even the most determined of Iron Butterflies will be able to change herstory into a different story for the Era of Women.

DEMAND ECONOMIC EQUALITY

Remember little Ada Aharoni who opened this chapter? Even at a tender age of seven, she tried to change the story of limiting women's potential. For a while, Ada's family lived in Egypt with Ada's paternal grandmother, Esther. Her mother, who loved playing the piano, made a little income for herself as a piano teacher. Esther would criticize her daughter-in-law for this, telling her to stop playing the "blasted thing," and shouting, "Your husband is coming home from work. Come on, go cook for your husband!" She would seize any opportunity to belittle Ada's mother, which would infuriate the willful Ada, especially when her mother bore this treatment in silence, bemoaned her fate, and fled to her room to cry. Ada herself refused to succumb to such a destiny vowing, "You make your fate."

When her father, whose first wife had died, forced her mother to sell the piano, arguing that a married woman did not need her own money, Ada watched the demise of her mother's spirit. When Ada told her that she was going to go to work when she grew up, her mother said, "But you will be a woman, and they don't allow women to work in this country." That didn't phase Ada at all. One day she would, she promised her mother, buy her a house and a piano.

The more grandmother Esther mistreated Ada's mother, the angrier Ada grew. One day seething with rage, the young girl went to visit her cousin and told her that grandmother Esther poisoned Ada's father's first wife! That story went straight back to her grandmother. "So little," she screamed at Ada, "and already a viper. Bad girl! I don't want to see you in this house again." Crying, Ada pleaded with her mother to move out. Surprisingly, her mother gave her husband an ultimatum. Either he make arrangements for Ada and she to live in their own house or the two of them would move to her mother's. When her father said he couldn't afford two houses, Ada's mother stood her ground, and before long Ada and she were knocking on the door of grandmother Regina's house.

When grandmother Regina opened the door and saw the two of them standing there with their bags, she exclaimed, "What? You want to come and live here? I can't keep you in this one room, with my sick husband,

and I just have a very small pension. Be smart. Go back." And with that, she closed the door.

The two sat on the stairs all night. Ada's mother cried, longing for her lost piano. Why had she let the man sell it? With it she could have given lessons and earned enough money to rent a room. Grandmother Regina would, from time to time, open the door and exclaim, "You're still here?!? Go back to Esther." Eventually grandmother Regina sat down on the stoop with them and joined in the lamentation. In the end, however, knowing they could not sit their forever, Ada and her mother returned to Esther's. Eventually, Ada's mother convinced her husband to move. As Ada recalled, "Why did my father agree to go? Because, in the meantime, my mother had given him a son."

Complete economic dependence on men at the price of personal freedom has plagued most women until very recent times. The colonial United States, following the law of mother England, placed women's property under the control of their husbands, and not until 1900 did married women hold any substantial rights with respect to their own property. And this is in "the land of the free and the home of the brave!"

Women have made certain strides economically, but we have not, nor should we pretend we have, attained full economic equality. Even today in the United States, when a man makes a dollar, a woman makes seventy-six cents, and the amount is even less for African American women, Asian women, and Latinas, according to the Institute of Women's Policy Research. Another study performed by the same Institute showed that, in actuality, women, over the course of their careers, earn 44 percent of what a typical man makes, a fact that underscores the labor market's discriminatory treatment of women. At the rate of progress achieved between 1989 and 2002, women wouldn't achieve equality for more than fifty years, a hundred years after President Kennedy signed the Equal Pay Act into law in 1963. The same holds true in the United Kingdom. Thirty years after legislation guaranteed equal pay for women, a woman continues to earn 87 pence for every pound a man earns; and part-time women workers earn 59 pence per hour for every pound a full-time male worker receives.

This pay differential produces long-reaching effects, as Teresa Heinz, chairman of the Heinz Family Philanthropies, pointed out: "Lower wages leave women with less to save or contribute to an employer's retirement plan, and only 30 percent of all older women can count on a pension, compared with 47 percent of men. In addition, more that half of all women sixty-five or older are widowed, divorced, or never married. On average, these older women rely on Social Security for 71 percent of their income, compared with 64 percent for men in similar circumstances."

No wonder a recent survey by the Heinz Family Philanthropies showed that more than 40 percent of women ages twenty-five to fifty-five fear they will live their retirement years at or near poverty level. Heinz concluded, "America shouldn't be a nation where a lifetime of work can leave a woman poor."

We also see economic discrimination in the global feminization of poverty, where, according to the Global Fund for Women, 70 percent of the 1.6 billion people living in extreme poverty are women and children.

All those cold, hard facts should propel us to stand for fairness and speak up whenever we witness wage discrimination. For instance, in 2008 the Supreme Court ruled in the Lilly Ledbetter case that a worker has to sue within six months after her first unequal pay. This means if a company pays you less for the same work and can keep the wool over your eyes for six months, you can't sue them when you find out you've been discriminated against. Congress tried to restore some protection, but Republicans balked because, as Senator John McCain stated, it would open us up to lawsuits for all kinds of problems. So should we worry about too many lawsuits rather than preventing discrimination that generates those law suits? President Obama didn't think so when on January 29, 2009, he signed the Lilly Ledbetter Fair Pay Act, which supersedes the Supreme Court decision and states that each paycheck that delivers discriminatory compensation is a wrong actionable regardless of when the discrimination began. If you or someone you know has done the job and put in the time, yet takes home a paycheck smaller than a man's, both men and women should object.

The principle doesn't just apply to the workplace. It applies to the economy of the household, where women provide the lion's share of care-giving and the economy of volunteer community building, none of which involves the exchange of hard currency, even though the work required to sustain these endeavors is as valuable as any paid work on the planet. According to the UN Development Program (UNDP) Human Development Report, more than two-thirds of the world's unpaid work is done by women, the equivalent of $11 trillion, or almost 50 percent of the world GDP, yet women receive only 10 percent of the world's income and own an astonishing 1 percent of the means of production. As Riane Eisler said in a 2008 interview with Peace x Peace, "The fact that human capital is largely produced in households is completely ignored in conventional indicators like the GDP. Yet people and nature are the real wealth of nations. So we must give visibility and value to caring for people and nature."

HOLD ON TO THE DESIRE FOR WHOLENESS

Barbara Kingsolver, esteemed and world-renowned author and environmentalist, grew up in rural bluegrass Kentucky, where nothing in her world suggested that a mere girl could ever become a writer, or much of anything except a wife, mother, or daughter. But the unyielding desire that helped her find her way was, as she recalls, "A person wants to be whole."

This girl in search of wholeness grew up in a very poor community abutting Appalachia. Although her father was a doctor, a rural doctor does not get wealthier than his patients, who often as not paid for his services with chickens and baked beans. Still, Barbara didn't lack her heart's desire: books and more books. But she longed for a life beyond rural Kentucky.

Remembering high school, Barbara said to me:

> I saw so much self-destructive behavior all around me with the girls in high school. I realized I was not the only one thinking I was worthless. I was just too scared to act on it as thoroughly as they were. It wasn't because it was a poor community that I had this insatiable hunger to get away; it was that the prospects seemed so limited. And I thought if I got out of there I might have better chances, but I was really afraid that it might not be true. As far as I could see, all the important things were being done by men.

Even she felt depressed and devalued.

Barbara did dream, however. She wanted to write even though she didn't think she was allowed to be a writer. Was there some place where she could write to her heart's content and make a living from her work, some place far away from a world where most girls ended up barefoot and pregnant?

Fortunately for Barbara Kingsolver and her million of readers, she did break free, find that wholeness she longed for, and do something truly magical and amazing, her writing. "I'm lucky that there was nothing that really overwhelmed or stopped me like the 50 percent of my classmates. I wish a woman could have been there, though, someone who could have said to me, 'You, little girl in the second row, you can do something magical and amazing.'"

Unlike Barbara's, too many baby boomers' stories do not end up with a dream fulfilled. Dr. Justina Trott, director of Policy, Research, and Education at Women's Health Services, in Santa Fe, New Mexico, a Robert wood Johnson Health Policy Fellow, and chair of the New Mexico Governor's Health Advisory Council grew up in an Italian household, a typical male-dominated, female-run household where her mother wasn't allowed to work outside the home. Although Justina loved playing music and wanted to take piano lessons, her father would only pay for accordion lessons. It made no sense to her. She nagged and finally convinced him to buy an old upright for seventy-five dollars. "I would go down in the basement and play piano for hours," Justina told me. "I never had lessons, so I had to make everything up. I composed things because I knew how to read music from being in the school band and choir."

A proficient student, Justina wanted to go to college. Her father thought she should take a job as a secretary and then get married. "Second-generation people, like myself, usually are very ambivalent because in order to do what you want, you have to leave your family. It's a really big thing." When Justina confronted her father and told him she was going to college, he vehemently objected, but in the end he said, "Go. But you're on your own. Don't look for any help from me."

Justina confided to me:

> I remember the day I made up my mind to go to college. I was with a friend, telling him it would be a struggle, but I was going. He asked what I wanted to major in. I said, "I want to become a conductor." He innocently said, "I don't know any women conductors." I just remember being totally silent, not knowing what to say. Hearing him say this, although he was a very supportive friend, made me think, maybe this is not possible. Effectively I shut down the creative part of me. I started to think I was not good enough. I felt the attainable for me was hard-core science.

Without anything to support her own heart's desire, Justina, like many women in similar situations, began to doubt herself, undermining her self-confidence and her dream. Nonetheless, Justina did go on to accomplish great things with her life as a successful medical doctor specializing in women's health. But I just can't help imagining her waving a baton before a philharmonic orchestra. After all, her dream was not foolish or impossible, just a long time coming. During the 1998–1999 season, JoAnn Falletta became the director of the Buffalo Philharmonic Orchestra, claiming the title of first woman conductor. And then not until 2007 did we see a woman conductor, Marin Alsop, take her place with the Baltimore Symphony Orchestra.

I tell these stories because they illustrate our recent past, not some long-lost, dim era of inequality. Baby boomers know firsthand about sexual discrimination, having personally felt the limitations that can stymie a woman's longing for wholeness. They ended up making compromises—and compromises, after all, make good umbrellas, but they make poor roofs. Many younger women have not experienced this overt discrimination simply because they haven't yet climbed high enough on the ladder to hit today's slightly higher glass ceiling. Being told all options are open to them, they can be more idealistic and think they are living in a post-feminist era where gender doesn't matter. They may need to think again.

To see just one example of what I'm talking about, consider a 2006 American Bar Association report. A young woman lawyer should think twice about her future in her chosen profession. Forty-eight percent of law degrees were awarded to women as compared to 52 percent for men. That's progress to be sure. Yet only 17 percent of women hold partnerships in major law firms compared to 83 percent of men. Only 15 percent are federal judges and only 10 percent of law school deans are women. A 2007 study by the MIT Workplace Center in conjunction with other bar associations revealed that female lawyers face intractable challenges in their attempts to become partners, causing them to abandon law firm careers, and even the legal profession all together, at a dramatically higher rate than men. Even when they do make it to the top, women lawyers are paid less than their male counterparts. According to a 2006 survey done by the National Association of Women Lawyers (NAWL), a $90,000 annual pay disparity exists between male and female equity partners. What are the consequences of fewer women ascending to leadership positions? The pool of women qualified to become judges, law professors, business chiefs, and law firm managers shrinks. The inflexible schedules, the demanding drive for billable hours, and the total disregard for a family-work balance contribute to this trend. If it continues in this direction, women will lose ground, and all of us who might need a capable lawyer will be the losers.

Discrimination has also taken on more subtle forms in the legal workplace, as Lauren Stiller Rikleen, senior partner at Bowditch & Dewey in Framingham, Massachusetts, told the *Boston Globe* in October 2003: "Discrimination is still a barrier. Female associates do not have the same access as male associates to mentors, to high-profile or high-end projects or cases, or to the business development opportunities inside the firm." When women must operate outside the buddy system and do not gain valuable experience from winning and losing high-risk, tough assignments, they do not develop their knowledge skills as much as their male colleagues. In some ways, they are set up to fail by the time they get to the level where they have the potential for senior leadership.

And of course, there is the Supreme Court, where Ruth Ginsberg stood alone as the only woman after Sandra Connors retired and before Sonia Sotomayor was appointed. Given the fact that women make up 52 percent of the US population, and receive half of the law degrees, shouldn't we have an equal number of women deciding the law of our common land?

BE A PROUD FEMINIST

Barbara Kingsolver took a major step toward her dream when she left the hills of Kentucky and went away to college. There she discovered feminism and its language for framing the oppression of women and the limited opportunities it created. She devoured works by Gloria Steinem, Robin Morgan, and Germaine Greer.

> There was this whole world of women who were working on this issue, who were thinking about the same things when I thought I was the only one thinking about them. I was part of them and I could never go back to being ignorant. There was no turning back; it was the feeling of finding religion for me. It was an awakening, and the transformation was rapid and complete.

Through feminism, Barbara learned that other women shared her longing for wholeness. Hers was not a lonely and unique quest after all. How comforting and inspiring it must have been to connect to a community of like-minded thinkers who gave her the support and encouragement she needed to realize her dream.

As with other women's issues, times have both changed and not changed on college campuses. First of all, academia has not unburdened itself of sex discrimination. According to a 2006 National Academies report, women faculty members in science, math, and engineering generally receive lower pay, follow a slower track to promotion, are rewarded fewer honors, and hold fewer leadership positions than their male colleagues. The report states that "these discrepancies do not appear to be based on productivity, the significance of their work, or any other performance measure." I call that gender discrimination, though the report chalked it up, rather euphemistically, as stemming "from a number of issues that are firmly rooted in our society's traditions and culture."

According to a report by the American Association of University Women (AAUW), women hold lower-ranking positions in academia, earn lower salaries, and are less likely to win tenure, even though women constitute more than half of college and university instructors and lecturers across the country, and nearly half of all assistant professors. In spite of this, only one-third of associate professors are women and only 27 percent of tenured professors are women. Why? According to the AAUW, unclear standards and biased decision making infects the tenure process.

But you can't ignore the good news. Women now head major universities such as Princeton, MIT, Brown, Harvard, and others. These women display a more feminine leadership style that wins admiration from faculty and students, both male and female. For instance, Harvard president Drew Gilpin Faust's nonconfrontational, welcoming style and spirit of openness has brought stability to a campus rocked by Lawrence Summers's stormy arrogance.

But what about the female students? When Barbara discovered feminism, it was an "awakening"; she could never go back to not knowing the injustices women face. Do female college students still experience such an awakening? Maybe, maybe not. For instance, when Shirley Tilghman was appointed president of Princeton University, she actively promoted women to dean positions at a majority of the schools at the university. Consequently, she has brought greater gender balance to positions of power in her institution, a move that has sent a positive signal about women's leadership capabilities. But how did some alumni respond? "Why don't we just call it Princesston?" A local paper, the *Daily Princetonian*, suggested that Tilghman had imported gender-based affirmative action to the Ivy League school. In other words, since women cannot lead as effectively as men, this was the only possible way you could justify appointing a woman. It surprised Tilghman when the women on campus did not rise up to protest this implication. "Have these young women internalized the idea that women really do not lead?" she asked. "There was a time when that kind of thinking would have inspired outrage." Yes, where is the outrage? Have younger women internalized the notion that women make inferior leaders, reverting to some sort of 1950s style of prefeminism?

Professor Lynn Layton teaches a women's studies seminar on psychoanalysis and gender at Harvard. The course includes a relationally oriented approach to women's psychology. When she began teaching about masculine development and its propensity for autonomy, she was met with a surprise. One of her women students raised her hand and said she could finally relate to something. She related more easily to male development rather than female descriptions of development. Are women unknowingly swallowing and accepting a masculine autonomy at a cost to their feminine side? Are women internalizing messages that they should act and think more like men, because doing so will get them more securely on the path to power and acceptance? Do they not realize the danger of this subtle dismissal of feminine skills and perspective? Do they not recognize it as profound discrimination?

Associate Professor Rhonda Garelick of Connecticut College fears that the fires of feminism may have burned down to ashes under the influence of careerism. As she watches her female students display a general lack of reflection and critical thinking with respect to gender issues and biases, it appears as if they take equality for granted. Have these young women realized that the dominant male-centered groups are getting most of the resources and defining most of the priorities and policies, and just accepted that without questioning its negative effect on women's priorities? Do they see that the powerful define the events and the powerless have to go along and get along with rules written to benefit the powerful?

Without question, younger women enjoy more options than ever, but as we've seen in this discussion on discrimination, we have not reached the ultimate destination of full equality. Expanded options reflect the hard-won battles of feminism, which opened doors for equal access to education and job opportunities. I have to say my jaw dropped when I read twenty-something Sara Kliff write: "A female president does not seem like change. . . . Now in our early twenties, most of us have not yet made any trade-offs between family and career; we're doctors, investment bankers, and lawyers in training. That makes a female president seem hardly revolutionary or cool." Obviously, young Sara has not climbed high enough. How quickly we forget how women struggled. When I hear younger women insist they are not feminists or even disdain and dissociate themselves from feminism, I scratch my head in wonder. What are they thinking? Exactly who has succeeded in pigeonholing feminists as hairy-legged, man-hating harpies, or as conservative pundit Rush Limbaugh has labeled them, "femi-nazis?" The media? Right-wing radio commentators? Men who dislike or fear women? Women who dare not offend men? All of the above? Genderless humanism will elude us all until we add a fully realized feminism to it.

And it's not only younger women distancing themselves from feminism; I've seen the ambivalence in older women when asked if they are feminists. "One of the more ironic spectacles," writes author and columnist Anna Quindlen, "is listening as conservative women trash the women's movement, the movement that made their lives as activist lawyers, lobbyists, and pundits possible." Have we forgotten Gloria Steinem's definition of feminism? "A feminist is anyone who recognizes the equality and full humanity of women and men." I really like the definition

Timothy Lassonde, a pipe fitter for a mechanical engineering company in New Hampshire, told me, "Feminism has been portrayed as a male-bashing, self-centered, and fanatical underground cult. It's anything but that. As global ecosystems merge in the twenty-first century, women's role in leadership will emerge to become the savior of humankind." Isn't it time to reclaim the f-word?

Or do we fall into the complacency decried by Susan Faludi, author of *Backlash*, when she spoke at Radcliffe College in 2005, "Women were passionate about changing society. This is what jumps out at you when you look at 1974. . . . In comparison, we now seem relatively complacent—not the next wave of feminism, but the receding trough after the wave has crashed."

Have we come to a point in our materialistic society where we prefer comfort and complacency over discomforting change? The very successful thirty-year-old Paula Carrico, a vice president in investment banking told me, "The previous generation of women had a clear objective of what they wanted to achieve for women. They paved the way for us. But my generation is less clear of what we want. Maybe we are just more comfortable with what we have, so we have no clear agenda as to what we need to achieve as women."

Do we stop and settle on the plateau we have reached? Deborah Rhode, professor of law at Stanford University, fears we might. "The central problem is the lack of consensus that there is a significant problem. Gender inequalities in leadership opportunities are pervasive; perceptions of inequality are not. There is a widespread belief that full equity is just around the corner." Have we resigned ourselves to "that's just the way it is"? As twenty-something Jenny told me, "It's almost as if women have resigned themselves to being 'almost equal?'" Come on, girlfriends! Do we really want to discriminate against ourselves? Do we want to live in George Orwell's barnyard where "all pigs are equal, but some pigs are more equal than others?"

When Senator Barbara Boxer spoke at the 2004 Democratic Convention, she said, "Women have to fight and work for our freedom, and every generation has to do it again. If you want freedom, we cannot rest." We cannot rest and turn a blind eye to sex discrimination or whitewash inequities against women or take for granted the gains we have made. We women of all generations cannot rest by accepting discrimination as the unbreakable norm, and dominance and the injustices as the natural order of things. We cannot rest until we realize author Riane Eisler's vision that reinstating women and feminine values to a central and social and spiritual place is the single most critical issue of our time.

I do believe that complacency and resignation are real issues for women, of all ages. However, I am excited to see younger women making feminism more accessible with magazines such as *Bitch*, *Bust*, *Bamboo Girl Zine*, and *Make/shift*, whose subtitle is "feminisms in motion," meaning feminism shouldn't have a single voice but rather should take lots of different forms. Danielle Maestretti, who posts on ninety feminist blogs, absolutely agrees and made this observation: "Thousands of people are maintaining their own mini-feminisms, writing about whatever they deem important. Some think that reproductive health is the day's most critical issue. Others write about pop culture, or parenting, or sexual violence, or science fiction. Moving from one voice, one subject, one discussion to another, it's clear that today's feminism is about everything." And that includes eight-year-old girls. *New Moon*, a fifteen-year-old feminist magazine for girls eight to fifteen, has hit the Internet and started a new online community.

I also admire the younger feminists such as Jennifer Baumgardner and Amy Richards who, in their book *Manifesta* published in 2000, rethought feminist goals to engage the minds and hearts of Generation X. They also elucidated a concern that there was a disconnection between generations of women in the feminist movement, that older women were not seeing younger women's accomplishments and activism. Lisa Jervis, cofounder and publisher of *Bitch: Feminist Response to Pop Culture*, who describes herself in the demographic of third wave responded to this generational disconnect in this way:

> This is what we need to recognize so that we can all move on: Those in their 20s and 30s who don't see their concerns reflected in the feminism of the elders are ignorant of history; those in their 50s and beyond who think that young women aren't politically active—or active enough, or around the right issues—don't know where to look. We all want the same thing: we want gender justice.

I like the scene in the movie *One True Thing* in which the mother, played by Meryl Streep, is talking to her rebellious daughter about true happiness. "Your father always tells me 'Less is more.' It's not. 'More is more.'" When it comes to gender equality, whether we are first-wave, second-wave, third-wave feminists, post-feminists, angry feminists, or shoulder-pad feminists, we should never settle for less.

We can all follow the example set by Janice Cook, an artist living in London, who told me, "I will fight people's automatic decision about what a woman is, what a woman should be doing. I will fight against women's power, women's intelligence being manipulated. It isolates me at times, but there is strength and integrity when you are isolated, because you start to know who you are, what is true for you, and what you believe in. It's about establishing yourself with yourself." But let's not do it in isolation. Mothers, daughters, sisters, aunts, grandmothers, let us join together to achieve nothing less than a social transformation that eradicates the phrase "almost equal."

Chapter 4

CHOICES

Pursue Your Passion

Gussy up your makeup, put on your shoulder pads, start your engines, and get into third gear, because, ladies, we are on a mission!

Barbara Mikulski, Democratic Senator from Maryland
at the Democratic Convention 2004

I agree with the honorable Elijah Muhammad when he said, "A nation can rise no higher than its women." If women cannot fully participate in every aspect of society, that society wastes at least half of its potential talent. Whenever women exercise their right to participate in society and pursue their passions, they make significant inroads into traditionally male dominated professions. Just a few decades ago, women who aspired to a professional career could only aim their sights at traditionally female pursuits such as being teachers, nurses, or librarians. The women's movement opened the pathway for women to enter male-dominated professions, jobs that usually paid better salaries, had better benefits, and held more respect and prestige.

As women headed into more lucrative and prestigious positions, such as doctors, lawyers, and business executives, the numbers of nurses, teachers, and librarians dwindled, although women still dominate these professions. With more and more women entering once male-dominated realms, will more and more men enter the once female-dominated ones? Hardly, according to Karen Nussbaum, director of the Working Women Department of the AFL-CIO, "It's not worth it to them," she said. "The pay is too low and the work is too hard." If in the Era of Women, we as a nation were to value and pay properly for the contributions these activities make to society, such jobs would acquire the respect they so fully deserve. If we respect and reward our caregivers, nurturers, and teachers as much as we do our sports heroes, attorneys and CEOs, we'll create a better world for all.

Of course, that will require a greater obliteration of gender bias than has yet occurred, even in the wake of the women's movement. To make it in a man's professional world in the 1980s, a woman found greater acceptance if she acted more like a man. However, developing their masculine side usually exacted a high price in terms of lost feminine power, attributes, and skills. Even today business books like *Seducing the Boy's Club* by Nina Disesa urge women to manipulate men as if that is the only way a woman can assert her power.

Still, we cannot ignore the progress we have made. More and more women are entering the old male sanctuaries without leaving their femininity at the door. More and more women are exiting the old corporate male bastion to launch their own entrepreneurial enterprises where they are assured of getting a fair wage. Either way, women's presence is transforming the professional landscape. With their growing participation, the antiquated career paradigm keeps shifting toward a greater balance of power in the workplace.

In the previous chapter we discussed women breaking into the areas of law and academia. Here we will restrict our exploration to progress women have made in the realms of politics, sports, the media, and business. We will also encounter the resistance they face as they challenge the status quo, and we will witness their courageous vulnerability as they press on and pursue their passions.

SECURE THE BALLOT BOX

Women began grumbling about their lack of political participation in colonial times when Abigail Adams implored her husband and future president John Adams to "remember the ladies." While Adams was drafting the Declaration of Independence with the Continental Congress in 1776, Abigail wrote to him pleading that the men put women on more equal footing.

"Do not put such unlimited power into the hands of husbands," she urged. "Remember all men would be tyrants if they could. John, I warn you that if particular care and attention are not paid to the ladies, we are determined to foment a rebellion, and will not hold ourselves bound by any laws in which we have no hand or representation." Of that bold declaration, journalist Eleanor Clift asserts in her book *Founding Sisters and the Nineteenth Amendment*, "Maybe we can credit pillow talk for the gender-neutral language of the Declaration of Independence. . . . It [the Declaration] established democratic principles upon which the suffrage movement was based."

Later on in our history, women waded into the political pool as abolitionists, fighting against the evils of slavery. In the wake of this work, women like Elizabeth Cady Stanton birthed the suffragist movement when they championed the cause for women's civil rights. Its adherents finally fomented the rebellion Abigail Adams had promised, insisting on their right to vote, to obtain an education, and to influence governmental and legislative decisions that affected their lives. At the same time such demands represented radical thinking. Who could have imagined that women would get involved in politics as something more than mere extensions of their husbands? Even in the years shortly after the suffragist movement began in 1848, women didn't imagine themselves as leaders, given the strict taboo against women speaking in public or attending universities. There were no women's organizations to support any brave woman who might wish to violate such taboos. When I talked to Dr. Eileen Hoffman, a physician and author of *Our Health, Our Lives*, she summed up the attitude toward women during this time in this way:

> There was a theory called the zero-sum energy theory that said there was only so much energy in the system, and for a female, it had to be used for reproduction. If you used it for something else, it would make you sterile. This sexist pseudoscience said that mental exertions would draw blood away from women's ovaries. This allowed doctors to play a big role in preventing women from getting higher education in the eighteenth century. Scientific studies showed that the majority of inmates in insane asylums were women, which has always been true, and a majority of them had some degree of higher education. So not only would she go sterile if a woman used her brain, but she would also go crazy!

The struggle for women's right to vote met with enormous resistance, abuse, and sacrifice. When the suffragists picketed Woodrow Wilson's White House for the right to vote, they were wrongly arrested for obstructing sidewalk traffic, and they fought and kicked all the way to the jail cell. Forty-three prison guards wielding clubs went on a rampage against thirty-three women during what came to be called the "Night of Terror" on November 15, 1917. The warden at Occoquan Workhouse in Virginia had ordered his guards to teach a lesson to the suffragists. They beat Lucy Burn and left her hanging with her hands above her head chained to cell bars. They hurled Dora Lewis into a dark cell, smashing her head against an iron bed and knocking her out cold. Her cellmate, Alice Cosu, assuming that Lewis was dead, suffered a heart attack. When one of the leaders, Alice Paul, embarked on a hunger strike, the guards tied her to a chair, forced a tube down her throat, and poured liquid into her until she vomited.

Honoring their courage, a young Katherine Hepburn presented the "Jailed for Freedom" pins to the eighty-one suffragists who suffered so much for all their American sisters. The HBO movie *Iron Jawed Angels* brilliantly depicts the battle these women waged so that all women could have a voice in deciding who gets to set the rules. Reflecting on the courageous vulnerability of these women, Anna Quindlen wrote, "Those suffragists refused to be polite in demanding what they wanted or grateful for getting what they deserved. Works for me." Stanton worked for fifty years to win women's right to vote, and she died before she herself could reap the fruits of her labor. On August 18, 1920, the Nineteenth Amendment granted women the right to vote in all US elections.

But the battle did not end with that legislation. As late as 1962, Fannie Lou Hamer, the African American activist who said, "I'm sick and tired of being sick and tired," underwent similar abuse when she tried to exercise her right to vote. The granddaughter of slaves and the daughter of share-croppers, Hamer was shocked to discover, at the age of forty-four, that African Americans could, according to the Constitution, exercise the right to vote. When she went to register to vote, she was jailed, beaten, and left bleeding and battered in her cell. Afterward, even though she received constant death threats and actually got shot at, this Iron Butterfly boldly traveled around the country speaking out and registering African Americans to claim their civil right to vote.

For most of us, it's hard to imagine a time when women couldn't vote. Far from receiving this right as a natural benefit of birth in a great democracy, women, for seven plus decades, had to struggle long and hard to gain it. And not all women joined the battle. Some didn't particularly care if they could vote or not, and others vigorously opposed the movement for fear they would lose their special protections as the weaker sex. Even Susan B. Anthony, the woman who was most associated with the cause, felt extremely skeptical about it. Whatever lesson you take from this episode in American history, you can rest assured of two things. One, those who hold power will not give it up easily. We must always fight for change, and no matter how hard we fight for it, it will most likely come much more slowly and more painfully than we would like, but by the same token, once women and like-minded men stand together, we can achieve most anything. Two, never take your rights for granted.

Today we see women facing the same struggle in such places as Afghanistan. Before the election in October 2004, the Taliban worked to disrupt the balloting process, specifically targeting women with harassment and intimidation at polling centers. Two Afghan women were killed and thirteen wounded by a bomb that exploded on a bus filled with female election workers. Consequently, only a very courageous woman would venture to register.

In developed nations, the right-to-vote issue has evolved into the struggle to get women elected into public office. To paraphrase a famous ad, "we've come a long way, baby," from those suffragist days. Today we see women leading their countries: some recent examples are Michelle Bachelet of Chile, Ellen Johnson Sirleaf of Liberia, Mary McAleese of Ireland, Angela Merkel of Germany, Gloria Macapagal Arroyo of the Philippines, Tarja Halonen of Finland, Christina Fernandez de Kirchner of Argentina, Helen Clark of New Zealand, Luisa Diogo of Mozambique, Yulia Tyoshenko of Ukraine, Emily de Jongh-Elhage of Netherlands Antilles, and Pratibha Patil of India, and Tzipi Livni of Israel. Segolene Royal came close to becoming France's president. We also saw the price a pioneering woman political leader can pay when assassins struck down Benazir Bhutto, former prime minister of Pakistan. We should study and emulate this collection of accomplished and independent-thinking female leaders who amplify rather than hide their feminine values.

In the United States, Carol Moseley Braun, the first African American in the US Senate, ran for president in 2004, an undertaking that invited much more unforgiving scrutiny than her male opponents faced. Rather than welcoming a woman's perspective, political pundits smeared her campaign and the *New York Times* dismissed her attempt as a "vanity affair." Would the media say that about a man running for office? Her agenda would not be questioned if not for her gender.

And then, of course, there was Hillary Clinton and her very close run for the presidency. Hillary has described herself as "the Rorschach test" for people's assumptions and fears about powerful women. One thing did become clear during her bid for the presidency, and it applies to any woman who aspires to high office, and that is the fact that female candidates must deal with frustratingly restrictive gender stereotypes. Marie Wilson of the White House Project described the dilemma this way:

> Women struggle with the cultural paradox of packing the right stuff yet being the wrong sex to unpack it and put it to work. When a man leads with the same attributes, it's seen as formidable. In a woman, it's seen as weak. People complain that top women today often don't demonstrate collaborative traits. They can't. They are too busy proving they are man enough for the job. To succeed, they fit into the male model of "command-and-control" leadership, which in men is seen as heroic, and in women as hellish.

The ultimate irony came when her rival for the Democratic Party's nomination, Barack Obama, could get away with displaying a more feminine style of leadership for which Hillary was pilloried. Hillary knew she had to prove her "commander-in-chiefness" by playing the tough fighter in the race while Barack Obama could comfortably embrace a more collaborative, gentle, feminine approach that, when delivered by a mellifluous baritone, appeared to be more palatable.

Entering a man's world of politics requires a thick skin and an acrobat's sense of balance as US Representative Eddie Bernice Johnson of Texas can attest. Eddie Bernice Johnson holds many political firsts, including the first African American woman elected to any office in Dallas, the first African American woman representing Dallas in the Texas House, and the first woman Representative from Texas since former congresswoman Barbara Jordan, to name just a few. Being a black female from a southern state has been a political challenge for her from the beginning, especially when she first won office in 1972. For instance, the Dallas Chamber of Commerce would invite the Dallas County delegation for meetings, and assuming the group would consist of all men, they always had their get-togethers in men's clubs. When Eddie Bernice showed up at the private clubs, she was turned away. She held her ground though and came right back at them, declaring, "I have an invitation to this meeting; I am part of the delegation and you have an obligation to allow me in. In fact, I'm going in." She took that stand so often that eventually the chamber of commerce realized Eddie would not take no for an answer and changed locations for their meetings and even altered their policies. How did Eddie Bernice do it? "Just by showing up, not kicking up a lot of noise, but persisting, and it fell into place. Breaking ground is not a new experience for me," she told me.

It can be lonely. It can be frustrating. It can be intimidating and insulting. It has been all of that. I have tried very hard to continue to respect other people's opinions because I want them to respect mine. Women have to appear confident and strong in what they believe in; otherwise, they get talked out of it. I gained respect for being a person who insists on thinking for herself. If you initiate something that you feel you are entitled to, then you have a responsibility to set out and do it and you don't allow people to discourage you. If I became discouraged and stopped every time I've been challenged, I would still be trying to finish elementary school.

In spite of the obstacles women have already overcome, many still block the path to full political equality, and not just in third world countries. In terms of representation of women in politics, the United States, the supposed leader of the free world, ranks seventy-first in the world. Eighty-four nations boast a greater percentage of participating women, including both our neighbors, Mexico and Canada. Women hold only 13 percent of the seats in the US Senate and 15 percent in the House of Representatives. At this rate, it will take until 2354 before the United States reaches Sweden's 45 percent female representation. Guess who holds the world record for female representation? Rwanda, with women making up 49 percent of its lower houses of government. Ironically, after the overthrow of the Taliban in Afghanistan and Saddam Hussein in Iraq, the United States required that those countries reserve at least 25 percent of legislative seats for women, while we don't even have that here in the United States.

Fortunately, Iron Butterflies are addressing the need to increase women's presence in the political arena: Marie Wilson and the White House Project, a national, nonpartisan organization dedicated to advancing women's leadership at all political levels including the United States presidency, have among other things developed a political training program for women called Vote Run Lead; Revolutionary Women, an organization headed by Barbara Lee, campaigns for women candidates; Emily's List has been supporting women Democratic candidates for twenty-five years; Emerge provides training for Democratic women wanting to run for office; and former governor Christine Todd Whitman established the Whitman series in New Jersey, one of nineteen similar programs nationwide that provides women with leadership programs.

Statistics show that the majority of US presidents used a state governorship as a stepping-stone to the highest office, good news for women governors such as Kathleen Sebelius of Kansas and Janet Napolitano of Arizona, but still, we have only nine women governors.

Washington State has earned the distinction as the "girl" state because it elected, after a long protracted fight over the vote count, a woman to the state house, Governor Christine Gregoire. Two other women, Patty Murray and Maria Cantwell, represent Washington in the US Senate. Together the three have produced greater electoral gains for women per capita than in any state in the country.

These women also reflect a larger trend among women in politics: women run for office because they are issue driven, not ego driven. Nearly every woman in Congress, when she tells her personal story, the first thing she says is that she had no intention of running for office. Instead an issue or a movement led her into a more national role. For example, Senator Patty Murray, a homemaker, was so angry at the inadequacy of the education budget, she got herself elected to the state senate. Governor Christine Gregoire started her career as a clerk typist, put herself through law school, and became a crusading antitobacco attorney general. Most women with political power are there because of what they wanted to *do with* that power. Iron Butterflies don't want to *have* power, they want power *for* improving things and effecting a direction or outcome, which makes them less susceptible to corruption. A study by David Dollar, Raymond Fisman, and Roberta Gatti, sponsored by the World Bank, found from numerous behavioral studies that women are more trustworthy and public spirited than men, suggesting women should be particularly effective in promoting honest government and lower corruption.

When Murray and Cantwell ran for Senate, many people, not just men, discouraged them from pursuing their passion for politics. Why would sisters do that? Because they bought into the stupid myth that only a man should be doing that job. Time to retire that myth. If you do not desire a political office yourself, cheer on those who do. If you want to enter the political arena, don't let anyone discourage you; and if you win an election, never forget to reach back and help other women behind you.

Women in the town of Pittsfield, Massachusetts, provide a great example of women bringing each other along and together achieving success. Fed up with the all-male council and their bickering, local women created a political action group called WHEN—Women Helping Empower Neighborhoods. Putting all their strength behind three women candidates, they managed to get all three elected.

State and local politics could also use a little myth busting. Only 22 percent of state legislators are women. At the state level, female candidates often encounter such huge obstacles when trying to raise money and secure key endorsements that they must go outside the political system to garner support, which comes so much more easily to men. In my opinion, we should focus a lot more of our attention in terms of volunteering and contributing funds at this level and electing women locally because the women who win these offices have the opportunity to enter the pipeline to the national level. Here again we see a shifting tide when in 2008 New Hampshire was the first state to have a majority of women in the state senate.

Women's participation in political processes makes a difference in many ways, but perhaps in no more important way at this point in history than by shedding light on issues that men might not bring up. For instance, even in Afghanistan, a country still run by warlords—the mujahideen, who commit sexual abuses, violate human rights, and kidnap and traffic women and children—we see a thread of hope for women. Twenty-seven-year-old Malalai Joya, a member of the Afghan parliament, was elected as a representative of the Farah Province in 2005, winning with the highest number of votes among all candidates. Malalai rose to fame in 2003 when she won a seat on the Constitutional Loya Jirga, or tribal grand council, where she spoke out publicly against the domination of warlords, denouncing them as criminals who should be brought to justice rather than leading groups in discussing the Constitution. When she raised the issue of discrimination against women, her remarks stunned the audience and forced people to take notice of women's suffering under the mujahideen. However, as so often happens when a woman speaks out for justice, she paid a certain price for her courage. She has survived four assassination attempts and must travel in Afghanistan under a burqa and accompanied by armed guards. Malalai's courageous vulnerability, standing up for what is right at great personal risk, should inspire us all and serve as a guiding light for all women as they enter the political arena. Malalai spoke up not only for herself, not only for Afghan women, but for all of us. In spite of the threats, she held to her vision and her promise: "I swore to my people that one day I would raise their voice for them."

PLAY BALL

Andra Douglas makes her living as a freelance graphic artist in New York City, but she spends a lot of time pursuing another passion: football. She doesn't just watch games from the sidelines; she gets right out on the field, shoulder pads and all. To look at this slender woman in her midforties, you would expect to see her swatting tennis balls rather than intercepting passes. But she not only plays the sport, she even owns her own woman's football team.

Growing up, Andra played football with the boys in the backyard, but when it came time to go to high school and try for a spot on the varsity team, she wasn't allowed to play. Although some of her young male friends petitioned on her behalf, the door remained firmly shut. "It still pisses me off," Andra told me. "I was as good as they were, better than some." When she realized that she would never play in the NFL, she decided to become a cartoonist and attended Pratt Institute. After graduation, she worked as creative director for Atlantic Records, then as a vice president of creative services for WarnerVision Entertainment, and then in 1998 she struck out on her own as a freelancer. Throughout all this time Andra played ball for the Long Island Sharks, a local flag football team.

One day in 1999 Andra got a call from the Women's Professional Football League, which had just formed two women's tackle football teams, the Minnesota Vixens and the Lake Michigan Minx. They had heard about the flag-team Sharks, winners of a national title in their sport, and they wondered if Andra's team would like to suit up and play against their teams in a full-contact football game. When the Sharks accepted, the league sent pads, helmets, and all the other equipment the women would need for a full-contact contest. With only two months to convert their flag team into a tackle team, the Sharks practiced hard, but all too soon found the all-stars of the two teams riding a bus heading to New York City. Game day dawned cold and windy. Amazingly, before a sparse but enthusiastic crowd of three hundred fans, the Sharks shocked Minnesota by defeating them 12–6. Women's tackle football had arrived.

To become part of the Independent Women's Football League, the Sharks needed to find a formal owner within a certain time frame. Potential buyers did not exactly break down the door with cash in hand. Undaunted, with the clock ticking and no buyer in sight, the girls kept practicing, believing *somebody* must want them. At the eleventh hour, with still no buyer, Andra saw the writing on the wall. If the Sharks were to move forward as a football team, Andra herself must find a way to push the ball into the end zone. She picked up the phone, dialed the league's office, and offered $20,000 that she got from her 401K plan; the offer was accepted. Andra became the proud mother of a brand-new bouncing baby football team! "I love my girls," Andra said proudly. "And it's a good thing because owning a football team is one of the hardest things I've ever done. It's like hitting my head on a brick wall. No one donates money, no one gives us a break, and we beg and borrow from mom and pop stores trying to get sponsors."

In an era in which star male performers in the NFL pull down megamillion-dollar salaries, a Shark must pay $750 to take the field. The staff, even medical personnel, volunteer their time. These women take care of their families, work full-time, and bust their butts to raise the money so they can play. They scrape it together for the love of the game. Their rewards? A stadium full of ardent fans? Hardly. The Sharks often get stonewalled when trying to just get a field to play on. Written up in the *New York Times* sports section? Forget about the media. "I watched a jump rope championship on ESPN and I couldn't believe it," Andra told me. "They show this, but they won't show Sharks on TV?" During an interview on a radio talk show, the host asked Andra why colleges should allow women to play football. "Because women don't have a team of their own," Andra replied. "They don't want to play with the men, or prove they are men, they just want to play football."

"Do women play like men?" I asked her. She smiled. "You can't coach women in the same way you coach men. You can't tell them to suck it up. They get upset when they hurt a player or mess up a play. You have to deal with their emotions. You gotta love them for getting out there because they approach the game with a lot of innocence, a purity that the men just don't have. No one expects money or glory, just fun."

Any advice to girls who want to play sports in a man's world? "Put on your armor and go for it," says Andra. "If you have a passion, don't sell it out, keep forging ahead. What we are doing today is going to make it easier for girls ten years down the line." No matter how much degradation or ridicule comes their way, the Sharks keep lacing up their pads and strapping on their silver helmets, pony tails poking out, not only for the fun of it, but because they are paving the way for future generations of women to gain from sports what men have always gained: an appreciation for the power of teamwork, the love of strategy and the thrill of competition, and the satisfaction and enhanced self-esteem that comes from winning, not to mention the lessons that come with losing.

More and more women have been reaping those benefits. Place kicker Katie Hnida made the team at the University of Colorado. However, she found this road into a male domain as bumpy as an unpaved road in the wilds of Africa. When Katie claimed that fellow players had sexually assaulted her, her coach responded, "It was obvious Katie was not very good. She was awful. You know what guys do? They respect your ability. Katie was not only a girl, she was terrible." Does her level of skill justify harassment? Apparently just being a girl is cause enough for harassment among these entitled athletes, who are often led to believe they are above the rules. Coach Gary Barnett ultimately lost his job in the wake of a three-million-dollar settlement in the case.

Hnida did not hide away in shame and degradation, and revealed that she suffered more than harassment. She was on the receiving end of that age-old strategy of violence used by men to keep women in their place: she was raped. What an inspiration to see this Iron Butterfly step forward and speak out, exactly the response all perpetrators of violence wish to silence. As she herself has said, "I need to talk about it. There are too many women who are out there suffering in silence. Unfortunately, the subject of rape and sexual assault is still taboo. And it's really a shame how our legal system always ends up attacking the victim." Katie ended up kicking more than a football. Her example of courageous vulnerability prompted six other women to come forward and accuse the University of Colorado football players of rape.

Needless to say, Katie did not escape unscathed. She went through a dark time with bouts of depression and self-doubt, but her journey of healing crystallized when, with the support of her family, she walked onto the University of New Mexico football field as a team member. "I had some initial flashbacks to all the horrible stuff at Colorado," she said, "but almost immediately at New Mexico I was treated like a real person. I love those guys. They have been the best teammates I could have ever asked for."

In spite of the continuing sexism and the cruelty that accompanies it, women's progress in the sports world is nothing less than revolutionary, as we see in the Olympic Games. Originally, the Olympics excluded women, so in 776 BCE women formed their own games, the Games of Hera, in honor of the Greek goddess. Finally, in 1900 women were allowed to participate in Olympic competitions. In the 2004 Olympic Games in Greece, 44 percent of all competitors were women, the highest percentage ever, and for the first time we saw two women host and organize the Olympics. The American delegation represented the results of Title IX, the legislation that required equal funding for women's athletics on high school and college campuses. Since Title IX went into effect in 1972, the number of women playing sports in college has increased by more than 400 percent and the number of young women playing interscholastic sports in high school has increased 847 percent.

In spite of such numbers, in 2002, the Department of Education created the so-called Commission on Opportunity in Athletics to review Title IX. Stacked with opponents of Title IX, the commission recommended weakening enforcement of the requirement. When feminists and women athletes cried foul, the Bush administration ended up reaffirming Title IX in a quiet announcement in 2003.

Title IX forbids sex discrimination in all programs at schools that get federal aid, although the controversy and furor relates mostly to athletic programs. Take, for example, Roderick Jackson, a high school girl's basketball coach, whom officials fired when he complained that the girls' team did not get equal treatment as the boys' team. Initially, a US district court judge ruled whistle-blowers do not enjoy protections against retaliation under Title IX. But when Jackson took his case to the US Court of Appeals and then on to the US Supreme Court, the justices ruled that whistle-blowers should receive protection. Former justice Sandra Day O'Connor, speaking for the majority, wrote, "Retaliation against a person because that person complained of sex discrimination is another form of intentional sex discrimination." Jackson was delighted with the decision and said, "I didn't have any other choice but to stand up for the young ladies. I would want someone in the educational spectrum to look out for my kids." We need more supportive men like Jackson looking out for our girls' rights on the playing field.

GRAB THE MICROPHONE

Women's participation in the media has grown a lot since Pat Mitchell, former CEO of PBS and the first woman to hold that position, started out. When Pat came to television in 1974, few women worked in the media, and those who did were advised to avoid stories about women and children, lest their work never appear outside the women's pages. "The fact was there were no stories on women and children," Pat told me, "because the men weren't going to do them, and if the women weren't suggesting them, then there were none. There had not been a single story on any single newscast, certainly not at the network level, on wife abuse, on divorce, on property laws having to do with women's rights."

In spite of the discouragement and hearing time and again "we don't do those kinds of stories" or "who cares about that stuff," Pat Mitchell believed there was an audience for these stories. After all, women were 52 percent of the viewers. She and other women at WBZ in Boston went to management with the idea of doing a whole day of programming for women. Because they asked to try it for just one day and secured their own funding at no cost to the station, they received approval and went on to create "Yes We Can" Day. For twenty-four hours, a woman performed every single job in the station, with all-day programming on women's issues, broadcast live from Boston's Hines Auditorium. On what turned out to be the coldest day of the year, the station's executives figured nobody would show up in seven-degree weather just for a lot of "women's stuff." Imagine their shock when seventy-five thousand women showed up! That day marked a new beginning for women in television and the female audience.

Since the 1980s, women's programming has blossomed not just on the major channels with shows like Oprah but also on numerous cable channels, such as Lifetime and Oxygen. Women's programming has extended as far as the Middle East with *Everywoman*, a new English-language Al Jazeera TV program from Doha, Qatar. Hosted by Shiule Ghosh and produced by Marie Devine, this half-hour weekly program has produced over two hundred short documentaries that expose the hardships and triumphs of women, from a Kurdish Yezidi girl being dragged out of her house and stoned to death simply for planning to meet a boy, to an all-women de-mining team clearing cluster bombs in southern Lebanon. The enthusiastic response from women reflects how deeply they resonate with these issues and how grateful they feel to see their stories chronicled and telecast. *Everywoman* rivals major-league magazine programs in popularity. Every episode is posted on the AJE channel on YouTube (watch it at www.youtube.com/aljazeeraenglish).

Today, we have Katie Couric, who became the first woman solo network news anchor in 2006 when she took the helm at CBS's *Nightly News*. Katie may have come a long way, baby, but her appointment to this position resurrected conflicting perceptions of a woman operating in traditionally male terrain. On the one hand, here was a trusted and authoritative woman; on the other hand, here was a woman scrutinized physically as if she landed a modeling job. Rather than questioning Katie about her interviewing techniques, her drive, her intelligence, her journalistic credentials, the media focused on her panache, and whether she had lost weight, or if her skin was too tanned. Would they have put a man under such a microscope? No, they would have studied him with a telescope.

However, the rise of young female newscasters is a growing presence. According to studies by the Radio-Television News Directors Association, nationally 57 percent of anchors are now women. As male industry veterans with large salaries leave, stations turn to younger female anchors who now draw viewers, but who are also paid less and cut costs.

Although women have established a greater presence in media, it does not overshadow the fact that men continue to exercise more control and therefore the media remain male centered. Consider this simple question: To whom does the media turn when it needs an expert on any subject? According to Who's Talking Research conducted by the White House Project, only one out of ten guest speakers on Sunday morning political talk shows are women, and out of those only 7 percent are repeat guests. Over half of all Sunday morning news talk shows on the five major television networks don't include women, and women make up only 14 percent of the guest appearances overall. Surely, there must be more women "experts" than that. These figures reveal a disturbing fact of life in the media and reveal a profound message, as Marie Wilson, of the White House Project, said:

> They tell us who can be trusted to deal with complex global issues. When women are rarely shown in the hot seat, two things occur. First, women fail to be seen as authorities by the millions of viewers tuning in each weekend. Second, only the opinions of men are heard, thereby losing a female perspective. It affects not only the way the country views women but also the manner in which problems are solved, limiting the range of solutions by limiting the variety of opinions.

Watchdog group Media Matters found white males overwhelmingly dominate the prime-time guest lineups of the three major cable news networks (CNN, Fox, and MSNBC). The percentage is as high as 95 percent on some shows. I love John Stewart, Stephen Colbert, and Bill Maher, but when I watch their shows with a critical eye, their guest lists follow the same trend. Come on, boys, you can handle more women on your shows! And girls, let's pay attention to who's running the show!

These patterns occur on radio and in printed media as well. On the radio, women only host 15 percent of the top hundred talk shows, and they host only about 8 percent of music shows during prime listening hours. Even my beloved NPR could use a boost in its female representatives. The Media Matters study found, probably not coincidentally, that women's listening has also declined. However, women are making some intriguing inroads with such entrepreneurial efforts as radio R-LOG airing out of Dorchester, Massachusetts. Cape Verdean, Latina, and Haitian girls, fed up with negative labels, crude pick-up lines, and derogatory statements toward girls that pollute so much contemporary hip hop and rap music, started their own station. With an intent of creating a sisterhood in the community, their motto is "Where the voices of young women are heard and respected." They play all sorts of music, including reggae and neo-soul, that doesn't put women down. The ages of these bold entrepreneurs? Thirteen to eighteen.

As with other media, newspapers also fall sadly short when it comes to female representation. Women constitute only 17 percent of opinion writers in the *New York Times*, 10 percent at the *Washington Post*, 23 percent at *Newsweek*, and 13 percent at *Time* magazine. Doesn't this imply that women's opinions matter less than men's? The *New York Times Book Review*, enormously influential in deciding which ideas and books the reading public should buy, prints the critiques of twice as many men as women. I find this ironic when research consistently shows that women buy far more books than men.

In the mainstream film industry, few female directors enjoy the status of their male counterparts. Most women must raise money and make their films independently. In the history of the Oscars, only two women directors received nominations—neither was from the United States and neither won. That's the bad news. The good news: in 2003, women directors made a big splash with such films as *Monster* by Patty Jenkins, *Lost in Translation* by Sophia Coppola, and *Whale Rider* by Nikki Carr. All three won Oscar nominations. *Monster* and *Lost in Translation* won Oscars, but not in the category of best director.

Women directors tend to tackle topics seldom explored by men, such as the uneasy and often disturbing world of adolescent girls as they search for their place in the world, as portrayed in *Blue Car*, *Thirteen*, *Mean Girls*, *Juno*, and Deepa Mehta's *Water*, which captures the unsettling world of twelve-year-old widows in India. Also on the plus side, Sherry Lansing became the first woman to run a major studio, 20th Century Fox. Before her ascendancy, she herself thought no woman would ever get that far in the industry. "Today," she said in a January 2005 *Newsweek* interview, "I'm convinced there will be a woman president of the United States in my lifetime."

The medium is the message and Iron Butterflies are expanding that message.

GET DOWN TO BUSINESS

Candice Carpenter Olson founded iVillage, a leading online network for women, acclaimed as one of the best online women's communities and the third-best community site overall on the Web. She later founded the Transitions Institute where she serves as the managing director. Her book, *Chapters: Create a Life of Exhilaration and Accomplishment in the Face of Change*, urges women to conquer all obstacles with energy and joy. True to the title of her book, Candice has lived many interesting "chapters" in her life.

She started her leadership training as an instructor in an outward-bound program, National Outdoor Leadership School (NOLS), when she was nineteen. "Being smart and good looking," she told me, "were irrelevant. It was all about character. I discovered an enormous depth of character I didn't know I had." This insight played a pivotal role in helping her overcome her battle with anorexia. She spent years out in the wilderness mountains, living a sort of tribal life, sleeping in tents. As a leader in physically challenging endeavors, she began to learn the importance of kindness and generosity, of serving people, of inspiring people so that they would willingly cross the desert with her. Leadership, she discovered, came naturally to her.

Then Candice decided to change course and applied and was accepted to Harvard Business School. The shock of entering this foreign culture felt like ice water thrown on her face. "It was my first dance with disillusionment," she confided. At Harvard she found that she needed to find a way to deal with an unfamiliar breed of cynical and selfish people, who felt entitled to life's rewards as members of an elite and exclusive club. To hell with the common good. She found her approach to leadership stonewalled time and time again. "I ran into our dominant culture; business school is the holder of that culture. I was at ground zero and it was disgusting, dinosaur stuff. But it prepared me for later."

That "later" dawned when she progressed to the corporate world, taking a job at American Express, where she worked for twelve years. Working in an organization is like being part of a family in which each person develops his or her unique version of his or her experiences there. I've talked to women who felt that American Express gave them a fantastic opportunity to grow. Others felt pressure to bury their femininity and act more like men in order to succeed. For Candice, it was a mixed bag. Yes, she enjoyed opportunities to grow, but she found herself growing in the most male-dominated culture she had ever encountered. For a woman to succeed, she needed to go undercover and act like and look like a man. This phenomenon did not just occur at American Express; it was happening all across the American corporate landscape, where most 1980s career women wore dark suits, white shirts, and neck bows (not a dress in sight anywhere), had perfect length hair, and donned a certain kind of Tiffany jewelry. One woman at American Express wore two bras so that her nipples wouldn't show. "I thought that was the best metaphor for misogyny I have ever heard," Candice recalled. "I saw her recently, and she's still dresses the same damn way. There isn't any sexuality in my behavior, but I'm not taping my breasts."

Although Candice maintained a strong desire to perform and please, she would ultimately never become one of the oxymoronic "American Express girls." Instead she imported a lot of her former "tribal culture" to her business life, treating problem solving as fun, relying on her intuition, and building a sense of community with her team. Even when accomplishing a serious undertaking, her team would burst out laughing in the process and find themselves escorted from the floor lest they distract fellow workers. They were having too much fun. "We were not part of the culture," she reflected, "so they were right to protest, because that is what cultures do—they reject interlopers. I was in trouble all the time."

The sort of female leadership that Candice demonstrated seldom meets with enthusiastic acceptance in corporate and political worlds where domination prevails, where assertiveness, aggression, and control overrule soft persuasion and playfulness. Looking at the cover of any major business magazine or in the business section of a newspaper, we usually see the picture of what I call the "Lone Ranger": the middle-aged white man, the all-powerful hero who saves the day single-handedly. We'll talk more about this image and the perception and behavior it symbolizes in the next two chapters.

Why do we see so few women's pictures in the business press? It's not that reporters and photographers can't find any worthy women. Given the fact that in 2006 women owned two out of every five privately held firms, businesses that generate $1.9 trillion in annual sales and employ 12.8 million people nationwide, you would think we would see some more of their faces on the covers of *Fortune, Forbes*, and *Business Week*. Between 1997 and 2006, women-owned firms grew twice as fast as all privately held firms. In light of that fact, it deeply disappoints me to learn that only 9 percent of institutional investment deals, 4 percent of corporate contracts, and 2.2 percent of federal contracts go to women-owned businesses.

Of course, fewer women make the covers because, in fact, not enough women have made it to the top of old-guard American corporations. Catalyst, an organization that tracks women's progress in business-leadership jobs, reported in 2005 that women held only 16.4 percent of corporate officer positions in Fortune 500 companies. Only 3 percent of Fortune 500 companies are led by women and only one leads a Fortune 50. More than one-half of the Fortune 500 claimed fewer than three women corporate officers. At this rate it would take seventy years for women to fill half the seats.

Can corporate America wait that long to reap the benefits of women's leadership? In 2003, the Glass Ceiling Research Center found that the twenty-five Fortune 500 companies with the best track record for promoting women to high positions were 18 to 69 percent more profitable than the median companies in their industries. The nine Fortune 500 companies presided over by women CEOs (that's up to twelve in 2007) outperformed the broader market by a substantial margin. The women racked up a 52 percent gain versus a 27 percent gain for the index of all large companies. Women can and do improve the bottom line!

According to Corporate Women Directors International, women also occupy only 10.4 percent of the seats on corporate boards in the world's largest two hundred companies. And yet, in 2007 Catalyst found that those Fortune 500 companies with the highest representation of women board directors attained significantly higher financial performances than those with the lowest representation. If there had been more women in boardrooms, we might not have seen such irresponsible risk taking that precipitated the global banking crisis. Maybe Howard Archer, chief European and UK economist, is right when he said in a February 2009 *Boston Globe* interview, "You can argue that the men have made a right mess of it, and now the ladies should have a go."

Apparently Norway recognized this unrealized female resource when it announced in 2006 that publicly traded firms must meet a 40 percent requirement for female board membership by 2008. Businesses, predictably, cried foul. Karita Bekkelmellem, Norway's minister of children and equality, stood her ground and proclaimed, "The government decision is to see to it that women will have a place where the power is. I do not want to wait 20 to 30 years for men with enough intelligence to finally appoint women." Sweden soon followed Norway's example. Vice Prime Minister Margareta Winberg announced that the government would take legal action unless the number of women on the boards of publicly listed companies rose from 8 to 25 percent, arguing that at the current rate of increase it would take 150 years until women occupied half the Swedish boards.

It just comes down to basic common sense: if we exclude women from top jobs, we squander half the nation's talent. But for more women to participate at higher levels in business, some changes that have begun to take place must unfold even more rapidly. Women have learned to play the game, and now it's time for women to change the game. In particular, they are leading the way into conversations about two topics that can transform the workplace: conscience and flexibility. Conscience transforms self-interest into a collective interest; flexibility transforms a rigid career paradigm into a more organic, holistic approach to work. With these two transformations, women needn't act like men and men needn't fear acting more like women.

BE A VOICE OF CONSCIENCE

Women's presence can disperse the testosterone cloud of omnipotence that has corrupted our institutions with so much immoral and unethical behavior. How many women went to jail over such dung piles of corruption as Enron, Tyco, WorldCom, and Adelphia? Research supports the fact that in general terms women tend to behave more ethically than men. One study found that women students expressed significantly less tolerance for questionable business practices. But we don't need a study to tell us this, just look at those who are blowing the whistles, women such as Sherron Watkins at Enron and Cynthia Cooper at WorldCom. At the FBI, Colleen Rowley, like Sherron and Cynthia, exposed herself to bullying and threats but never backed down. Bunny Greenhouse, the highest-ranking civilian at the US Army Corp of Engineers, blew the whistle on Halliburton and its subsidiary, KBR, and got demoted for challenging their illegal practices. Marie deYoung, a logistic specialist for KBR, discovered that most of the contracts had nothing to do with servicing US troops, but rather KBR was building houses, gyms, and rec centers for itself. In the end, these ethically empowered women helped bring down some of these houses of corruption and, along with them, their entitled alpha executives. Unlike their male counterparts, they spoke up and awakened the corporate conscience.

Although studies on moral judgment often produce conflicting results, they do underscore that women and men often differ in their moral reasoning. Psychologist Carol Gilligan summarized the difference in her book *In a Different Voice*: men tend to define morality in terms of justice and individual rights, whereas women's terms revolve more around care and responsibility. Since women generally concern themselves more with relationships and community, they would naturally tend to be more service-oriented toward clients, more nurturing toward co-workers, and more attentive to maximizing benefits for the majority rather than just for themselves. A woman's participation positively affects business and corporate culture whenever she raises the ethical bar, encourages restraint and accountability, and supports a much-needed balance in the corporate world. Boys always behave better when girls are around.

CHALLENGE THE CAREER PARADIGM

Corporate culture centers on a "work is primary" model, an idea proposed by Rhona Rapoport, Lotte Bailyn, Joyce Fletcher, and Bettye Pruit. This model derives from two assumptions: (1) men make work primary while their wives tend to home and family duties, and (2) organizations exist in a fairly stable marketplace. These two realities have gone the way of transistor radios and typewriters. Markets have grown more complex and dynamic; the "organization man" is dead. With the rise of working women and mothers, the percentage of mothers staying at home has dropped from 76 percent to 28 percent in the past fifty years. However, in 1998, 41.3 percent of mothers with infants stayed home, a significant rise after years of increases in the numbers of working mothers. According to Reach Advisors, a marketing and research firm, 84 percent of Gen X stay-at-home moms are considering returning to work. However, even though the conditions have changed, many corporate cultures still cling to a paradigm where work takes preference over everything at all times.

Many Iron Butterflies in the business world object to this paradigm. They are less willing to jump to the corporate dictate and relocate, or put in the endless hours on the job, or identify themselves only with their job title—all the old standby requirements for an upwardly mobile career. They are losing faith in old-style employers and institutions, questioning the very values that have driven them for decades, and challenging the assumptions of how companies must function. It's not that women don't want status. A study done by Simmons College School of Management in 2004 surveyed a hundred women managers and found that 47 percent wanted top leadership positions. Fifty-five percent of women under thirty-five wanted top jobs. But for many women, that doesn't mean marching in step with the old assumptions.

Some younger women have been shying away from those executive positions when they see the price women pay to gain a corner office. Twelve of the most senior women in a multinational company of 90,000 employees hired consultant Susan Boland to answer a key question: "How were women moving, or rather, not moving through the ranks?" At entry level, the company hired about 50 percent men and 50 percent women. By the time people got to higher management levels, the story changed. At director's level, 3 percent were women; at vice president level, 1 percent. Susan discovered that it wasn't the guys at the top holding women back. She concluded, instead, that "women were dropping out."

She discovered that women would try to go sideways rather than upward because they felt they couldn't take on any more responsibility and sustain any sort of meaningful life outside of work. Seeing what was happening to women who moved up through the ranks, they didn't want that for themselves. Women at the lower levels who knew the twelve senior women who initiated the study shook their heads saying, "Look at the lives they have. This one is divorced; this one has a delinquent child; this one is doing OK, but she has a stay-at-home husband raising the kids." Susan said, "They didn't see role models they liked." Not wanting to find themselves in the same predicament, they would refuse promotions time and time again, though not without a certain amount of apprehension because they knew they could deter promotions for only so long before they would find their careers stalled or even backsliding.

"When I talked to the senior women about what I was hearing, I thought I would discover a real sisterhood," Susan recalls. "I didn't. Instead they dug their heels in saying they were able to manage all the responsibility without help and so should these women. They weren't sympathetic. They thought of themselves as self-made women."

During a final meeting of the project, the executive women came up with twelve action items. "They were afraid to look at the systematic issues," Susan told me. "Instead they turned into cheerleaders. 'You can do it. We'll have an Olympic athlete come in and give a seminar!' Taking a serious look at what was really happening, why women weren't climbing the ranks, was too painful. They wouldn't go there."

So what's holding women back? I could argue that there are as many answers as there are unique women in the workplace, but I think most long for a new career paradigm. Rather than rigid career paths where a person must slave away in a particular place for a specified number of hours at a particular time of day, they want a flexible work schedule in their day-to-day work lives that would allow for telecommuting, job sharing, and family-friendly programs. This shift could also benefit the organization because researchers have linked flextime usage to increased performance and productivity. If, however, a company offers flextime and does not alter its career paradigm to accommodate these changes, it will most likely penalize women for their choice. In fact, in most cases, women pursuing the more unconventional options found their advancement hindered because the powers that be regard them as less serious about their work.

Women also want flexibility over the course of their career, to be able to take time off from the career track, usually to bear and care for children, and then to return to the workforce without suffering severe penalties. Pursuing this approach challenges the assumption about an uninterrupted, nose-to-the grindstone career path. Fortunately, business schools and businesses have been making efforts to help women rejoin the workforce, for no other reason than a realization that women leaving the workforce represents a brain drain and a loss of an investment. For instance, when Deloitte and Touche, a professional services firm, realized too many of its talented women were walking out the door, it chose to make some fundamental changes, not just stick a Band-Aid on the wound. The firm designed a new career paradigm consistent with the new realities in the workplace, a move more companies might emulate. Why does welcoming a woman back after maternity leave make good sense? Because returning mothers bring back a heightened sense of responsibility and caregiving, and exercise good judgment, attributes that do not automatically come with a brand-new MBA.

Harvard Business School, Penn's Wharton, Tuck's School at Dartmouth, and others are developing programs that will help women reenter the workforce. Over the course of her career, Myra Hart, former executive vice president of growth and development at Staples and professor at Harvard Business School, often found herself the only woman in meetings, yet she rose to the top in a man's world. She struggles with the idea of women not making it like she did. "All of us are torn between two things," she told me. "One is realizing we have extraordinary gifts, opportunities, which make us unique, and on the other hand, why can't everyone be like me? I did it. Why can't they do it?" These questions have led her to create more choices for women. She calls one of her many projects Working Options. "We're thinking about how to restructure work so that women have choices. If they choose to leave work to have a family, how can we help women keep themselves current in their skills, keep them connected to the marketplace, and help them back in the marketplace when they are ready to return." Iron Butterflies like Myra help women along professionally.

REDEFINE COMMITMENT

Underlying all the progress toward flexibility is a transformation of the meaning of commitment. In their book, *Beyond Work-Family Balance*, Rhona Rapoport and her colleagues have written that commitment, "remains rooted in a traditional concept of the ideal worker as someone for whom work is primary . . . [and whose] time to spend at work is unlimited. . . . Anyone (male or female) who has outside responsibilities is disadvantaged." This outdated meaning of commitment excludes a balanced life, which most contemporary women and men want as much as a paycheck. Let's bring the definition of commitment up to date: we can be committed to our work *and* also have a life outside of work. Commitment isn't a ball and chain that binds you to a desk in a cubicle; it's a bungee cord that allows you to stretch and bounce with creativity.

Susan Pinker, author of *The Sexual Paradox*, argues that women may not have ascended to the upper echelons of the corporate world because they are hardwired to resist the demands of the old domination paradigm. Because women are genetically and hormonally wired for empathy, they broaden their fields of interests, think more in terms of a service orientation, and maintain a holistic view (an idea we will revisit later). When seeking status in a domination-driven culture doesn't correlate with women's instincts toward building a balanced life, they will often trade the longer hours needed to gain higher status and bigger paychecks for more harmony in their lives. Corporations must eventually alter some of the underlying assumptions and structures that existed when middle-class men worked full time and their wives stayed home. Otherwise, both they and our society will suffer.

The United States lags behind Europe in its support systems for a balanced life. By comparison, Americans receive less in terms of paid maternity and paternity leave, and paid sick and emergency leave. Believe it or not, until the Family and Medical Leave Act (FMLA) in 1992, maternity leave fell under disability protections! Also, Americans put in a full three weeks more work than the British, and nine weeks more than the French and Germans. Does that extra time contribute to a better quality of life than theirs? And what about childcare? Here Americans find little help from the corporate world. For example, finding good backup childcare poses a huge problem for most working parents, and although parents lose an estimated five to eight days annually due to childcare breakdowns, only 9 percent of companies offer backup care, and that's down from 14 percent in 2001. Who suffers most? Women, men, children, employers? I'd say everyone ends up in the loser's column. Americans espouse family values; well, let's put our money where our mouth is.

Men deserve a mention here because the old model assigns men the role of earner and provider, and no option for flexibility. To measure a man's worth, you must measure his paycheck and his occupational success. But a 2000 a study done by Radcliffe Public Policy Center found Generation X men expanding their identity. Men between the ages of twenty-one and thirty-nine said they wanted a work schedule that allowed them more time with their families. According to research from the Families and Work Institute in New York, fathers in 2002 spent 2.7 hours each workday caring for children, an hour more than in 1977. Working mothers spent 3.3 hours a day. Even though the gap is narrowing slowly, these figures mark a significant break from the old paradigm for men. It will, however, take both men and women banding together to pressure corporations to recognize and include a work-life balance as an essential element of corporate policy because doing so benefits everyone.

Iron Butterflies realize that we must engage men in this social transformation. Since more couples are sharing family tasks than ever before, although women still carry the brunt, it's important that men support and promote more flexible, ethical work and career models. They, too, can enjoy more options and more balanced lives, and thank the Iron Butterflies that demanded them.

This shared goal holds the potential for a convergence. In one of the most comprehensive reviews of current research on families and work, Monahan Lang and Barbara Risman found more similarities than differences in what men and women want, a shift toward what they call, "gender convergence," an ever-increasing similarity in how men and women live and what they want from their lives.

As a collective force, men and women can change the conduct of business. As professor of geography at University of California, Los Angeles, Jared Diamond wrote in his book *Collapse: How Societies Choose to Fail or Succeed*: "Businesses have changed when the public came to expect and require different behavior, to reward business for behavior that the public wanted, and to make things difficult for businesses practicing behavior that the public didn't want." If we steer our consuming power or offer our talents toward companies that reflect our values, corporations will take notice. Take it to the bottom line and you'll gain their attention.

The Center of Women's Research did a study on success strategies by women business owners. Ninety-four percent cited patience and perseverance. John Quincy Adams wrote that "patience and perseverance have a magical effect before which difficulties disappear and obstacles vanish," as Iron Butterflies discover as they pursue their passion.

Chapter 5

GLADIATORS

Dealing with Mucho Macho

> The greatest part of our happiness or misery depends
> on our disposition and not our circumstances.
>
> Martha Washington

Does the name Metis ring a bell? How about Zeus? I suspect most everyone has heard of Zeus, but Metis? You'll understand why you don't know the name of Zeus's first wife once you hear her story. I love myths because like cultural x-rays, they expose themes that have formed the backbone of human life and civilization. As Joseph Campbell wrote in the *Power of Myth*, they reveal "the deep inner problems, inner mysteries, inner thresholds of passage." The myth of Zeus and Metis offers a glimpse into our innermost beliefs about power, masculinity, and femininity.

Metis was the daughter of two Titans, Oceanus and Tethys, and was regarded as the wisest of all gods and men. The upstart god Zeus, intent on overthrowing the ruling order of divinities to which she belonged, pursued Metis so aggressively he eventually caught her and made her his first wife, despite all her efforts to escape his clutches.

Zeus came from a long line of sons who overthrew their fathers. Zeus's father, Cronus, deposed his father, Uranus, by castrating him. Cronus, afraid that one of his own son's would depose him as well, swallowed his children. His wife Rhea, however, determined to save her sixth child, Zeus, fooled Cronus into swallowing a stone wrapped in swaddling clothes instead.

In order to overthrow the Titans, Zeus needed to free his brothers from his father's belly so they could help him. When he turned to Metis for counsel, his brilliant wife devised a plan whereby Cronus drank a concoction that made him regurgitate his five children, which included two boys, Poseidon and Hades. Then Zeus, together with his brothers and other allies, defeated the Titans after a ten-year war. And, true to his lineage, he slew his father with a lightening bolt.

When Metis became pregnant, the earth oracle told Zeus she would bear a girl now and a boy in the future. Afraid that future son would supplant him as he had supplanted his own father, Zeus seduced Metis with clever words and guile, tricking her into becoming small, and then he swallowed her. Metis was never heard of again. The crafty Zeus appropriated all her attributes and power as his own, including childbirth, and gave birth to his daughter, Athena, out of his head. Athena, the warrior goddess of wisdom, never could recollect her mother. In the end, triumphant Zeus sat alone atop Mount Olympus with his lightening bolt in hand.

Now you know why you don't know Metis. She vanished. A man stole her powers. We'll revisit the swallowing of feminine wisdom throughout the book, but here I want to look at the heart of this myth of domination and conquest, and in particular, at men exercising their power by making women small. Although Zeus triumphed, he could not maintain his position without constant vigilance. Always fearful of losing his throne, he trusted no one, not even his wife or the son she might bear.

In this chapter, we will look at the contemporary version of the domination game, a toxic phenomenon. I call it the gladiator culture. We will see the gladiator defense and how gladiators try to make women small. Unlike Metis, however, Iron Butterflies do not allow themselves to be tricked into making themselves small. In fact, their grace and poise in dealing with degrading behavior, such as public humiliation, reveals an inner strength that is admirable. After reading their stories, I think you will agree that the Iron Butterfly is truly the strong one and not the gladiator.

REJECT A GLADIATOR CULTURE

Twenty million people watched *The Apprentice* starring Donald Trump. Welcome to the gladiator culture televised. In a work environment that follows Trump's Rule 5 for success ("I love pitting people against each other. My whole life is based on that!") brawls among contestants inevitably broke out. In this adrenaline-rushing, testosterone-driven, chest-thumping culture, gladiators celebrate aggression, posturing, and physical prowess. Epitomized by narcissists like Trump, gladiator leaders are ego-driven, arrogant, often downright bullies. To all the gladiators who define the world as a battleground, women should say, "You're fired!"

Unfortunately, the show provides a microcosm of the real and increasingly toxic world of far too many contemporary organizations. Somewhere along the yellow brick road to success, greed has transmogrified from a vice into a virtue. Many of today's hard-nosed institutions have little in common with corporations of twenty-five years ago. Instead of serving different constituencies and employees, today's companies and their (mostly male) leaders are obsessed with maximizing stock prices over all else.

In "Memo to: CEO," an article in the December 2002 issue of *Fast Company*, Robert Simons, Henry Mintzberg, and Kunal Basu capture the predicament succinctly in reference to Enron: "Glorification of greed is causing a disconnect between the interest of the few and the well-being of the many." It seemed clear to me at the time of the article that this disconnect and selfishness inevitably would be the undoing of many of our major corporations. And that indeed has come to pass. In 2008 and 2009 we witnessed Ponzi schemes, toxic assets, credit-default swaps, and other arcane financial instruments designed to generate quick, easy (and very risky) profits, strategies that led to the collapse of giants such as AIG, one of the largest insurance companies in the world. And the United States taxpayers were left holding the bag and bailing them out.

If you want one simple, surefire way to detect a gladiator culture, look at the way an organization lets people go. Downsizing may at times become a business necessity, one that poses difficult decisions about who to retain and who to dismiss, but it need not devolve into a dehumanizing, mean, and rude process. During a time of downsizing at Motorola, Vice President Janiece Webb noticed that women vice presidents found out about their dismissals via messages on their voice mail. Janiece finally went to the CEO's office and told him, "You've got a problem. You have guys flushing women down the toilet in the rudest ways. Stop this. You are losing the balance in the company."

Stacy Blake-Beard, an associate professor at Simmons School of Management, recalled a time when she worked at a large technological firm that laid off a number of employees. Without any warning, company representatives escorted people to their desks, gave them a cardboard box, and asked them to empty their desks, turn in their key, and then go. "It was disturbing to see," she said in a *Boston Globe* interview. "It created anxiety, a survivor syndrome where the people who remained had to deal with the dehumanizing way people were dismissed. They had to deal with the psychological ramifications of whether their own jobs were secure." In this kind of atmosphere, people quickly learn that their livelihoods depend on doing whatever it takes to survive. Keep your head down, remain inconspicuous, make safe decisions, stay off the radar screen, play your cards close to the vest. In other words, become small like Metis and hope you don't get swallowed. This is not exactly an environment conducive to innovation and productivity. People running scared do not make for a fast company.

Think twice before you place your talents and energy on the line into this kind of mean-spirited environment with all of its aggression, intimidation, and control. Gladiator cultures are exclusive, secretive, and self-protecting. They are closed systems that abide by the DAD strategy: decide, act, and defend. Rather than encourage dialogue in the quest for solutions, a closed system issues edicts, resists regulation, suppresses criticism, and limits access to information.

In a gladiator culture, dichotomies splinter reality into conflicting views. It treats those who oppose it as the enemy, dehumanizing them with name-calling. That tactic magnifies the importance of the gladiator tribe by denigrating others; and it invariably leads to scapegoating, which further unites the tribe. Sociologist Patricia Hill has referred to this good guy/bad guy tactic as "controlling images," a set of false images that cement each group in its place in order to protect the status quo and thwart attempts to alter the culture's belief system. It follows Lenin's logic that if you tell a lie long enough, it becomes the truth. We often absorb these images about others and ourselves without even realizing it. The Bush administration applied a number of controlling images to unify its cause, from "axis of evil," to "you are either with us or against us," "cheese-eating coward" (in reference to French president Jacques Chirac), and "unpatriotic" (all dissenters). The rulers of a gladiator culture suffer little angst, at least on the surface, because, in their eyes, reality is crystal clear, and all the complexity and uncertainties of life are just bulldozed through. That way no one needs to pause for reflection or ever question why things work or don't work in the organization. Grand illusions of conquest trump facts. Loyalty conquers competence. Power is seductive. You get a little, you want more. You get more, you want it all. Eventually, you become so power crazed you will do whatever it takes to get the absolute power that corrupts absolutely. It's a culture that consumes its people, demanding nothing less than their lives, and callously spits them out when they are done with them.

We all know what happened when a gladiator culture ran rampant at Enron, which ruthlessly ripped off employees' pension funds without a single blink of conscience. The company's leaders only cared about raising stock prices, which they rewarded with outlandish pay packages. Not surprisingly, this culture of greed wanted it all so badly, its leaders resorted to aggressive and illegal accounting practices and fictitious transactions. Dishonesty became the best policy because as long as you maintained the illusion of growth, it didn't matter what you did to get it on paper.

We saw it on Wall Street with the mergers-and-acquisitions rush. "Some studies show," writes Dan Fost in his article "Mergers a Rite of Passage in Life of U.S. Companies," "that 50 to 70 percent of mergers fail in that they don't live up to their financial promise." They failed because they were not created for the welfare of employees, customers, and stockholders, but for the gratification of executive egos and the expansion of their own personal wealth creation. They were more about domination than combination. Business has long served as the arena where men fight it out.

I recently spoke with the female president and CEO of a leading independent investment bank that disdains that old model. About the shortfalls of a gladiator approach, she told me, "A lot of mergers were done by . . . people who wanted a boost in their stock price. Investment bankers convince people to merge by focusing on the huge financial benefits, and they get so wrapped up in it that they don't see whether or not there is strategic benefit. Typically a lot of deals are done very quickly, and certain things don't get looked at. Is there real compatibility between the people? How are they going to work together? Is it possible to keep the people motivated?"

Unfortunately, an obsession with financial benefits often obliterates the people factor, a critical element to any successful merger. If you don't see the world of relationships, you don't think twice about shredding the web of connections and ignoring the consequences of dismantling a community, even if that results in a demoralized and detached workforce.

Given the poor odds of merger success, why do so many business leaders pursue them? My opinion? Gladiator hubris. It's the modern way to seize the throne atop Mount Olympus. When assistant professors at University of California Berkeley Ulrike Malmendier and Geoffrey Tate studied mergers and acquisitions, they uncovered shocking overconfidence among many chief executives. CEOs were almost twice as likely to pursue merger or acquisitions than a control group. The researchers also found that overconfident chief executives were two and a half times more likely to pursue a diversifying merger or acquisition, a strategy with an even poorer track record than mergers. In other words, we cannot assume gladiator CEOs act rationally. The gladiator's arrogance convinces him that he can beat the odds.

STOP THE BULLIES

To explain this male high-risk aggressiveness, anthropologist Helen Fisher of Rutgers University believes that evolution has selected men with a taste for risking everything to get to the top of the hierarchy. Those males get more reproductive opportunities, not only among primates, but also among human beings. So men want to be more competitive with others. Women, although just as competitive, don't get as big a reproductive payoff by reaching the top. In other words, men who display prowess through power and money will win their share of wives, as Donald Trump's marital record illustrates.

Women not only fail to get a big reproductive payoff by reaching the top, but studies show that the more success and education a woman achieves, the fewer marriage proposals come her way. Elaina Rose, an economist at the University of Washington, termed this trade-off the "success gap." But after examining the 1980, 1990, and 2000 Censuses, Rose has determined that while the success gap still exists, it has been rapidly narrowing.

Helen Fisher's statement implies that women won't become gladiators. Generally speaking, they don't. In recent years more women have opted for the tactics of what I call the "Amazon," a development we'll discuss in a later chapter. However, some women, identifying with the slash-and-burn style and pledging allegiance to the hierarchy, have selected the gladiator option. They choose to act as Athenas—ambitious women who identify with their fathers, feel an affinity with men, and look down on less-aspiring women. And, perhaps like Athena who could not recollect a mother, they have disassociated themselves from the maternal and the feminine within themselves. These women, who muscle it out to survive in gladiator cultures, seldom realize the tenuousness of their position until they lose a mentor's support, hit the glass ceiling, or discover their mentor or the organization does not reciprocate their loyalty.

Playing the gladiator game carries a cost, as Janiece Webb told me. "I have muscled it out big time, but you pay several prices. You ignore and stop nurturing your soul in order to survive these cultures. Either physically, emotionally, [or] spiritually, women are going to burn out from being in the flight-and-fight positions for years." Janiece considered a promotion to a job where she would be working for a boss whom she described as "combative to a sin, pits his people against each other and celebrates warfare and gladiator sports every day. He focuses on macho, aggressiveness, burn the barn down, ignoring ethics and disrespecting people. His ego is on the line and he wants to be Jack Welch in the worst way. This guy is not in touch with himself." Janiece declined this higher position, shocking her colleagues, who believed that she had just killed her career. "I'm not going to sell my soul," Janiece insisted, "and I would have had to sell my soul to work with this guy."

Top dogs with the gladiator's hubris care little about serving the organization as an effective leader or even about getting bottom-line results. If they did, they would combine determination and humility to generate a more human-centered culture as Jim Collins, author of *Good to Great*, has pointed out. We also know from Jeffrey Pfeffer's research and his book *The Human Factor* that organizations that practice human-centered management perform better financially than their coldhearted counterparts. If success does, in fact, hinge on treating people right, why do people, mostly men, become gladiators to achieve success? Egos. Gladiator leaders certainly possess generous amounts of determination, but are short on humility. The sort of balance that Collins recommends eludes them. As Janiece pointed out to me, they have lost touch with their better selves, the selves who could bring courage and vulnerability to the corner office.

Narcissus looked into the pool, saw his own reflection, and fell in love. As CEO Larry Ellison of Oracle once said, "The difference between God and Larry is that God does not believe he is Larry." Sadly, the gladiator culture rewards this sort of narcissism. Even though organizations talk about teamwork, few actually promote it. Corporate culture, not to mention the American culture at large, promotes and rewards the star. And generally narcissists aspire to stardom because their grandiose sense of self-importance and their sense of entitlement require excessive amounts of admiration. They tend to exaggerate their achievements. By the same token, narcissists lack the capacity to empathize with others and to appreciate how their own behavior harms other people. Remember the former CEO of Sunbeam Corporation, Albert Dunlap? His slash-and-burn style with the weapons of layoffs and restructuring earned him the nickname "Chain Saw Al."

Dacher Keltner, a psychologist at the University of California at Berkeley, and his colleagues Deborah Gruenfeld and Cameron Anderson, conducted an experiment to test their hypothesis that power makes people less sensitive to those around them and concluded that those who gain power may actually grow to be less cognizant of others and, as their power increases, they become less and less attentive to those around them. Power is associated with low levels of cognitive complexity (black and white thinking), and a lack of careful thought about the potential consequences of one's own actions and responses.

Since gladiator leaders act with certainty, even when full of doubt, they will seldom admit to making a mistake or allow room for error. Not admitting mistakes, however, leads to incompetence because if you do not learn from your mistakes, you doom yourself to repeating them. This sort of arrogance supplies a weapon for holding back or sabotaging competent people whom gladiators view as a threat to their power. Andy Litinsky, a contestant fired on *The Apprentice* but later hired by Trump, observed that people who were arrogant were the biggest hindrance to success. If you are not willing to humble yourself and ask dumb questions, then you are not really a smart person.

Belinda Board added an interesting study to this topic. After she compared personality traits of thirty-nine high-ranking business executives in Britain with psychiatric patients and criminals, she found that both criminals and executives demonstrated narcissistic personalities: grandiosity, lack of empathy, exploitativeness, and independence. They also shared traits associated with compulsive personality disorder: stubbornness, dictatorial tendencies, perfectionism, and excessive devotion to work. Executives differed in that they significantly more often displayed a histrionic personality: superficial charm, insincerity, egocentricity, and manipulativeness. "The reality," Board concluded, "is that sometimes the characteristics that make someone successful in business or government can render them unpleasant personally. What's more astonishing is that those characteristics when exaggerated are the same ones found in criminals." The wave of corporate scandals continuing to make headlines proves her point: we have seen how thin that line is as we watch executives become criminals.

If not engaged in criminal activities, many gladiators exhibit what I can only call childish behavior. Take CEO T. J. Rodgers of Cypress Semiconductor, who likes to clip and display articles written about his rants and uses what he calls his "drooling psycho face" when he wants to intimidate an employee. Sounds like the behavior of a two-year-old to me. Or how about Bonnie Fuller, editorial director of American Media, well known for throwing temper tantrums if her coffee falls below her exacting standards. Psychologists call this Intermittent Explosive Disorder, a ten-dollar word for five-cent behavior. Some might call such behavior bold, but I call it bullying, and I see no more excuse for bullying in the corporate arena than I do on the playground. When women encounter this behavior, they should say what they would say to a child, "Grow up, boys. Stop pushing people around!"

Unfortunately, bullying occurs quite naturally in a culture that rewards aggression. A study at Wayne State University revealed that one in six workers experience bullying or harassment every year. Workplace Bullying Institute and Zogby International conducted 7,740 interviews with American adults in 2007 and found 37 percent of workers had been bullied, 72 percent of bullies were bosses, 57 percent of the targets are women, 62 percent ignore the problem, 40 percent never report bullying, and only 3 percent sue. Women bullies target women 71 percent of the time; men target men 54 percent. Bullying is four times more common that harassment, which is illegal. Forty-five percent of the targets had stress-related health problems.

The behavior has grown so rampant that it has gained increased attention from human resources specialists, who often find these gladiator tactics directed toward the nicest, hardest-working people. Suffolk Law School professor David Yamada not only promoted a "healthy workplace bill" around the country as a way to protect bullied employees but also started to establish legal implications of workplace bullying. Gary Namie wrote a book called *The Bully at Work: What You Can Do to Stop It*, and he and his wife started a foundation called Campaign against Workplace Bullying. Bullies may keep their jobs because they achieve results, but they do a lot of damage in organizations because their tactics create cynical and apathetic employees and ultimately they erode democratic processes by excluding and silencing different perspectives.

Iron Butterflies do not tolerate such behavior. If they can stop it, they do; if they can't, they exit the organization. Given the specter of talent drain, one of the major problems plaguing companies in desperate need of innovation, can any organization afford to lose its best and brightest women?

RECOGNIZE THE GLADIATOR DEFENSE

The gladiator defense protects the gladiators' dominance and shields them from attacks on their weaknesses. Unwilling or unable to admit their vulnerabilities, gladiators fend off and avoid these feelings by externalizing and projecting them onto others in order to establish what psychologist Judith Jordan calls "forced vulnerability." She argues that "forced vulnerability involves the exercise of power over others, sometimes including humiliation, being rendered vulnerable against one's will. . . . And in a stratified and oppressive society, those at the bottom are continually forced into places of vulnerability and then reminded of their vulnerability, partly as a means to intimidate and control them." By forcing their own feelings of vulnerability onto others, gladiators endow others with all their own perceived negative attributes and weaknesses, which they proceed to attack. In sport speak, "The best defense is a strong offense."

When a gladiator attacks, he attacks a hidden part of himself: Eliot Spitzer, crusader against prostitution rings, gets caught having spent a fortune on a prostitute; Reverend Ted Haggerty, defender of the faith, denounced gay rights, only to see his own homosexual affair make headlines; Representative Mark Foley, a battler for laws against Internet sexual exploitation, ends up text-messaging sexually explicit messages to minors working as congressional pages.

Oftentimes women subjected to this defense become so vulnerable and confused they wonder what they have done wrong, thus becoming unwitting participants in the tactic. When a woman shoulders a gladiator's vulnerability, she takes on an oppressive burden she cannot possibly carry nor should she. Only when she recognizes the defense can she put down that burden and reject all the vulnerabilities the gladiator would foist on her because he refuses to acknowledge them in himself.

TRANSCEND HUMILIATION

How would you describe a strong leader? I doubt that anyone would list "manipulative, controlling, mean, aggressive, narcissistic, and intimidating" as prized attributes. No, those traits describe the classic bully, an insecure person. I want to look at the most extreme version of the gladiator defense, publicly humiliating people. As you will see in the following stories, a woman's stature or position does not exempt her from this behavior. In fact, the stronger and more powerful a woman is, the more she may experience it because she poses a greater threat to the gladiator's place of dominance. Iron Butterflies subjected to the gladiator defense demonstrate an inner strength and unlike Metis will not be diminished or made small.

They show us strong leadership in how to deal with mucho macho: walk away with their integrity intact, resist playing into the domination game, adhere to feminine values and don't apologize for them, survive and thrive in the lion's den but don't stay too long, and hold on to their truth when they are being talked out of it. When women behave in this way, they disable the gladiator defense and help disempower the gladiator culture.

KEEP YOUR INTEGRITY INTACT

Dr. Carolyn Bennett, a medical doctor and a Liberal Party member of Canadian Parliament, knows all about gladiators. When Carolyn had complained to then prime minister Jean Chretien because he had reduced the number of women in the cabinet when the country actually needed more, he scolded her for discrediting him. Uh-oh. She forgot that you don't challenge or criticize gladiators. When they met again, she came armed with a scathing analysis of the central party's financial plan, questioning its financial accountability and demanding to know what the party was doing for her constituency.

> He wasn't paying attention, as usual. He was signing books and then his head snapped back. He said, "The central party got you elected, Madam. You can run as an independent if you want." And then he went nuts. He became so angry, some people thought he lost it. He threw everything including the kitchen sink at me and just wouldn't stop going at me. It's like being mad about the burnt toast and throwing in the overextended Visa card and the dented fender in the same argument.

After the meeting concluded, people came over to Carolyn to offer their sympathy and decry Chretien's behavior. "I was toughing it out, but when I heard all that compassion, I cried. I am blessed with these friends. They wipe your neck with a white towel and send you back in the ring. The media said I gave as I got."

If anyone challenges a gladiator's dominant position, as the prime minister felt Carolyn had done, and the challenge touches a sore spot, expect a major outburst of the gladiator defense. It's not easy dealing with the fury of a gladiator or reminding yourself where it's really coming from—not from what you are saying or doing necessarily, but from some feeling of vulnerability stored deep in the gladiator's heart. Carolyn did not allow Chretien to intimidate her into silence because she knew in her own heart that not speaking up would have done more harm in the long run. "For me to have said anything less would have led everyone who sent me to Parliament to think that he bullied me into things and that I couldn't say the obvious. My credibility is the only thing I came into this job with, and I don't want to leave without it." Ultimately, Carolyn's power grew, despite her adversary's effort to make it smaller. Refusing to let him humiliate her, she walked away from the situation with her integrity intact and even became a darling of the media for having weathered such a bruising assault.

NEVER APOLOGIZE FOR YOUR FEMININE VALUES

Cuban-born Judge Maria Lopez, the first Latina to sit on the superior court bench in Massachusetts, went to law school after fighting for civil rights and women's rights because she saw "law as a vehicle for social change." Maria, a woman unafraid to speak her mind, has managed to keep and act on her feminine values in the highly adversarial, aggressive legal world, a world where she saw "men fighting about principles that were tied up with their egos rather than conflict resolution." That's not to say that Maria can't play hardball with the boys, especially when she must keep order in her court. Her feminine values permeate her dispositions, which reflect her reliance on her intuition. "There are more than two sides to every story," she told me. "There are the witness's version and then the real version somewhere out there. I have a good shit detector."

As a superior court judge, Maria strives to enforce the law, but never without weighing the context of a person's life. "I really do believe that people aren't inherently bad; bad experiences can make people go bad. I think there is always something salvageable. When given a choice between punishing someone and giving them a chance, I'd rather give them a chance."

Maria's philosophy, however, got her in hot water when her penchant for empathy and sensitivity ran afoul of the traditionally punitive environment of the court system. The trouble began when Maria sentenced a defendant to one year of home confinement with an electronic ankle bracelet and five years probation in an alleged child abuse case, rather than the eight- to ten-year jail sentence the prosecutor had demanded. The media created a political firestorm, alleging that Maria had violated numerous ethical rules governing judges, including rudeness to those who appeared in her courtroom. The gladiators gathered their forces and demanded nothing short of her removal from the bench. Maria's attorneys, Silvergate and Good, called it a classic witch hunt masquerading as a legitimate inquiry. When I talked to Maria before the hearings began she agreed.

> It is a witch hunt. I think it's because I yelled at a man, the prosecutor, and I'm a woman. Why? Because he was lying. I had asked him a question and he gave me an answer that he knew and I knew was not true. I said, "You're being disingenuous," and then I turned around to listen to

the defense, and the prosecutor stood up and tried to argue with me. I told him to sit down. That happened twice. And then I yelled at him and said, "If you don't sit down, I'll have my court officer sit you down." He deserved it.

The prosecutor was a narcissist and couldn't handle anyone disagreeing with him. I see plenty of these twenty-eight-year-old prosecutors who have all this power to take away people's liberty and have no judgment or life experience. They're full of themselves.

The fact that a woman yelled at a man publicly triggered a media frenzy. There was a recent judge who had some criticisms directed to him over some comments he made, and he was a white Irish male, and he didn't receive the attention I received. It's very interesting.

The case that plunged Maria into the cauldron of public humiliation was a combination of unfortunate circumstances and a lot of complexity. The charge: kidnapping and assault with an intent to rape a child, whose age the media misreported as eleven rather than just shy of thirteen. The alleged perpetrator: a twenty-one-year-old transgender female. The defendant, diagnosed with gender identity disorder, displayed a history of repeated beatings at school and came from a broken home where his mother was a drug addict and his estranged father had died. A psychiatric social worker concluded that the defendant was remorseful and would not likely repeat his crime. Incarceration would be a disaster for her. Since she was still physically a male, she would be sent to a men's prison.

The outrage at me, a woman, not being sensitive to a child abuse victim and sympathetic to a transgender person was the only story they wanted to see. The press perceived the judgment as lenient because the whole case was misperceived. The prosecutor put it out there that Ebony was a man dressed as a woman for the purpose of luring kids into her car. Ebony was dressing like a woman since she was thirteen. In my mind she was more of a public nuisance than a threat. She admitted to picking up younger males and performing oral sex on them. She never admitted to paying them although there was an unresolved issue about $50.

The victim said she wanted the victim to perform oral sex on her. I knew that was not possible or true because a transgender female with a penis, a source of shame and embarrassment, was not going let her penis play a role in whatever sexual activity was taking place. She wanted that penis removed, she just couldn't afford it. She was acting out her sexual identity issues with this young male and she was committing a crime, but more akin to statutory rape situation than the predatory pedophile they were trying to make her appear. We needed to get her off the streets, but to send her to a male prison where she could have been killed, raped, and certainly emotionally abused would be tantamount to a death sentence for her. It's not that I didn't sentence her. It was a decision that grasped the nuances of male-to-female transgender sexuality and not wanting to impose a cruel and abusive punishment. I was threatening the status quo, threatening business as usual, by not just throwing this kid in jail. Most judges would have just rubber stamped whatever the DA's office wanted. And they're not letting this go.

And they didn't let it go. It was a firestorm fueled by a number of forces including her enemies—people she had ruled against in other cases. They brought formal charges against Maria and held the disciplinary hearing, usually done behind closed doors, in a rare public display. The hearing officer's decision was that she should be suspended for six months and apologize to the prosecutor and the victim. It was the first step of a three-step process, going before the judicial conduct commission for approval and then before the supreme judicial court. Over the months, Maria suffered the glare of the media as the prosecutors launched scathing attack after attack. Maria remained true to her values and issued her own blistering attack on the ethics of the prosecutors and the lawyers who investigated her. "In my view," she said, "this is one of those situations where an elephant gun was used to shoot a mouse." Then she went on to sound the alarm that the treatment she had received would cause other judges to think twice before making unpopular decisions. She asked that all charges against her be dismissed.

In the end, Maria believed she wouldn't get a fair hearing and quit her judgeship after the first phase. How could she possibly perform her judicial duties while under continuous public scrutiny? When I spoke to Maria months before the hearings, she had already begun thinking about reinventing herself, perhaps devoting herself to work in Cuba. She did reinvent herself, but in a surprising way; she starred in a nationally syndicated daytime court show called *Judge Maria Lopez*. From media target to media celebrity! "How I handled things as a woman and as a Latina was alien to the system in Massachusetts," she said. "But my style of handling things has led me to this, and I'm having the time of my life. Oh, the irony."

Today she is a visiting scholar at the Women's Research Center at Brandeis University and writing her memoir. I spoke to her again and asked what she had to say in the end. "I'm glad I'm not part of that institution anymore. It's a sad statement. I'm completely disillusioned by what happened to me and how the process worked. It's not what I bargained for in becoming a lawyer for social change, to be kind and fair and sympathetic. That's not what it's about. It's all about politics and watching your ass."

Whatever you think of the circumstances that sent Maria's career in a new direction, you must admire her strength: she held to her feminine values and didn't apologize for her beliefs, for her nuanced thinking that informed her choice of punishment even while the witch-hunters clamored for her hide for daring to challenge them.

RESIST THE DOMINATION GAME

Let's return to the story of Janiece Webb, the Motorola vice president whom we met in the discussion on bullying. Her initiation into a gladiator culture was a baptism by fire. Like many of the highly successful women I interviewed, Janiece's parents left her pretty much to her own devices as a child. Growing up in an alcoholic family with little structure or order and not much care, she was at once given significant responsibilities but also regarded as of little consequence. Janiece recalled a defining moment when she was ten years old and walking alone across the desert in the dark. She was frightened and kept repeating to herself, "I'm not going to be like my family. It's not going to be like this forever." She left home at the age of sixteen. But the destructiveness of her family and their unwillingness to see her capabilities, she would discover, was not left behind. She rediscovered it in a gladiator culture at Motorola.

By the time Janiece was in her late twenties, this petite dynamo had already achieved an impressive level of stature in a very macho domain at the company: she was the person in charge of developing a missile's most crucial component, the guidance system. When she was to give an important presentation to three hundred admirals and commanders, she found herself a bit intimidated by the experience, even though she had worked with men her whole career. But she chided herself, as she had so many times before, "I can do this," and walked up on the stage. An admiral, assuming she had come to set up the audiovisual equipment, said, "Honey, I think we're all set there. You can get down now." Janiece replied, "I am the program manager and head this project." Taken aback by this diminutive woman's position, the admiral shouted, "What the hell is the world coming to that Motorola would send some broad to talk to me about my ordinance!" He turned his back to her, laughing out loud, with three hundred men joining in. Resisting feelings of humiliation as she stood there alone, Janiece had to think fast on her feet and figure out how to dig herself out of this man-made hole. After a brief pause, she spoke firmly, "Sir, I will do my best to earn your respect. I think if you give me a chance, you will find I can do this job, and if not, you can fire me." He turned around and said, "That's pretty gutsy. Let's hear what you have to say."

"It became a side show for three years," Janiece recalled. "Whenever I spoke, the room would fill up. I have put up with things that I would never put up with today. I have had things said to me—people would be arrested for saying them now—the crudest things. I could tell you stories that would make your hair fall out. Today, I wouldn't stand there and tough it out. I would simply walk off, or say, 'Admiral, I'm here to give you a presentation. I would really like you to turn around and listen, and if you can't, I will leave.' I wouldn't have jumped over the rope and let them keep raising it. I would say, 'I don't want to play that game.'"

One feisty little woman versus one big, bad admiral. Which would you follow into battle? I'll always prefer a leader who accepts her vulnerability over one who buries it in a hard heart. And what about the rest of the boys who laughed along, a gallow's laugh, terrified at the prospect of being in her shoes?

Janiece's brainpower and achievements rattled the status quo. It reminds me of a scene in the movie *The Secret Lives of Dentists*, where the bicycling husband, with his terrified wife-to-be sitting on the handlebars, goes barreling down a hill. Later, as their marriage seems about to dissolve, she asks her husband, "Why did you scare me like that?" He does not skip a beat. "Because you scared me. You were so smart and powerful." Deborah Kolb, a professor at the Simmons Graduate School of Management who studies workplace interactions, calls this a gender test, meaning a situation in which someone denigrates another person or puts her work under a microscope just because she is a woman. It frequently occurs when women take jobs usually held by men.

Janiece has managed to thrive in this environment even though, as she confided to me, "I have had two decent male bosses, and one male colleague who I could talk to in thirty years! Talk about being isolated. You develop internal strengths that most people don't have." Those strengths sprang to some extent from her determination to prove herself, to shake off her family's low expectations of her, and to establish herself as a person who could handle anything and everything that came her way. Many Iron Butterflies, like Janiece, develop inner strengths because they lack external support and must reach deep inside themselves for it. As women, we should make this less necessary by providing for each other the external support that makes it easier to resist the domination game.

SURVIVE AND THRIVE IN THE LION'S DEN

Things were shaping up nicely for Diana Twyman, now president of her own consulting business. She was working on her PhD and had won a very lucrative grant in a tough competition, enabling her to study head injuries at a large trauma center. In the midst of all this progress, she was also having conversations with the president of a small medical equipment company about how to use his technology in her research. Diana saw potential in using his equipment in medical diagnostics and in research, whereas the company had at that point used it only for health and wellness purposes.

Then a convergence of events would steer Diana in an unexpected direction. The grant she had won, she learned, would be very difficult to implement in the hospital. She decided to go ahead with a divorce. Just when life began to look very uncertain, the president of the medical equipment company called her and invited her to work for him and develop the new markets she had envisioned for his technology. He also offered to pay her 50 percent more than she was currently making. As a single mom, it seemed the right time and the right opportunity to get into business. She accepted the job.

It was not long before Diana began to note her boss's management style. "He was a bully," Diana told me. "His MO included shunning people, public humiliation, and pitting people against each other. Sometimes he wouldn't talk to an employee for weeks. He also made promises that he never intended to keep like paying bonuses as a way of motivating people."

She also discovered that the president hadn't been completely honest with her about the state of the company, failing to tell her they faced new competition they didn't know how to deal with, and that sales had dropped 50 percent. In the president's eyes, Diana was the golden girl who would get them out of this mess by developing new applications.

However, he used Diana's golden-girl status to set up a horse race between her and the head of sales. In self-defense, the sales director would point out to the president that golden girl had not increased sales, the phones were silent, and the problems were the same. "It's true, the phones weren't ringing yet, but I was actually making good progress in a short amount of time," Diana reflected. "I was designing new software, consulting scientists around the country, and developing the new research applications I envisioned. In addition, I was improving the existing products to be more powerful and successful." However, when progress wasn't immediately apparent, the president began to buy into all the innuendoes and suggestions the sales director whispered in his ear. Maybe he did make the wrong decision in hiring her; maybe Diana's strategies weren't going to work after all.

After a few months, the president called her to a meeting before the entire company. "The meeting," she recalled, "was designed to point out publicly that sales had not improved as a result of my efforts. It was designed to humiliate me and make me the fall guy for the problems the company was facing, problems that had existed before I got there. By this time, I had figured out how he operated; he was manipulative and controlling. I stayed calm as he pointed the lack of response to my programs. I listened to him like he was talking about someone else."

When he finished, Diana looked him in the eye, and at the rest of the group, and asked if there were any questions for her. There weren't any so she said, "I guess we're done here then," and she walked out the door. "In some ways, he was easier to deal with him than most because his maliciousness was overt. Backstabbing is often veiled with corporate niceness, which makes it harder to understand. It's challenging to hold up in terms of self-esteem, especially for someone new since they are usually in less powerful positions. But I already saw him for what he was."

In a stroke of divine justice, the day after this failed attempt at humiliation, the phones in the sales department started ringing with orders from eager customers. When the president saw that her strategies were working, he did a complete turn around and once again Diana was the golden girl. He fired the sales director and put Diana in charge of both sales and marketing. In time, Diana turned the company around, bringing in sales to where they had been when the company was at its peak.

I asked Diana how she could work with someone who had attempted to publicly humiliate her:

> I could work with him because he needed me. I was successful. I had the opportunity to learn and advance my career. If things hadn't improved as dramatically as they had, I wouldn't have stayed there. Being in the lion's den is a sudden-death situation. As long as you win, you survive, and you're a hero. But that's an exhausting way to live. I wouldn't recommend staying in that situation for very long.

After several years, Diana realized that if the company was to get to the next level in its maturation, it needed to develop strategic partnerships with some large companies. Publicly, the president would support Diana's proposed strategy of different agreements and relationships. Privately, he knew this approach would require him to give up more control than he was willing to do. "There was a very important and strategic relationship with another company I had been working on for some time that was coming to fruition. The president made a commitment to this partner, and then told me privately that he had no intention of honoring his commitments. That's when I decided it was time for me to go."

Some time later, Diana bumped into the president at a convention. He was with the sales manager, whom he had rehired. They both expressed their regrets about the past, acknowledging that they had treated her badly. "The president seemed to be seeking absolution," Diana recalled. "It was clear to me that I had moved on, and that nothing had changed for him."

Gladiators keep many sharp arrows in their quivers: personal attacks, ridicule, sabotage, and treachery, to name a few. These weapons promote self-interest at any cost. The sales director, threatened by Diana's competence, tried to sabotage her by diminishing her in the eyes of the president. To her credit, however, Diana did not take the attacks personally because she knew they sprang from their own deep-seated vulnerability. By distancing herself emotionally from the situation, she protected herself from the gladiator defense and refused to play their game. "I never let it get to me and drag me down to a similar way of operating. I never went after the sales guy because, at some level, I saw that he was just as vulnerable as I was."

HOLD ON TO YOUR TRUTH

Capturing the 1997 Nobel Peace Prize for her work on eliminating land mines didn't exempt Jody Williams from the wrath of gladiators. Jody is a woman who doesn't mince words and calls it as she sees it. Her story shows how some gladiators will stop at nothing in their efforts to diminish a strong woman who has outshone them, even to the point of threatening a campaign that could save thousands of lives.

> Some people involved in the campaign were vicious after I was named the Prize recipient. It was at once a horrible time personally and a terrific time for the campaign. But there was a group of men, whom I do think were sexist, who resented me receiving the Prize, although they were happy to let me coordinate the campaign and make the Mine Ban Treaty happen. These big talkers would go yapping that we should do this or that. If it had been left to them, we wouldn't have had shit happen, because they didn't do anything that they were yapping about. When I was individually named recipient of the Nobel Prize, other tensions that were in the campaign were also given free rein.

The tensions included a terrible run-in between Jody and her boss, Bobby. Bobby, a disabled Vietnam vet, had approached Jody in 1991 to create a land mine campaign. Since Bobby's plate was full with several other projects, he handed full control of the campaign to Jody. They became very close friends until a year before she won the Prize, when their relationship fell apart for several reasons, among them Bobby's hiring consultants to tell him how to run his foundation. In a stunning defiance of logic, the consultants saw the land mine campaign and Jody as valuable assets but felt strongly that Bobby should pull the reins on Jody and insist that she treat him as a boss rather than a colleague. "Instead of telling me clearly that he wanted me to treat him like a boss, he started acting very differently toward me and we had a couple of fights in front of the staff," Jody recalled. "I was rather fired up and he later said I had treated him disrespectfully. That is beyond the pot calling the kettle black. He even curses more than I do, so it was clear that something much more complicated was going on."

The summer leading up to the successful negotiation of the Mine Ban Treaty and then the totally unexpected Nobel Peace Prize, he gave Jody her first-ever job evaluation. Continuing the pattern of cutting off your nose to spite your face, Bobby praised her as the most brilliant organizer he had ever seen and awarded her a $10,000 raise. Then he went on to say that he would be parting ways with her at the end of the year, once the treaty fell into place. "He told me I was 'too big' for the organization. I was stunned and sad. I kept trying to persuade him that it was not a good thing to do."

The day of the announcement of the 1997 Nobel Peace Prize, which went to Jody as well as the International Campaign to Ban Landmines, Bobby grew furious when she refused to immediately jump in the car and drive eight hours to Washington, DC, for a press conference he planned to arrange with a Senate champion of the ban and others. Bobby didn't want to hear that even at that hour—5AM—there were already five journalists waiting on the stairs outside her house, at the end of an unmarked dirt road in Vermont, and more were on their way as they spoke on the phone. Enraged, he called all the executive directors and founding members of the campaign and vilified her as a self-promoting liability. "If you read any of the press from that time," Jody said, "you will see that it is all 'we,' 'we,' 'we,' when I spoke, never 'I.'"

Imagine being upset enough over her achievement to risk destroying the whole campaign by attacking her publicly! "I can't get my mind around that," Jody mused. "You can be pissed with me personally, you can hate my guts because I was recognized, although, 'Hello,' I did the work and he was more than happy to let me do it. But to risk this incredible thing we'd created? I struggled hard to keep the moral high ground. Only one time did I say publicly, 'This is male ego.' Eventually all the assholes quit. We just kept doing the work."

At the Nobel ceremony, Bobby walked past his former friend and then called her a cunt within earshot of her mother. So let's add insult to the gladiator's arsenal. When Jody returned home from the ceremony, she was hand-delivered a termination letter giving her two weeks' notice. Standing her ground, however, Jody continued on as coordinator of the International Campaign to Ban Landmines and then was named Campaign Ambassador. She has been working for the campaign pro bono ever since.

Although the stories of women working in gladiator cultures may seem like a sad commentary on contemporary organizations, they also illuminate the power of Iron Butterflies. Iron Butterflies reject victimhood, even while under the fiercest onslaught by those who would devalue and demean them. They do not whimper. They do not whine. Nor do they turn aggressor and try to humiliate the gladiator in return. Instead, they simply refuse to play the aggressor/victim game. Iron Butterflies, courageous and vulnerable, display their strength by taking the high moral ground. Rather than casting stones, they sow seeds of respect.

Chapter 6

TEARS

Heal the Hidden Wound

I'm not afraid to show my feminine side—it's part of what makes me a man.

Gerard Depardieu

"I thought you might be interested in this story," Katie Dealy, a friend of mine, told me as she handed me a page from *Metropolis*, a local free paper. "Isn't this what you're writing about?" she asked me. Indeed, it was. The small autobiographical piece written by a boy named Doug Lang is worth retelling. Like most kids in junior high school, Doug battled with insecurity and awkwardness and wanted desperately to be popular. And, like most boys in our culture, he quickly learned that the gladiator defense not only obscured his insecurity but also gave him the approval he so desperately sought. On the playground he'd pick a fight with a wimpy misfit, then pummel the hapless victim until a cheering crowd had gathered to watch the brawl. As the playground supervisor hauled Doug off to the principal's office, older kids would pat him on the back. "It was glorious," he recalls. "For a few days at least I'd be a hero." Then something happened to crack his gladiator's armor.

One morning on the school bus he picked out another weaker classmate and beat him up. Late that night, lying in his bed, his conscience caught up with him. Crying, he woke up his mother and told her how he'd attacked a kid who had done nothing to deserve the attack. "But," as Doug recalls, "the lesson didn't stick."

Doug kept picking fights, and although he still hadn't learned the lesson, it continued to bubble away in a corner of his conscience. One time, gripping a boy in a headlock and preparing to knee him in the face, Doug just couldn't bring himself to do it. "It haunted me for years, this limitation," he said, "and still does, in a way."

Eventually he stopped picking fights and took up football, a new battleground where he discovered "a new level of macho assimilation. We learned controlled rage, and how to be stoic. If you were hurt or tired, you didn't show it. This was all about being a man."

Doug still struggles with the societal association between aggression and manhood. "After decades of mentally straddling the worlds of bully and the bullied, of 'manliness' and sensitivity, I can still empathize with the contempt for weakness that makes men violent. And when I contemplate dying of cancer, as my mother did, what haunts me most is that people will know how scared I am, and see me cry."

I think Iron Butterflies have developed a special antenna for detecting the scared and sensitive boy lurking in every man who, like Doug, does not want anyone to see that fear or watch him burst into tears. That explains why the Iron Butterflies I interviewed did not want me to overemphasize aggressive and debasing male behavior. While some denied or whitewashed abusive actions, others thought that awarding them too much attention might only further empower the gladiator. Still others feared that confronting bad behavior would only exacerbate a bad situation. Eventually, I concluded that many women defend or overlook gladiator behavior because we naturally wish to protect the men in our lives. I myself belong to a generation of girls who were told not only to protect the male ego but also to boost it up. That was actually one of the rules of attraction. I never thought to ask why we needed to treat men's egos like fragile birds' eggs, but looking back on my younger self I realize that many of us instinctively sensed an invisible wound on men's souls. At some visceral level we grasped that all that male assertiveness, aggression, or rudeness didn't stem from strength but from insecurity, that although we perceived men as the powerful sex, they often masked their feelings of powerlessness with sheer bravado. Those feelings arise, I now think, from the way domination-based societies define the very essence of masculinity.

The story of Zeus and his ascendancy to power also provides some insight into how we perceive masculinity. After swallowing his wife, Metis; killing his father, Cronus; birthing his daughter, Athena, from his head; and finally vanquishing the Titans after ten years of fighting, the action hero Zeus achieves his goal: to sit alone atop Mount Olympus, lightning bolt in hand. Zeus epitomizes an idealized image of masculinity: emotionally detached, omnipotent, and autonomous. For all the power and the glory it portrays, this image of a powerful man limits all the males who buy into it from fully realizing themselves. Hidden behind the gladiator façade lingers a gaping wound inflicted by a domination culture that requires that a real man must appear as invulnerable as Zeus.

The moral of Zeus's story? Manhood is a precarious achievement a male must constantly prove and defend, oftentimes by severing relationships, as Zeus did, between father and son, mother and daughter, husband and wife. In essence, to become and remain a manly man, the gladiator must repudiate any form of dependency. Zeus and his gladiator disciples turn themselves not only into Lone Rangers but also into lonely rangers, often living in a world of isolation.

In *The Birth of Pleasure*, psychologist Carol Gilligan writes, "Masculine often implies an ability to stand alone and forgo relationships whereas femininity connotes a willingness to compromise oneself for the sake of relationships—both entail loss of relationship." This dynamic destroyed the relationship between Zeus and Metis. In order to stand alone with all his power intact, Zeus abandons his relationship with Metis, who colludes in the game by becoming small for the sake of their relationship, only to end up getting swallowed and forgotten. When masculine and feminine social constructs like the ones Gilligan describes rule behavior, they can prevent both men and women from realizing their true selves.

This story of interpersonal disconnection also contains a story of emotional disconnection. Zeus expresses no remorse, shame, uncertainty, or any consideration for how his actions may impact others. For all the power and privilege gladiators may wield, they suffer from constricted emotional lives that impinge on their ability to relate intimately with both women and other men. To compensate for their emotional limitations and lack of intimacy, they anaesthetize themselves with power and success.

In this chapter, we will explore three concepts that define the meaning of masculinity in a domination culture: femiphobia, emotional detachment, and invulnerability. We will then invite a new way of looking at manhood that allows men to embrace their more feminine realities and fulfill a better destiny to hold love, be loved, and be beloved.

RECOGNIZE FEMIPHOBIA

What does it mean to be a man? According to clinical psychologist Stephen Ducat, author of *The Wimp Factor*, "The most important thing about being a man is not being a woman." This leads many men to fear the feminine, an attitude Ducat calls femiphobia. Ducat points out that while its severity varies from man to man, it leaves "no man . . . completely unaffected." Feminine conjures up all those uncontrollable and messy intangibles in life, such as emotions and, according to author Caitlin Matthews, passion: "Fear of the feminine is often fear of the chaotic and ecstatic nature of sexuality itself in which men and women temporarily lose control of their rational, ordered being." Throughout history, societies have designated weakness, powerlessness, and inferiority as feminine territory. Why on Earth would any man ever venture there?

Femiphobics fear powerful women not only because they threaten male dominance, as we saw in the previous chapter, but also because they reduce their autonomy. Women exude the mother aura, which a gladiator will disdain or attack because he fears that it might augment his sense of dependency and undermine his self-reliance. Certainly, from birth to age three or four years, a child's whole world revolves around his mother. Most of us have experienced the great mother, who holds our well-being, for better or for worse, in her hands. To defend himself against the memory of his dependency on mother, which he sees as a weakness, the gladiator demeans and devalues the feminine in himself and others. He disassociates from his feminine realities by scorning soft-heartedness as touchy-feely and unmanly. He splits away from aspects of himself by not admitting any physical or emotional dependency on others. By denying the feminine, gladiators hope to inflate the masculine and deplete any feelings of envy by deeming feminine realities as worthless. A man who believes he must dominate to prove his manhood not only severs interpersonal relations but also intrapersonal relations, that is, a relationship to aspects of himself.

How do you recognize femiphobia? Sometimes it takes such a subtle form, you need a microscope to see it. I remember speaking to some consultants in London who worked for a very progressive organization that focused on enhancing adaptability in organizations. They showed me a report about key strategies for achieving that goal, strategies that clearly fell under the label "feminine activities": more inclusion, relationship building, and collaboration, less hierarchy. But I could not find the word "feminine" anywhere in the document. When I pointed this out, they told me, "Yes, we know these are feminine qualities, and we argued back and forth about it. But in the end we decided it would be too bold to use the word because people would find it threatening." Threatening? There it is: the fear of a simple word that conveys interconnection and interdependence because it threatens the masculine illusion of independence and autonomy. I say illusion because even Zeus, the ultimate Lone Ranger, couldn't have achieved his goal without his brothers' aid or Metis's plan to free them. Like Zeus, who swallowed Metis, these consultants wanted to swallow feminine wisdom and hide it behind the old masculine façade.

Femiphobia can also take the form of blatant misogyny. Take Cynthia Papageorge's story, for instance. While working as a successful district manager at Mothers Work, Inc., a maternity clothes retailer, Cynthia became pregnant. During her third trimester a vice president paid a surprise visit to her office, and when he laid eyes on the obviously pregnant Cynthia, he recoiled in horror at the sight of her round belly and the sensible sneakers she wore to ease her swelling ankles. The vice president repeatedly referred to her pregnancy and asked whether she could do her job in her "condition." As she said later, "He made me feel like he was disgusted." This man told Papageorge's boss, Jan Dowe, to fire Cynthia, which Jan refused to do, so he fired both Jan and Cynthia. What a sad irony. Instead of viewing Cynthia as a walking advertisement for the company, this maternity clothes retailer made her disappear. But she did not go easily into Zeus's belly. Cynthia filed a discrimination complaint that was settled on the first day of trial. The court barred Cynthia and Jan from speaking with the media or publicly discussing the case, and it sealed the terms of the deal. But they did win an important, if silent, victory over a femiphobic.

Even the fiercest gladiators will, despite all their weapons and armor, feel attracted to women, which can and does cause problems for them when their proximity to the objects of their desire connect them to their own fears of impotency and the unruliness of passion and desire. Nikki Watkins, who at the time was an internal consultant for a software company in England, is an attractive woman in her thirties, with long, lush chestnut hair and incredibly blue eyes. After she wrapped up one of her workshops, a male participant approached her and asked if she wanted some feedback. Of course she did. "It's about your dress code," the man said to her. "I feel vulnerable with the way you look." All Nikki could think was, "Why vulnerable? And what's wrong with feeling vulnerable?" He went on to say that her skirt was too short, her hair too long, her makeup too enticing. He concluded that "a bunch of us boys got together and talked about our vulnerability." Our vulnerability? Indeed.

In this awkward situation Nikki felt, as so many women would, that male vulnerability had become her problem. When Nikki confided her feelings to a personal coach, the coach advised her that by dressing conservatively, pinning up her hair, she could progress more rapidly in her career. If she refused to abandon the look and style that made the boys feel vulnerable, she must accept the fact that her blatant femininity would put her on a slower track. In other words, the fast track depends on protecting men from feeling their own vulnerability. Which path did Nikki choose? She opted to continue dressing as she always had because she refused to accept the notion that it's a woman's job to protect men from perfectly normal feelings.

RECOGNIZE THE TABOO ON VULNERABILITY

Beneath femiphobia and the gladiator defense lies a denied wound, a tender sore caused by the age-old taboo on men revealing their vulnerability. Vulnerability, perhaps the most human of all traits, has unfortunately become gender-coded as feminine and therefore shameful to gladiators. No one likes to feel vulnerable, but if a gladiator must constantly feign invulnerability, or always battle to control his environment in order to avoid vulnerable feelings, then he can only embrace half of his human traits, leaving whole dimensions of himself unknown. Unknown, these softer sides become frightening and unwanted and hated. But by avoiding vulnerability, its emotional pain, and its resolution, men limit their own humanity, and that ultimately limits their understanding of the world. Instead, they physically, emotionally, and mentally camouflage their needs and dependencies with the mask of invincibility. Physical invincibility shows up as bravado when gladiators willingly take physical risks that put them and sometimes others in danger. On the other hand, they take few emotional risks as they force themselves to become emotionally detached, unshakeable, and fearless. Mental invincibility takes shape as the hubris gladiators employ to avoid admitting failures, mistakes, wrongdoing, or a lack of knowledge. How many women have ridden in a car with a man who refuses to stop and ask for directions?

Masculinity defined as invulnerability can only lead to emotional underdevelopment in men who must struggle to deny all weakness, fear, uncertainty, ambivalence, dependency, and pain. "The mass of men," observed Henry David Thoreau, "lead lives of quiet desperation." For countless men, desperation leads to depression. According to a *Newsweek* article, six million men were diagnosed with depression in 2007, with millions more suffering silently and undiagnosed. Prohibited from expressing his suffering, a depressed male may commit suicide. That helps explain why the suicide rate among men is four times greater than among women.

Therapist Jonathan Stillerman, former director of Men Can Stop Rape, told me, "All men are quite aware at some level, probably more on the subconscious level, of the fear they have of their own feelings." Gladiators avoid looking deeper into their emotional selves because they fear that what they will see there might erode the very foundation on which they have built their identities. Fearing that their long suppressed vulnerable feelings might overwhelm them, they demean personal reflection and avoid internal work. As long as he disavows and disowns his vulnerable feelings, a man will remain emotionally unstable because his denied feelings do not evaporate and, in a sad twist of irony, become controlling factors in his life. They control him to the extent that they force him to develop the gladiator defense. And men learn to do this at an early age.

EMPATHIZE WITH OUR BOYS

Psychologist William Pollack, codirector of the Center for Men at McLean Hospital, has studied boys for decades. In the *Wimp Factor*, Stephen Ducat's definition of what it means to be a man echoes Pollack's definition of what it means to be a boy. In his book *Real Boys: Rescuing Our Sons from the Myths of Boyhood*, he writes, "Being masculine is defined as avoiding the feminine. Being a boy becomes defined in the negative: not being a girl." Boys, he argues, are separated from their parents, and especially their mothers, much too early in their lives. "They are often being pushed toward pseudo-independence before they are really ready." Forced to cut mother's apron string, often by age five, they lose the close and dependent relationship with mother that might imperil their masculinity and invite derision as a "mama's boy." This separation denies them any feelings or behaviors the culture might consider feminine. Pollack calls this repudiation of the feminine side in a boy's personality "the boy code." As they grow up under this code, boys deemphasize their need for comfort, opting to take care of themselves even while they pursue high-risk endeavors to prove their manhood. It's John Wayne or Gary Cooper proclaiming, "I can take care of myself," while staring down another gladiator's gun barrel.

The boy code observes strict rules: be cool and stoic, avoid shame at all costs, and never show weakness, dependency, warmth, or empathy. Under great pressure to emulate strength, boys work hard to hide their true inner feelings and show the world only their heroic, tough, action-oriented side. In order to live up to the gladiator definition of masculinity, they split off parts of themselves, but, without access to all human aspects of themselves, they end up with fragile self-esteem. And as bullies do, they mask that fragility with boasting, bragging, and, all too often, their fists.

Studies show that children learn about gender as early as age three. By the time they reach age six, they already know the characteristics and behaviors their culture associates with each gender. Girls play with dolls; boys line up their toy soldiers on an imagined battleground. Girls, however, enjoy more latitude than boys. For instance, it's OK for girls to be tomboys and play rough and tumble, but it's not OK for boys to be sissies and play with dolls.

Our society continues to raise gladiators because our *domination culture does not sufficiently empathize with boys.* As much as any society needs boys and men to provide food and shelter and defend against enemies, it actually treats them like disposable commodities. In Sparta, boys were removed from their homes at age seven to prepare them to become warriors. "The less a boy valued intimacy, life, and love," writes Warren Farrell, author of *The Myth of Male Power*, "the more he would allow himself to be disposable. We bribed him to do this by offering him respect." Farrell goes on to say that "the wound that unifies all men is the wound of their disposability. The wound of believing that they're loveable if they kill and die so others might be saved and survive. . . . We don't call male killing sexism, we call it glory." Like the gladiators of old, we treat our boys as tools of war where major powers sustain their influence with the blood of young men. As Farrell points out, if a fetus has a right to life but eighteen years later has an obligation to death (with the draft), which sex is it? A boy, of course.

In order to prepare for this role, boys learn that they must toughen up. Just think about all the soul-hardening messages boys hear every day. All too soon they are told "Boys don't cry," "Suck it up," "Tough it out," "Be a man," "Don't act like a girl," "Stand up and take your medicine like a man," ad nauseum. Can a boy suffer more shame than to earn the label "sissy" because he throws a ball or runs the bases "like a girl"? Or described as "so gay" because he prefers to help his mother fix dinner rather than participate in a rough-and-tumble game of tackle football in the backyard? The list goes on: pansy, henpecked, and pussy-whipped. Governor Arnold Schwarzenegger added his own term to the list, "a girly man," when he chided the men in the California legislature. Guess all that bodybuilding isn't armor enough.

Disparage the feminine in boys, and they quickly come to believe that the feminine, and therefore girls, are weak and unenviable. A 1991 Michigan Board of Education study asked boys and girls how they would react if they woke up one morning to find themselves the opposite sex. Fifty percent of the girls found the idea exciting and interesting and spoke of advantages they would enjoy. On the other hand, only 7 percent of the boys saw any advantage to living as a girl, and the vast majority gave extremely derogatory responses. An alarming number of boys said they would kill themselves. Even now, no one thinks twice about calling a mixed-gender group "guys," but no one, absolutely no one, calls such a group "gals." Except as a joke.

Female genetics no more predispose girls to feel vulnerable than male DNA dictates a tendency toward feelings of invulnerability. In fact, male children display very strong feelings. Studies revealed that boy babies start out more emotionally expressive than girls. Take Yoga guru Victor van Kooten, for example. Unlike most boys, Victor did not give up his feminine side as a youth and liked to play with his favorite doll and jump rope. As he told me, "I had my antennae out and knew the boy role was going to crumble. I had an inner conviction; something warned me against this behavior and made me stand up to it." He also offered this observation: "I see more vulnerability in boys than in girls. They are much more easily victimized. Boys cry faster than girls; their whole world falls apart. When they hit bottom, they hit it really hard, because they don't have enough resources to draw on."

If more adult males, fathers and father figures, adopted Victor's point of view, and if more women saw the fearful and potentially sensitive boy inside all that gladiator armor, they could, I think, send our sons the liberating message that it's OK to feel and express so-called feminine emotions. An ounce of empathy could cure a ton of frustration and depression, not to mention aggression and abuse.

STOP THE BULLYING

Boys come under great pressure to act tough. If a boy's actions violate the boy code, he will slam into a wall of societal resistance. Join the club, or suffer the consequences. Boys find safety and security as members of the male in-group, that rigidly ordered clubhouse where they earn their stripes and climb up the ranks. Initiation into that club includes lessons on fighting and dominating, which equip him to thrive in a domination culture.

The clubhouse also uses a potent and pervasive tool to control boys from expressing a shame. Shame may be a vulnerable experience, but it is also an important emotion that regulates conscience, modesty, and morality. Shame becomes highly corrosive when it's used to indoctrinate boys into denying feminine realities through feelings of inadequacy, impotency, and guilt. Boys employ various verbal weapons such as insults, jeering, and taunting to shame each other into manhood. Humiliated, boys can run but not hide.

What do they do to defend themselves? They disconnect from their vulnerability. Shame is such a frightening possibility, they will do almost anything to avoid it. To avoid losing face, they tough it out, ultimately hardening themselves from feelings they associate with weakness and its sister, femininity. Doing otherwise would invite shaming. "Rather than expose themselves to this kind of potent embarrassment," writes Pollack, "boys in the face of suffering shame, engage in a variety of behaviors that range from avoidance of dependency to impulsive action, from bravado and rage-filled outbursts to intense violence." When shame needs to be inhibited, boys slide down a slippery slope, as psychiatrist Jim Gilligan found in his research with male prisoners. When shame had to be a secret, or covered up with bravado, it inevitably led to violence. And when a man inhibits feelings of shame, he also inhibits feelings of guilt, love, and fear.

Bullying is the bastard child of vulnerability and shame, an aggressive strategy men often transport into the workplace, as we saw in the previous chapter. Bullying in schools has become such an issue that many have launched antibullying campaigns. In 2002, the American Medical Association labeled it a public health menace. Across the country, children ages eight to fifteen reported bullying as a greater threat than racism or the pressure to drink alcohol or take drugs. One hundred and sixty thousand children a day don't go to school for fear of being bullied. Schools once overlooked bullying and dismissed it as common, even normal, behavior. But when educators learned that the children responsible for shootings in such incidents as the horrific massacre at Columbine High School had suffered at the hands of bullies, the whole world began to take notice. Will these new programs succeed? Only time will tell. Many school officials acknowledge the antibullying programs buck the norms of society that encourage the hierarchies so intrinsic to domination cultures. Boys encounter a dilemma. "Don't bully others," the new program insists, while the culture at large promotes and even glorifies the opposite.

We can all help change the meaning of manhood by telling our boys that they do not need to toughen up and suck it up whenever they begin to feel vulnerable and instead give them the empathy every human deserves. Yes, the big alpha dog may rule the pack in a dog-eat-dog world, but a better option exists, the option to feel your deepest feelings and express them as caring—caring for yourself and everyone around you.

WELCOME THE NEW MAN AT WORK

If we all encourage a more expansive and humane meaning of manhood, honoring rather than dishonoring the role vulnerability plays in men's lives, we may find the workplace a much more hospitable place for women. The research conducted by Robin Ely, professor of business administration at Harvard Business School, opens the window to envisioning a new man at work. She and her team ventured to the supermacho world of offshore oil platforms to study masculinity. Typically in such dangerous, male-dominated work settings like this, or like coal mining, firefighting, and military service, men gain respect by demonstrating and defending their masculinity and will go to great lengths to appear invulnerable in three realms: physical, technical, and emotional. This tendency can, ironically, lead to quite costly safety and efficiency problems, as Robin Ely pointed out in an interview with Harvard Business School's *Working Knowledge*:

> Efforts to appear invulnerable blocked precisely the kinds of actions that encourage safety and effectiveness. Covering up mistakes, for example, curtails learning and allows for the repetition and escalation of errors. In complex systems with high degrees of interdependence, small errors that go unrecognized can cascade into large accidents. Practices that conflate competence with toughness lead workers to ignore precautionary measures and take unnecessary risks.

However, Robin and her colleagues found something remarkably different on the oil platform—men who did not fear or shy away from feelings of vulnerability, who readily acknowledged their physical limitations, publicly admitted their mistakes so they could learn from them, and openly attended to their own and other's feelings. Predictably, these work habits produced deeper, more intimate co-worker relationships.

How did this happen? The organization emphasized safety and effectiveness above all else, a focus that generated "purposeful" behavior because it, as Ely observed, "involved making oneself vulnerable in order to achieve work-related goals," thus releasing men from social pressures to prove their invincibility and toughness. Ely identified three conditions in organizations that promote a shift toward what I call the "new man at work." Condition One: establish a clear connective purpose, what Roger Lewin and I referred to as "the soul at work" in our earlier book. By that I mean people in the workplace investing in a meaningful shared purpose that connects them to one another and to something greater than themselves. A macho self-image contradicts engaging the soul at work and striving toward the common goal of safety. Condition Two: create psychological safety that supports men who willingly take interpersonal risks, show their vulnerability, and do not feel diminished by doing so. Condition Three: decouple masculinity and competence. Bravery and toughness and other gladiator-style masculine traits do not ensure competency and, in fact, contribute very little to safer working conditions or improved effectiveness. By implementing these three changes, an organization can effect a profound shift from a situation where men are engaged in self-absorbed efforts to prove themselves, to conquer and rule, to one anchored in the real demands of the work and a more humane and honest idea of what it means to be a man. When we redefine masculinity in terms of connecting to others and sharing a purpose, we replace potentially damaging defensive processes with restorative and generative ones. It does not boil down to which is better, the masculine way or the feminine way. As Ely points out, "*How* people enact their gender identities—defensively versus generatively—may be more consequential than *what* traits they display."

Dick Knowles's story illustrates what Robin Ely observed and shows that when our culture and our institutions allow men to express vulnerability without incurring shame, everyone benefits. Dick Knowles, founder of the Center for Self-Organizing Leadership with his wife Claire, authored the book *The Leadership Dance*. As a "reformed" gladiator, Dick went through a personal transformation, then a cultural transformation, which reduced injury rates in an unsafe, macho environment by an astounding 95 percent.

Before he started his own organization, Dick worked for DuPont in Belle, West Virginia, where he managed the first commercial synthetic ammonia facility in the United States. The company had charged him with the task of turning around the troubled facility. Otherwise, DuPont would shut it down. Dick encountered a hugely challenging situation, a severely ailing environment "like a sick person needing healing." In a predominantly male setting involving highly dangerous work, the plant displayed all the symptoms of an organization ruled by the gladiator's commitment to invulnerability. People didn't express their feelings, and whenever a person felt abused or threatened, he would tend to harbor a grudge and wait for a chance to exact revenge. Managers abdicated their responsibilities and blamed everyone else for the toxic environment. Punishment and intimidation had replaced any sort of thoughtful, caring management. Consequently, people would rather cut off an arm than admit a mistake or blow the whistle on a serious safety problem. Of course, the injury rate escalated as workers watched out for themselves, rather than for each other.

Dick dedicated himself to changing all that. He immediately made safety an overriding issue and started holding people accountable for safety problems and resultant injuries, but he did it with gladiator-style command and control. He'd just tell the men how to get the result the company wanted. Period. No discussion, no debate. He admitted that he treated others at that time in a brutal, foul-mouthed, and demeaning fashion. For example, if he wanted to know the exact details of an injury, and the supervisor didn't offer an acceptable answer, Dick would erupt in a shouting rage. He made it clear the supervisor should know this information. But Dick went even further, ripping the person to shreds in front of everyone, humiliating him in a classic example of the "shame game." Unsurprisingly, managers avoided Dick's wrath by concealing even more bad news. Rather than opening communication as he truly wished to do, Dick only managed to shut it down even more.

As part of his effort to open communication, Dick scheduled biweekly meetings with the leadership group. At one such meeting with forty mechanics and their managers, a group that prided itself on its fierce independence and toughness, something happened to open Dick's eyes. Before the meeting the mechanics had met with their supervisor, who warned everyone not to make waves with Dick. Midway through the meeting, Dick asked for questions from the group. All forty guys just got up, turned their chairs around, and sat back down with their backs to the boss. Dick recalls that moment vividly:

I'm the boss for God's sake, the boss of the entire plant! I panicked. "God, what do I do now?" I said to myself. I knew if I walked, I was dead. If I lost my temper, I was dead. I just stood there, and finally told all the managers to get the hell out. So I'm in there alone with forty backs facing me, the place was silent. I got myself a cup of coffee, and sat down, looking at their backs. I don't know how long we all sat like that. It seemed like an hour, but maybe it was only a few minutes. I was sweating. And then I said in a soft voice, "You know, this is a real lonely job. Are you guys going to talk to me?" Within a minute they turned around, and we had a wonderful meeting, people being honest about their concerns, not just complaining. The back-turning stunt was the guys' way of punishing their bosses for having told them not to make waves with me. It was very funny afterward. We really connected.

Staring at those backs, Dick did not feel so tough and invulnerable. To his credit, he got the message, turned his own back on his inner gladiator, and allowed himself to express his vulnerability to the men by admitting that he needed their help. That reaction both literally and figuratively turned the mechanics around. Mark those words: "We really connected." Through his example he showed others that they could reveal their own vulnerability safely, without fear of shame. If you screw up, don't hide the problem, but own up to it, stop the blame game, and work with your colleagues to fix it. With that new model of behavior, the men began working together with a common vision of creating a safer and more effective plant. They welcomed a new man into the workplace, one who can freely express vulnerability physically, tactically, and emotionally, without fear of ridicule or retaliation. By the end of Dick's tenure, the plant's productivity had increased 45 percent and injury rates went down by 95 percent.

INVITE MEN TO HOLD LOVE

Inhibiting vulnerability limits a man's capacity to hold feelings of love. When we love someone, we open our hearts and are immediately vulnerable. We expose ourselves to being hurt as well as nourished, to being moved to our core. We abandon control. Love, in all its mysteries, can expand our lives with joy and awaken our most magnanimous self, but it can also scare us to death, resurrecting our deepest fears. For a man to hold love, he must willingly face his fears and vulnerabilities. If he does not, he risks sabotaging his chance at love and all the joy it can bring into his life and work. He must allow himself to feel small, uncertain, and insecure, and risk that he will receive comfort and joy rather than humiliation and exploitation. Without a willingness to let go of certainty and control, no human being, male or female, can achieve his or her full potential. When we grasp the opportunities of love, the chance it offers to be authentic and boldly truthful, we forge a deeper connection with other human beings. Women should encourage all the men in their lives to revel in the joy of intimacy and share one of life's central tenets. In order to hold love, paradoxically, you must let go.

Although love creates a sanctuary for nurturance through an exchange of feelings, it flies in the face of the gladiator definition of a man. Men, according to that code, should serve, not feel, perform, not reveal, and behave heroically, not humanly. Do your duty; do not waste time searching for emotional fulfillment. Men can march in a straight line, can frighten and intimidate people, can force their will on others with emotional outbursts, but they cannot cry, cannot show love or vulnerability. You want to feel something? Feel self-confidence and arrogance, anger and rage. Be aggressive. Above all, never let that fearful little boy peek out of your hardened heart. All these emotions and behaviors deprive our boys and men from nourishing relationships. We expect strength and certainty in all matters. We urge our men to conquer the world, and then we ask them to strip off their armor and reveal their softness. To learn to hold love and be vulnerable is men's door out of a limited meaning of manhood, a journey where they can claim their feminine realities and admit their needs for love. At the very least, we can allow men the feelings of vulnerability every woman has experienced.

I invite you to rent the movie *Shall We Dance?* In it Richard Geer finds a connection to a dormant and softer part of himself through dance. I would also recommend the wonderful movie *Million Dollar Baby*, starring Clint Eastwood, the leading man of celebrated spaghetti Westerns, the ultimate man's man. In this film he replaced the power of the .45 Magnum with the power of relationships. Wesley Morris, in his *Boston Globe* review of the movie, titled "Women Are Key in Eastwood's Growth from Macho to Mellow," observed that "Clint Eastwood the icon has leveled towns and stopped rapists and killers and thieves from further stinking up society. He's mocked himself, gone into outer space, and starred with a primate—twice. But who knew the bravest thing he could ever do was return a woman's love?" Older men modeling a different sort of manhood supply a model for younger men to follow. And there are young men also trailblazing a new path to the meaning of manhood. The mere presence of hip-hop star Kanye West, wearing a pink polo shirt and tight jeans and whose mascot is a teddy bear, is forcing rappers to rethink their ideas of masculinity and homosexuality. This new sort of manhood, as we see in Topher Sanders's story, reveals how tears can heal the hidden wound.

Topher Sanders's story appeared in "My Turn" in *Newsweek*. A beautiful, moving story, it details the fifteen-year-old Topher's experience when the mother of his friend Roland died. The boy did not know how to respond to his friend's loss.

I had faced a similar situation two years before when my grandfather died. I was closer to my grandfather than any other man in my life. It was a loss I should have mourned heavily, but I stood by his gravesite burdened with the misunderstanding of what it meant to be a man. I shed no tears. I was working so hard to maintain the kind of stoicism I'd seen in the movies—the kind that's permanently etched on the faces of leading men like Denzel Washington—that I didn't think about how *I* felt.

At the age of thirteen, Topher had already learned that a man should never display weakness. "It isn't long before this shell," he reflects, "begins to affect the choices we make and the relationships we have. We carry this unwillingness to confront, discuss or deal with emotion with us throughout our lives."

When Topher visited his grieving friend Ronald, whose pain-filled face moved him deeply, he found tears springing from his own eyes.

I had never witnessed a man comforting another man, and I wasn't sure what to do. Unconsciously, I pulled Roland toward me, and he responded by collapsing in my arms, as if that had been his desire all along. As I held him and our tears flowed, I found myself filled with a kind of freedom that my adolescent existence hadn't permitted before. When our friends entered the room, I saw the emotion swell in all of them as they surveyed the scene. Instantly, they joined me at Ronald's side, all of us crying. There we were: four teenage black males, all without fathers, all without examples of this type of expression. But for a few minutes, we were able to cloak our friend in love and support. For one night, as we huddled together in tears, we had refuted our erroneous ideas of masculinity. Our tears had felt right. They had felt responsible. And while many of my tears were for Ronald and his loss, more than a few were for my grandfather.

With the shedding of their tears, men learn the power of vulnerability to deepen their connections to themselves and to other people. As men redefine the meaning of manhood, women's perception of men must change as well. Women have received just as much indoctrination into the invincible image as have their men. Seeing vulnerability in a man can alarm some women, causing them to shrink back from it or to try to reason him out of those feelings. When women hold the wisdom, they recognize and appreciate the courage it takes to feel vulnerable when a man holds the love.

Chapter 7

SPLIT VISION

Dispelling Gender Distortion

Vision is the art of seeing the invisible.

Jonathan Swift

Visiting San Francisco not long ago, I saw a Calvin Klein ad for a white shirt plastered all over town: a picture of a braless model, leaning back with her shirt opened to her navel. She couldn't have been more than thirteen. My first reaction was to boycott Calvin Klein products. It was bad enough that ad men love to project their idealized fantasies of women to potential buyers of their products; but how dare they oversexualize a child and rob her of her girlhood.

But when I took a closer look at the picture, I wondered, "Is this supposed to make me want to buy this shirt?" Supposedly the advertisers had geared this ad toward the female consumer. Through whose eyes did they expect me to look at this product? Not mine. Men formulate eighty percent of ads for women, and the images of women they project teach us to see ourselves not through our own eyes but through eyes of fantasizing men. As a result, many women internalize a male perspective of themselves, which represents not our natural sense of ourselves but a sense of ourselves being appreciated by another. John Berger said it well in his 1972 book, *Ways of Seeing*: "Men look at women. Women watch themselves being looked at. The surveyor of woman in herself is male: the surveyed female." When this happens, we see ourselves in split vision: on one side who we are, on the other who others want us to be (or, more accurately, how they want us to look), a dual perspective that dilutes our wisdom by overemphasizing our looks. Instead of living in our skins, feeling our bodies, being embodied, we are prepossessed with a chronic self-observation. This emphasis on measuring a woman's worth in terms of her physical appearance distorts women's wisdom. In this chapter we will discuss this phenomenon and how unconscious cultural assumptions about women's competence and media bias undermine our perception of women as leaders. I doubt we women can fully realize our full leadership potential until we resolve the split-vision screen into a clear, focused picture of who we are and what *we* want people to see.

DON'T TREAT YOURSELF LIKE AN OBJECT

Given all the idealized, airbrushed images that bombard us every day, no wonder it's so hard for a woman to feel normal and attractive without feeling compelled to modify herself physically. I can't think of a better way to describe marketing to women than as an assault, a war waged on woman the purchaser. Just listen to marketing language: target audience, penetrating the market, point of entry, product positioning—all gladiator language. Although not as blatant as humiliation, this war diminishes women by limiting beauty to cookie-cutter perfection and basing a woman's worth on her sexual appeal. Women often fight a battle that they don't even know they are fighting, images of a woman, manufactured by others, that are not her images.

This sexualized perception of women paradoxically makes them at once visible and invisible. Objectification veils a woman's wisdom by spotlighting her sexuality; people see her but never know her. A veiled dancer, she cannot possibly emerge as a clearly defined leader. Skimpy outfits veil women's wisdom like power suits veil men's vulnerability. For both, their humanity remains concealed. Unlike our Islamic sisters whose burqas cover everything except for their eyes, Western women, sporting sunglasses and low-cut mini dresses, reveal almost everything *except* for their eyes. Both are seen and yet unseen.

Most visual advertising, rather than reflecting the confidence women feel in themselves, rather than celebrating their differences, projects images that divide women rather than unite women. With a few exceptions—such as the ads for Dove soap and for designer Eileen Fisher's clothing, which use normal women rather than painfully thin models—most images of women become a tool for self-policing, a constant comparison test that leaves the majority of women feeling inadequate to live up to these ideals. Never thin enough, young enough, and rich enough. And even if you are thin enough, young enough, and rich enough, you cannot escape these pressures, as I learned from actress and activist Jane Fonda. When I heard her speak in New York City at a conference on women and power in 2005, she confessed that she spent most of her life hating her body. Jane Fonda, like many of us, got caught up in the perfection curse, in obsessively over-scrutinizing our bodies and hating parts of our bodies, in being our own worst critics, until we become alienated from ourselves and disembodied.

This behavior has become so rampant that we even have a term for it, self-objectification. When women self-objectify, they look at themselves through the eyes of another, not those of an admirer or beloved, but of a scrutinizer and judge.

Those who self-objectify chronically monitor their physical appearance and measure their worth almost solely in terms of their appearance. Studies show that girls and women who self-objectify frequently suffer from depression and have low self-esteem and grave doubts about their capabilities. It even affects their capacity for pleasure, because during love-making they worry so much about how their naked body looks that they forget to take joy in the experience. As Caroline Heldman wrote in her article called "Out-of-Body Image," we teach a boy that his body is a tool to master the environment; we teach a girl that her body is a project that needs work before she can attract others. And we know the consequences when this is taken to the extreme—anorexia and bulimia. According to the National Eating Disorders Association, ten million Americans have an eating disorder; 90 percent of anorexics and bulimics are female.

Try this little experiment. What part of your body do you love? What part of your body do you hate? I would bet for most women hated parts would spring to mind much more quickly than loved parts. Does this happen naturally, or does it result from years and years of schooling in idealized images?

We absorb these images without even realizing it. When women remain unaware of the subtle messages that diminish them, they can easily allow the media to reduce them to hot babes posing in little more than body glitter and stilettos on the covers of men's magazine. Many women, unwittingly, find themselves perpetuating and supporting a system that looks down on them by transforming themselves into objects.

According to Ariel Levy, author of *Female Chauvinist Pigs*, women are adopting a model of female sexuality that comes straight from pornography and strip clubs. When women are regarded hot, according to Levy, "hot means two things in particular: fuckable and salable." If so, through whose eyes are we defining our sexuality? Now I'm not condemning sexiness, because sexy can be fun and afford a woman a certain sense of power, but let's not confuse sexual titillation with real feminine power, and let's not say we are empowering ourselves when we play the role or allow ourselves to be sex objects with no higher purpose than performing for men.

In an interview in the September 2005 issue of *Marie Claire* magazine, actress Reese Witherspoon, star of *Legally Blonde*, had this to say: "What gets me is how many women—young women—give up their power and their sense of self, thinking they're going to get more out of life if they take off their clothes and objectify themselves, instead of functioning on the principle that they're smart and capable." When asked about vacant-eyed starlets such as Paris Hilton and Jessica Simpson, she replied, "I don't think these women are stupid, I think they're selling a personality that's very marketable: 'Wouldn't it be fun if we were all gorgeous and didn't have a care?' But creating a cultural icon out of someone who goes, 'I'm stupid, isn't it cute?' makes me want to throw daggers at them!"

Whether knowingly or not, women like Paris Hilton undermine the progress the women's movement made when it created widespread awareness of objectification, that is, the treatment of women as objects of desire, as ornamentation, or as bait in promoting products—all ways of minimizing female wisdom and true power. As Witherspoon concluded, "My grandma did not fight for what she fought for, and my mother did not fight for what she fought for, so you can start telling women it's fun to be stupid. Saying that to young women, little girls, my daughter? It's not OK."

The fact that many women have bought into idealized images of themselves shows up in their willingness to alter their bodies surgically and cosmetically. Twenty-eight million Americans have undergone plastic surgery; 90 percent of them women. In 2003 alone, 8.7 million Americans spent 9.4 billion dollars on cosmetic surgery. In 2007 the number of tummy tucks went up 133 percent, Botox treatments 420 percent, and breast enlargement 55 percent. A survey in the British weekly magazine *Grazia* found that over half of the one thousand women polled, whose average age was thirty-four, expected to go under the cosmetic surgeon's knife in their lifetime. And consider all the "style" surgeries such as the toe cleavage and deboning so women can wear those Jimmy Choo killer high-heel sandals. In 2009, London's Harley Medical Group reported an astonishing 30 percent rise in nipple surgery over a twelve-month period and a "significant increase" in the sale of prosthetic nipples. As Ellen Goodman wrote in her op-ed piece in the *Globe* on December 11, 2003, "That should make you raise your brows, if your forehead hasn't been paralyzed with Botox."

Women as early as their twenties have been caught up in the fad for Botox and plastic surgery when they haven't even lived long enough to earn many wrinkles. Reality star Heidi Montag had ten procedures—including liposuction, breast augmentation, and a brow lift—in one day. She's twenty-three. Today a mommy makeover doesn't mean a facial and a manicure but liposuction, tummy tuck, and breast lift, with or without breast implants. Television programs such as *Extreme Makeover* reinforce the notion that women's worth depends on her looks. One participant on the show, after getting all her bits and pieces changed and rearranged, came home to her child, who cried when he couldn't recognize his own mother! There's even a children's book, *My Beautiful Mommy*, that helps parents explain to their young child why Mommy has a new nose. What on earth are we doing?! Do we really want to meld ourselves into sterile, airbrushed Stepford Wives? What if women didn't buy into these images? What if we rejected the ruse that elective surgery is a benchmark of self-determination that providers and promoters pitch? Imagine what women could do if they channeled all the energy and money they spend on enhancing their appearance into other areas and actualized their real power. And I'm talking about a lot of time, energy, and money—for example, the $12 billion we spent in 2007 on antiaging products alone.

In her book *The Beauty Myth*, Naomi Wolfe exposed the staggering amount of time, effort, and money that women feel compelled to spend on outward appearances in order to make themselves socially acceptable, employable, and marriageable. A recent study, done by sociologists Dalton Conley and Rebecca Glauber of New York University, shows that the pre-occupation with appearances is not a figment of the female imagination. They found that weight created a startling negative consequence for women's financial well-being and their career and marriage prospects, whereas a man carrying extra weight suffered no ill effects in those areas at all. Heavier women face grimmer prospects than thinner women. In just one example of that fact, a thinner woman with no college degree can earn the same as an overweight woman with a college degree. Conley concluded that women are held to standards of objectified appearances that men are not.

On the other hand, being both attractive and bright seems for some an elusive concept. The brilliant neurobiologist Susan Greenfield, director of the Royal Institution in the United Kingdom and first woman to hold the post, hosted her own BBC television show about the brain. She does not look like the stereotypical drab academic. She loves short skirts and red lipstick—and why shouldn't she? Why, like patting your head and rubbing your stomach at the same time, does intellectual brilliance and an attractive appearance seem incompatible?

> I was serving on a committee and the first woman to be appointed. When the chairman introduced me, he said, "I would like to welcome a new member of this board who will bring some glamour to our gathering." That was all he said. He would never have introduced a man that way and said, "We'd like to welcome John and look at his nice suit and how handsome he is." He just assumes he can say something like that about a woman. He meant well, but it did make me feel different. If he had also said that I would give valuable insights, that would have been OK.

By focusing so much on Susan's physical appearance, the chairman limits her power by overshadowing her wisdom. I suspect he did not realize the effect of his words, which come so naturally to men working in a domination culture. It's harder to address such behavior when it springs from a subconscious level. Had Susan looked dowdy with forty more pounds on her frame, that ingrained reaction would not have surfaced.

Iron Butterflies like Canadian fashion designer Linda Lundström challenge these distortions, such as the rail-thin version of beauty. "The whole fashion industry I'm involved in perpetuates women's feelings of inadequacy," she told me. "I love designing for curves and hips. I don't care what size you are. Marie, who works for me, is a gorgeous woman who walks right into my size 22. That's why I make everything from size 2 up to size 24." Linda emphasizes sensuality in her line of flowing, romantic summer wear that she calls Goddess Gear, because as she said, "Hikers have hiking gear, skiers have skiing gear, goddesses need goddess gear!" In 2002, she created the Authentic Women Model Search, an effort propelled by the philosophy that all women are beautiful and deserve fabulously fashionable clothes. Linda invites Canadian and American women regardless of shape, size, and age to submit a letter answering two simple questions: "What is important to you?" and "What makes you an Authentic Woman?" So far she has formed a group of sixteen Authentic Models, women from across North America representing a wide array of age, shape, and size. "I have had the privilege of watching their lives transform as they were taken on a journey of self-discovery and then given the opportunity to discover what it is like to be a fashion model, a real fashion model. The search was uplifting, proving that 'true beauty' comes from within."

Let's stop look-look-look-looking at our bodies and instead let's relate to our bodies in a different way, one that makes us feel good about ourselves, that amplifies the true beauty within each and every one of us. Let's eliminate negative body talk and teach our daughters to love their bodies because they see and hear their mothers speaking about their bodies in a positive way. Let's celebrate, listen, and love our bodies.

CELEBRATE YOUR BEAUTIFUL BODY

For hundreds of thousands of years prior to the modern era, human cultures honored women, and men deferred to women's judgment because they revered the female body. The female body contained many mysteries, especially the miracle of creating life and giving birth. Because women menstruate, "wise blood," their bodies undergo visible transitions within a natural life span in a way men's bodies do not. With menarche and the flow of the first blood, a girl encounters the primary mystery of womanhood, her ability to create life. With maternity, her blood mysteriously creates another being, a life she herself can fully sustain on her own with her milk. With menopause and the ceasing of blood, ancient people believed the no longer visible blood flow accumulated in a woman and made her wise.

Because the woman's body told the story of life, women were first to create rituals. For instance, a woman's body goes through cycles similar to those of the moon. During menstruation, once called moon time, women took time out from daily chores and went to special huts as Anita Diamant wrote in her novel *The Red Tent*. There they dreamt and prayed with a community of women, using that time to combine their energies to empower those dreams. They did not retreat because they were somehow dirty, but because they needed to engage with other women during this time of great power, a time when they saw the crack between the world, a time of cleansing.

I often think about the need in our hectic contemporary world for women to do the same, to fashion more rituals with which we can celebrate our bodies. Imagine having a monthly retreat called moon time when women of your community gather together away from daily routines to share dreams and help each other make them come true.

Better yet, let's celebrate by honoring the woman's body in existing rituals. Take bridal showers, for example. Although it's cute to make a wedding dress out of toilet paper, why not add a serious time to honor this transitional time from maiden to mother/woman. We could do the same with baby showers. Instead of focusing only on baby clothes, as cute as they are, and toys, we could honor the birth giver and share our own unique birthing stories, share lullabies, and offer words of wisdom that come with experience. When a young woman experiences menarche, we could seize the opportunity to celebrate the occasion and teach her about the glory and wonder of her body. Does anyone celebrate menopause? Why not? Rather than letting a woman go through this passage alone and depressed, her girlfriends could turn it into a moment of shared joy and camaraderie. As French actress Bridget Bardot, regarded as the sex kitten of the fifties, said, "It's sad to grow old but nice to ripen."

If you are planning to marry, celebrate your body. If you are expecting a baby, celebrate your body. When your daughter menstruates for the first time, celebrate her body. When you go through menopause, celebrate your body. Celebrating the wonders of a woman's body opens a portal into a deep spiritual connection between women, nature, and a higher power.

One of my favorite stories in Clarissa Estes's book *Women Who Run with Wolves* tells the tale of the Butterfly woman. An especially beautiful passage tells us how to replace split vision that criticizes the female body with a clear vision that loves it.

> There is no "supposed to be" in bodies. The question is not size or shape or years of age, or even having two of everything. The issue is does the body feel, does it have a right connection to pleasure, to heart, to soul, to the wild. Does it have happiness, joy? Can it in its own way move, dance, jiggle, sway, thrust? Nothing else matters. Is it afraid, paralyzed by pain or fear, anesthetized by old trauma, or does it have its own music, listening, looking with its many ways of seeing?
>
> It's the power of seeing what is *in* the body. The cultural power *of* the body is its beauty, but the power *in* the body is rare to see, for most have chased it away with their torture of or embarrassment by the flesh. Butterfly woman inquires into the numinosity of her own body, and understands it not as a dumbbell that we are sentenced to carry for life . . . but as a series of doors and dreams and poems through which we can learn and know all manner of things. In the wild psyche, the body is understood as a being in its own right, one who loves us, depends on us, one to whom we are sometimes mother, and who sometimes is mother to us.

When was the last time you looked in the mirror, and looked beyond your surface appearance and really looked deeply into your eyes? Try this experiment. Look deeply into your eyes, so deeply that you see the beautiful being, the amazing woman who resides within your body. And then speak to her and say "I love you." Say "I love you" until you mean it with your whole body. I think this exercise should be like brushing our teeth, something we do every day, a focus that will keep us on track with what's important. If you are diligent with this exercise, when you catch your reflection in a plate-glass window as you stroll past a department store window, you'll find yourself saying, "Hey, gorgeous, I love you!" Since our bodies are beautiful just the way they are, why not love them to death?"

DISPLAY CONFIDENCE IN YOUR COMPETENCE

Gender schemas, another distortion infused in our collective unconscious, also keeps women on the defensive and cloaks their wisdom. In her book *Why So Slow? The Advancement of Women,* Virginia Valian explored why women's advancement has crept at such a snail's pace and uncovered the world of gender schemas, culturally bound assumptions about men and women that are held by both genders. Gender schemas affect our expectations of men and women and how we evaluate their work and their performance as professionals. That in turn affects pay, promotions, and prestige. It's no surprise that in a male-dominated culture, gender schemas work to men's advantage and to women's disadvantage.

One unconscious assumption about men holds that they gravitate toward independent and autonomous behavior. In other words, men *act*, an attribute traditionally associated with leadership. In contrast, a powerful assumption about women associates them with nurturing, emotional expression, and concern for others—qualities not traditionally associated with leadership. Bottom line? We assume men make better leaders and women have to deal with the initial impression that they are not leaders.

According to gender schemas, women are first assumed incompetent until proven otherwise. Consequently, cultural biases consistently *overrate* men and *underrate* women. Everything a man does that reinforces his masculinity reinforces the perception that he's competent. As I mentioned in the previous chapter, domination cultures couple masculinity and competence. On the other hand, everything that a woman does that reinforces her femininity diminishes the perception of her competence. It's a nice little feedback loop. Marginalize and objectify women because perceptions define them as incompetent, and their perceived incompetence justifies marginalizing and objectifying them. In the eighties and nineties women set about defeminizing themselves and trying to look and act like men in an effort to counteract this perception of incompetence. Margaret Thatcher even underwent training in lowering her voice when she served as prime minister of Britain.

Assumed incompetence puts women on the defensive and their struggle to prove themselves keeps them on a never-ending treadmill. For instance, when people see an unarguably competent woman, they seldom say "Wow, she's a born leader" (something they would say about a man), but they will attribute her success to dumb luck or extraordinary effort: "Is she lucky!" or more patronizingly, "What a hard worker!" When she fails, they attribute it to her lack of competence, "Well, she was in over her head" or "She didn't really have the chops in the first place." The inverse comes into play for men. When a man succeeds, admirers attribute it to his competence and proclaim "He's a born leader," and when he fails, they shake their head and mumble "What bad luck!" I like how Simone de Beauvoir put it in *The Second Sex*: "Her wings are clipped, and it is found deplorable that she cannot fly."

But some women like Myra Hart, former executive vice president of growth and development at Staples, the office supply store, and professor at Harvard Business School, cleverly used this bias to her advantage. "I had a lot of advantages when negotiating real estate deals on behalf of Staples by virtue of being a woman," she told me. "Usually the person I was negotiating with discounted my skills. They assumed because of my exterior that I couldn't do math, while, in fact, I could do the numbers twice as fast. I just let them go where they wanted to go. I knew where we were going to end up. And we did. Actually it was to my advantage to be underestimated, but, of course, that's a short-term thing."

Both men and women fall prey to these schemas of assumed incompetence in women. You see it in self-assessment studies: women tend to evaluate themselves two points lower while men will evaluate themselves two points higher; or you'll hear men promoting the seven qualities they possess, while women apologize for the three they lack. So it should come as no surprise when Dr. Laura Schlessinger's book *Ten Stupid Things Women Do to Mess Up Their Lives* remained on the bestseller list for a year, but when she published the man's version, it fell off the list after a scant three weeks. Even then, as holds true for almost all self-help books, many more women than men bought the male version.

In one experiment called the "Goldberg paradigm" researchers asked men and women in one group to evaluate a particular article or speech supposedly written by a man. Then they asked a similar group to judge the same material, this time supposedly authored by a woman. In countries all over the world, participants rated the very same words higher coming from a man.

If women think they feel unblinking eyes scrutinizing them, if they think they must perform to a higher standard, they're right. No wonder women become preoccupied with their appearance, constantly second-guessing themselves and other women in a grueling struggle not to look incompetent. Split vision not only distorts how they see their physical selves but also how they see their talents and abilities.

Myra Hart describes how this defensiveness plays out.

> In general, women are more concerned about how they will be viewed and whether or not they are making a contribution. So they are likely to self-censor and only say things that they think will have high value. It may be because they still find themselves in a position fighting up the ladder and don't want to be perceived as lightweights. Whereas the guys, it's just a game, they throw their ideas in there and if people don't like them, it doesn't matter. I think this only happens in mixed-gender situations. When I am in an all-female group, then it's a level playing field and we don't have to worry about the perception. Women are willing to say what they think, but also more likely to say what they *feel*. Emotions are another level of communication, and women are willing to divulge them when it's a same-sexed meeting.

When women get together, they reveal an emotional side that does not take away from their power and wisdom. But in mixed groups it does, because as we saw earlier, gladiators dismiss or hide their feelings. When internalized assumptions of female incompetence undermine women's self-confidence, women often go to extremes to compensate, overpreparing for a job or assignment, gaining more experience than they really need to do it well, and demanding impossible perfection in themselves. Meanwhile, men feel free to learn on the way and expect that someone will help them along, and if they fail, pick them up and dust them off.

I must stress that women hold this schema of assumed incompetence with respect to other women. A lot of women, eager to succeed, do not doubt for one second their own competence, but still apply it to other women expecting their incompetence. This might explain, at least partially, why women do not champion themselves or other women as vigorously as men do; they have let images that are not *their* images silence their voices. Like the struggle against objectification, assumed incompetence is a battle we are fighting that we often don't know we are fighting. Only heightened awareness can pull us out of that mire.

DON'T LET ANYONE STICK YOU IN THE MARGINS

Because people unconsciously assume women are incompetent, women often find their wisdom ignored or marginalized. As Laura Liswood, secretary general of the Council of Women World Leaders, observed when we talked:

> You face enormous frustration when there are feminine ways you want to approach something and men aren't hearing, or not valuing and not giving consideration to it. I tell other women, "Don't let it affect you." But it does. You start to think, "Well, gee, maybe I don't have that leadership ability." You see men mirroring back to each other, but not to women. Since I have historically been in basically male fields, it was difficult for me to get that reinforcement. You just wonder, "Wait a minute. I'm bringing a lot to this table, but I'm not getting a lot of reinforcement."

Laura's image of herself splits in two, one lens focusing on her genuine competence, the other blurring her sense of competence with doubt when others do not fully recognize, respect, or respond to her competence. Men may not mirror Laura, but neither do women. The moral? Don't marginalize a sister and do not let her marginalize you. Stand up for yourself, stand up for her, and expect her to stand up for you. Acknowledge the importance of what she says and does, tell her publicly it resonates with you if it does, and she will join the community of support that will enable all of us and our competencies to be heard and counted.

The talented and widely admired Cynthia Trudell, former CEO of the Saturn Division of General Motors, rose to the top in the heavily masculine field of manufacturing. She has learned to balance feminine and masculine attributes, but, even so, she has experienced the split vision. "I've struggled with why is it not obvious to others what is so obvious to me," she told me. "When I see a people issue, people will often dismiss it because they haven't recognized it yet. It's very frustrating because I can drop the idea on the table, and it isn't picked up. Fifteen minutes later, a male version of what I said is on the table and it's heard loud and clear."

Relational issues, those that gladiators tend to marginalize, appear obvious to Cynthia. Ironically, when a man raises those issues, people pay more attention to those ideas than they would if they were coming from a woman. Like Zeus who internalizes Metis's wisdom as his own, women often find their ideas swallowed up, restated, and claimed by a gladiator. Laura and Cynthia demonstrate the difficulty of bringing feminine wisdom to the table. Why bother, if people will just ignore it or co-opt it as their own?

Virginia Valian points out another dilemma. A woman who aspires to success cannot ignore marginalization because each time colleagues ignore her comments, she loses prestige and those around her grow less inclined to take her seriously. Sociologists call this the "accumulation disadvantage." As Valian has written, "Very small differences in treatment can, as they pile up, result in disparities in salary, promotion, and prestige." When women find their words landing on deaf ears, they correctly infer that they are better off not speaking at all. Otherwise, they risk accruing a disadvantage and losing prestige. Yet rarely does anyone acquire prestige through silence either. A Catch-22.

No wonder, then, that so many women find it hard just to raise the issue of marginalization of women leaders. Swanee Hunt tells a story illustrating this predicament. Swanee, former ambassador to Austria, heiress to the Hunt Oil Company and founder of the Initiative for Inclusive Security, which includes the Women Waging Peace network, teaches at Harvard's Kennedy School of Government. A highly respected woman, she feels comfortable in the public arena and uses the podium to shed light on the roles women play in peacekeeping processes. During our interview, she recalled a meeting where the dean of the Kennedy School called the faculty together to talk about leadership.

"The first thing I do is check out the male/female ratio in the audience," Swanee told me. "I thought this meeting wasn't bad because it was half men and half women; the faculty is mostly men." The dean stood up and said he had asked Joe and Bill to say something about leadership. As Joe and Bill talked, each passed out three descriptions of students he thought displayed great leadership potential. All men. "So we have the dean who is a guy who calls on Joe and Bill who pass out six examples of men," Swanee recalls.

> The meeting was almost over, and so far only one woman had spoken at that meeting. Five minutes before the meeting was to end, I stood up and said, "I have to go on record because you brought me to this campus to address women in public policy and to change the culture of the Kennedy School. So I'm going to do it. The leadership issue is not just about how we encourage leadership among the students. It's also how we encourage leadership at the faculty level. The way this meeting was constructed, I am standing here as the second woman to talk in an hour." My heart was pounding. I could feel that my cheeks were red. I said, "I have had decades of experience in public speaking and it's taking all the nerve I have to confront this. Now why is that? How was this meeting set up?" The meeting went on for another fifteen minutes, and now finally the women started to speak up a lot.

My point was that there are so many subtle clues about what leadership *is*, and who leaders are, and even accomplished faculty members are unconscious of it. Even people with my background have a hard time confronting it. Before I stood up, I was thinking that they would think, "There she goes again. Completely predictable." I wanted these people to respect me, but every time I stand up for this, I risked them respecting me less. That's why I began as I did, that I was brought to this campus to do this. I have so much experience. But think about other people. I mean, I was hired to stand up! That is why we need to bring women together in a setting that feels safe to them, to let them get their confidence up.

If it is difficult for Swanee, a woman of remarkable power, prestige, and experience, and hired to address the very issue of marginalization, no wonder the rest of us want to hide at times rather than muster up the courage it requires to bring it up. "There she goes again" creates so much pressure not to point out gender bias and assumed incompetence in leadership that we develop an aversion to mentioning it at all.

Marginalization of women occurs every day, sometime subtly, sometimes not subtly. When suffragette Elizabeth Cady Stanton presented a bill to give women the right to vote before senators, the men sat before her reading newspapers, clipping their nails, and yawning. Whether blatant or subtle as a raised eyebrow, the marginalization and diminishment of women continues. If women don't call attention to it and bring it up, who will?

What's a girl to do? Keep silent? Get on the warpath? Neither tactic will change the situation in my opinion, but you can certainly speak up when you see women leaders and potential leaders glanced over. A soft, persistent objection to marginalizing behavior can help make everyone more conscious of all the unconscious assumptions that hold women back. When another woman objects or points out marginalization, support her in the moment; don't wait to tell her by the water cooler how you agree with her. Don't let feelings of vulnerability dissuade you. Let's refocus the split vision that so often distorts the true power of the Iron Butterfly.

WATCH OUT FOR BABES IN BOYLAND

The media, usually unaware of its own biases, sexism, and gender schemas, conspires in making women's wisdom and leadership invisible. Reporters and journalists share the same unconscious assumptions that associate masculinity with competence and leadership, and women end up coming up short in getting a fair representation. In fact, the media seems particularly immune to the fact that a woman leader can be both feminine *and* competent.

In a study by Catalyst, an international group of senior executives generally viewed women whose actions reflected gender stereotypes (for instance, women concerning themselves with people issues) as less competent. But if the women acted in ways that seemed more "male" (asserting themselves, for instance), the group tended to think those women were appearing unnatural or too tough. Another damned if you do, damned if you don't predicament. Act soft, and they'll dub you as a "marshmallow"; go hard, and they'll call you a "bull broad." Either nice and stupid, or smart and mean. You can't win. The more feminine a woman behaves, the more she runs the risk of seeming less competent. If a woman highlights her accomplishments, she comes across as a pushy braggart. However, if a woman is self-effacing, people find her unimpressive.

Hillary Clinton's run for president in 2008 made these biases against women leaders painfully clear and rattled many women into awareness of how much sexism is alive and well. The double bind women leaders find themselves in (if she is too feminine, she is weak; if she is forceful, aggressive, and decisive, she is not a good woman) expanded to a triple bind: if she complains about the double bind, she's playing the gender card and accused of taking unfair advantage of her disadvantage! Oy vey! What a challenge for ambitious women! It's an uphill battle to be perceived as both a good woman and a good leader.

When the media deals with this mix of femininity and leadership, it often devolves into a deep sexism that reduces a competent woman to being a "babe." Fortunately, Iron Butterflies, like Candice Carpenter Olson, challenge this perspective. Every time they take their place as a leader and bring their femininity along with them, they create new associations that link the feminine to power. Consider this story Candice told me about an interesting encounter with the press.

> All my life I didn't think there was an issue of sexism, but one incident made me realize how deep the sexism is. I was at the World Economic Forum in Davos, Switzerland, and a reporter wanted to interview me outside in the snow. I had this fur hat on. I got creamed by analysts and the press. They said I was supposed to be a CEO. How dare I wear a fur hat! I didn't get letters from stockholders that the stock prices sucked, which they did. That would have made sense to me. Instead, I got letters of outrage at how I was dressed, that I was wearing a fur hat. I didn't believe this could happen until it happened to me. Suddenly I couldn't make up a story that sexism wasn't an issue.

2

At this point, Candice swore that she would never let anyone force her to act like a boy in order to succeed in business. Instead, she would willingly pay any price to act like the full-blooded girl she is.

> I started to bring a lot of feminine touches to the way I dressed. I had these beautiful lace blouses, these sexy and elegant Versace suits. More and more I was expressing my femininity—my hair was getting longer, my nails were getting longer, my heels were getting higher. I felt like a gay guy coming out of the closet. I had come to a point where I thought, "The hell with it. If I can't wear what I want to wear as a CEO of a public company, I may as well hang it up."
>
> But I got so much grief about the way I dressed. I could feel the sexism all around me. I had a lot at stake, but I wasn't going to wear that grey flannel suit that made everybody happy. This coming out party that I was having with myself was more important than whatever the consequences were. In many ways it was like an explosion in me, I had no choice. It was just happening. I was radiating girlness.

By radiating her "girlness" Candice melded leadership with femininity, which violated the schema of masculinity being equated with competence and leadership. If enough women do that, dressing as they choose rather than as others expect, remaining true in appearance and attitude to their personal definition of femininity, perhaps the media and other observers will stop treating a woman leader as a sex object and pay closer attention to her words than to her lacy blouse or shade of lipstick. Perhaps more of us can keep a page from Candice's book. Whenever we find ourselves in the media spotlight, we can stand tall and proud and powerful *and* feminine all at the same time. Doing this, we forge a new association between feminine and power, women and competence.

Kim Polese, former CEO and chairwoman of Marimba and now CEO of SpikeSource Inc, a successful software company in the Silicon Valley, played her cards differently but with the same results. The media chastised Candice for playing up her femininity because competent leaders don't look like that. When Kim, on the other hand, played down her femininity, the media played it up as a way of discrediting her competence.

In 1997 *Time* magazine voted Kim as one of the most influential people in the country. Interviewers besieged her, but they couldn't quite figure out this very attractive, thirty-something who had excelled in the male-dominated field of technology. Kim remembers it clearly:

> As CEO, I had to be in the public view; I would be interviewed by all these magazines. I would talk exclusively about the company, the market,

the technology. But the articles would be all about me, in a way they didn't write about male CEOs. I knew I didn't look the typical image of a technology company. It got weird because of the undue amount of attention I got; I knew it had nothing to do with my merit. But this type of attention promoted a perception that I was going out there to promote myself—it took on a life of its own. It was unavoidable, and it was a factor of being a young woman in the technology industry. I just had to wait for it to die down, because it was so out of control.

When *Fortune* requested an interview, Kim agreed, but only on the condition that the article would focus on the company and its accomplishments rather than on her. The *Fortune* reporter said she completely understood. Before the interview appeared in the magazine, the reporter called to say, "You probably won't like how the article has turned out." She had written a version true to her commitment, but her editors made her rewrite it. "I have a problem with reporters who put their names on pieces that don't represent reality," Kim confided. "And she had made a promise to me and didn't keep it. That was not OK."

The *Fortune* editor, a man, had decided in advance what the story would be even before the writer had interviewed Kim. It's not uncommon for editors to write a piece with the intent of taking someone down who has been getting a lot of attention. The *Fortune* editor adopted the tired old sex-object angle, falling back on the bimbo image, and it permeated mainstream media. It was all about playing up Kim as the seductive vixen CEO. The title of the piece was "The Beauty of Hype." Kim bridled. "It was all about how I had set out to create this big hype machine around myself. It was amazing to see that appear in a publication the stature of *Fortune.*"

The article, which Kim could not alter or block, came out two weeks before Marimba went public. But this Iron Butterfly did not just sit back and swallow the bitter pill. After many Silicon Valley women raised a stink about the piece, Kim and the reporter who had written the story accepted an invitation from the University of California at Berkeley journalism school to talk about how the press treats women.

When the media encounters an anomaly like Kim, it resorts to the lowest level of stereotyping and degradation of the feminine by veiling her in images of bimbo and vixen. Some might excuse this behavior by claiming that it wouldn't happen if more women held positions of power, but why does the relative scarcity of women leaders give the media the permission to smear them? If you think misogyny is subtler now, think again. The *Fortune* article on Kim was clearly aimed at diminishing her and stripping her of her authority by objectifying her. You don't see that happening to male CEOs in the same way. Her story makes explicit how the dominant group sexualizes women to keep them in a subordinate position.

Split vision also applies to ability: how Kim perceived herself one way, while the media wanted to perceive her quite differently. The manufactured perception took on a life of its own. It had nothing to do with the true Kim. Apparently, seeing a young, beautiful, bright woman must have tapped into some feelings of vulnerability and inadequacy that propelled the editor to resort to the gladiator defense and make her vulnerable instead.

Degrading a woman to a babe and stripping her of wisdom also happens to women in the media. Ashleigh Banfield, cohost of *Courtside* on TruTV and formerly an NBC and MSNBC correspondent, offered this observation in a talk she gave about embedded journalism during the early days of the Iraq occupation: "We got rid of a dictator, we got rid of a monster, but we didn't see what it took to do that. . . . I can't tell you how bad the civilian casualties were." When she criticized the major TV networks for portraying the Iraq War as "glorious and wonderful," the NBC news president, Neal Shapiro, sharply criticized her, saying NBC News was "deeply disappointed and troubled by her remarks." This is the same network that offered no comment on MSNBC commentator Michael Savage's tirades and smearing epithets against Banfield, who went so far as to call her a "slut" and a "porn star." Rush Limbaugh had to lumber his weight into the smear campaign when he labeled her "hot tub Banfield." Why? "If she is going to be in hot water, let it be a hot tub."

What Banfield said took guts; she demonstrated courageous vulnerability. And what did she get in return? Condescension, verbal abuse, and reduction to the status of sex object. In a statement about her treatment, she plaintively concluded, "Free speech is a wonderful thing, it's what we fight for, but the minute it's unpalatable, we fight against it for some reason." For some reason? Would her male colleagues have sexually objectified her for any other reason than the fact that an "uppity" woman has asserted her moral authority and outrage? And would she have found herself under attack had she not pulled the scab off a gladiator vulnerability, reminding men that war is not just "shock and awe" but a devastating human loss? And why doesn't anyone hold the media accountable for degrading women for being women when it doesn't degrade men for being men? Have you ever heard a commentator say, "It's time to hang up your Superman cape"? When Richard Clark challenged the administration over its handling of 9/11, the media may have smeared his reputation and dragged his good name through the mud, but it did not put him in a Speedo swim suit.

A study on women leaders and the media undertaken by the White House Project shows pervasive media bias against women, particularly in the realm of politics. For instance, in six races for high state offices in 1998, male and female candidates received equal coverage in the press, in terms of *quantity* of coverage. But in terms of *quality*, the women suffered from the "babes in boyland" effect. Journalists far more often focused on the personal characteristics of female candidates, but when it came to male candidates, they emphasized their qualifications and achievements and stands on substantive issues. They quoted men backing their claims with evidence or reasoning to a greater extent, suggesting that women can't marshal the hard data and, by subtle inference, lack sufficient competence and credibility to hold office.

Many tremendously successful and effective women have felt that the media either cannot see or completely misunderstands their talents and capabilities as leaders. Experiencing the media's assumed incompetence can drive women nuts and get downright depressing, as ex–prime minister of Canada Kim Campbell, an international consultant and speaker, recalled.

When Kim served as the minister of justice of Canada and the first woman to hold the position, she engineered the passing of a piece of legislation on gun control. It took a huge effort. Although Canada has exercised gun control since the nineteenth century, it still remains a very contentious issue.

> When I was dealing with my legislation, I had a very good staff and we worked very carefully with my colleagues. I've always enjoyed getting the dissenting sides together to hammer out solutions together. I would have people sit with people who didn't always have the same views. I had to know when to push and when to pull back. Getting consensus required enormous amounts of consultation. Even when I knew I had the votes in the House, I would consult with colleagues who didn't agree with the legislation and negotiate the dissent. It was important to me to keep the solidarity of these people and of my own party. And it required a lot of very careful handling.
>
> When the gun control bill passed, by a very large majority incidentally, the press reaction surprised me. Instead of saying, "Kim Campbell did what she promised to do, and she got her bill through," it was, "Well, she must have watered it down. How did it possibly go through?" I couldn't understand why I was not getting the credit for a highly sophisticated process of getting a very difficult piece of legislation through the House of Commons.

The reporters couldn't see Kim's great skill as an interactive leader, not just because she exercised it in closed meetings and discussions, but also because she never trumpeted her accomplishments, didn't make all the noises or declarations that they recognized as leadership. There was a total disconnect between her manner of dealing with a very difficult piece of legislation and the success that she had. And the fact that she managed it all without creating a whole lot of enemies completely eluded them. "It was as if they didn't want to give me credit for having accomplished something," Kim told me.

This oversight did not really shock her, however. Before she became prime minister, she had developed an impressive track record as a front-running candidate. But when she finally declared her leadership of her party, the media called her a rookie. She asked her assistant to calculate how much cabinet experience the previous prime ministers had. Out of eighteen men, only eight could boast of more cabinet experience than Kim. "It just drove me nuts."

When Kim read something about female candidates getting less coverage than male candidates, she checked to see how fairly journalists had treated her in her 1993 election campaign.

> It was interesting because there was a theme throughout the coverage of that election about how unfair the coverage was! They would say, "Kim Campbell said such and such and we jumped all over her. And Jean Chretien said the same thing and we didn't say anything." But there was no attempt to really understand what was going on.
>
> I couldn't figure out what was going on myself. I was aware of the double standard. It wasn't until some time after that I began to understand I was fighting a battle that I had no idea I was fighting. When I said something that the media took issue with, the worst was assumed. If my male rival did the same thing, it was assumed he didn't really mean anything. I realized that the media had a framework of assumptions and expectations that they unconsciously brought with them. If, however, I were to say to these reporters, "Well, the fact of the matter is you brought a lot of gender bias to the issue," they would say it wasn't true and that I was a sore loser.

Kim's vision splits between what she actually does as a leader and what the press assumes and distorts and renders invisible.

And it's not just male journalists. A woman journalist wrote an excellent column praising the feminine consciousness Kim brought to politics and criticized the way the press treated her. Then, during the election campaign, the same journalist wrote a column in which she took Kim to task for wearing the same earrings all the time! Kim shook her head over that. "I thought, hmmm, would she criticize a man for wearing the same cuff links?"

Kim made it a personal mission to increase awareness of the media's gender bias, for both men and women, speaking regularly in Los Angeles at a course on media ethics. Whether you write a letter to the editor, add your thoughts to a blog, or e-mail reporters with your objections, you can join Kim's mission reminding the media to check their facts, focus on real issues, balance their coverage, and treat all their subjects fairly. Reporters all know they need to check their sources. What they also need to check out and chuck out are the unconscious biases and assumptions that can distort the truth about women's leadership abilities when covering the news.

DON'T GIVE AWAY YOUR POWER

When women adopt gender schemas, they unwittingly relinquish their power, saying in effect, "I'm a woman, what do I know?" It reminds me of a story Swanee Hunt told me about a meeting that took place after the massacre in Srebrenica, where eight thousand men and boys were killed in a town of thirty thousand, another horror story of disposable men in a domination society. A man and a woman came into her office and introduced themselves. To Swanee's amazement, the man said he was the president of the Women of Srebrenica! "The woman had given away her power, and he had no trouble at all in taking it," Swanee recalled. "So the guys have their inclination to seize power and the women are not there to refute it. We collaborate with undermining our self-confidence."

We collude with those who would undermine female self-confidence whenever we silently let anyone diminish or overlook us or our sisters. We collude when we allow others to objectify or marginalize us. We collude when we jump to the assumption we can't do it, and then project our power onto men saying they can. We collude when we fail to see and honor women's competencies. We collude when we hold ourselves back in self-doubt and think we are not good enough. We collude when we twist and contort ourselves in order to adapt, to make it right, to fit in, to fulfill someone else's expectations. When we collude, we make *ourselves* invisible by underrating ourselves. Only when we call a halt to all that can we emerge from our cocoons, spread our wings, and take the lead.

Chapter 8

CHRYSALIS

Shedding Self-Imposed Limitations

Loving ourselves is the miracle cure we are all looking for.

Louise Hay

When Candice Carpenter Olson worked at Time Warner, she successfully immersed herself in all the tasks at which she excelled, such as making deals and recognizing new talent. However, she soon learned that her boss, who wanted no contenders for his position, invariably found ways to get rid of people who began to shine too brightly. Candice anticipated that her time was coming up and, sure enough, one day the axe fell. While she was away on business in Hong Kong, her boss trumped up some false moral charges she could not disprove in person. Fortunately, other higher-ups at Time Warner liked Candice's work and wouldn't let her boss fire her. Instead, they gave her an option to get some coaching for high-potential people, which she did.

The coach, who became a profound mentor for her, taught her how to succeed in a gladiator culture and gave her one particularly helpful bit of advice: do not engage in battle with a gladiator when he functions from his basest instincts. "Basically, I was told to suck it up, make them feel important, and don't lose myself in the process; it would make my life easier," Candice told me.

I saw it as surrendering, but the coach said, "No, this is how you protect yourself. Make an offering to the gods." I realized it was a good thing to do.

I often advise younger women that if you choose a career in certain environments, and if you try to change the system too early in your career, you will kill yourself; you won't be a player. Hide out as a boy and let your masculine traits come to the fore. You have to keep your nose clean, keep your agenda well under wraps, until you are in a position of true power. The question, of course, is when is anyone ever in a position of true power? The hard thing is how not to lose the other parts of yourself in the process, which is a big challenge. Most of us probably did lose that balance at some point.

Losing your balance in a gladiator culture poses a very real danger. In this chapter I want to explore two strategies Candice mentions that women often adopt for surviving gladiator cultures, both of them perilous paths where women risk losing that internal balance between masculine and feminine attributes. In a domination culture, you always find two different players, the dominator and the dominated. When women adopt a more dominating role, they act as Candice advises younger women to act, "hide out as a boy" and play the man's game. I call women who do this *Amazons*, after the great, fierce, and mannish women warriors of legend, who purportedly would cut off a breast in order to use a bow and arrow more effectively. In contrast, I call women who opt for being dominated *Shape Changers*, who like Shape Changers of mythology, adapt and mutate to what others need. And as Candice's coach advised her to do, they offer themselves up to the gods. Regardless of which role a woman adopts, both rob her of a valuable part of herself. By accepting a gladiator's terms of engagement, women may think they have successfully adapted to a gladiator culture, but in reality they have merely fabricated a false self, just as the gladiator does. When women resort to self-imposed limitations on what they can reveal about themselves, whether as an Amazon or a Shape Changer, they end up displaying a constricted version of themselves to the world. In the previous chapter we saw how split vision distorts women and conceals their wisdom. Here we'll see how women conceal themselves and make themselves invisible.

RECOGNIZE AMAZONS, SHAPE CHANGERS, AND FURIES

Amazons and Shape Changers represent two ends of the spectrum, but while the two may seem diametrically opposed, they actually share more similarities than differences. One commonality they share is that both cause women to dissociate from aspects of themselves. Dissociation functions as a very effective defense because a woman quite often does not even realize she has disconnected from parts of herself. She goes blithely along thinking everything is fine, unconscious of exiled aspects of herself until something or someone comes along and rattles her into awareness. When either Amazons or Shape Changers imprison aspects of themselves, they cannot tap into the full range of leadership skills and resources produced by the internal, dynamic balance between the masculine and the feminine.

The two tactics involve different dissociations. Amazon women dissociate from their feminine realities in order to succeed. Embracing male autonomy, they sequester such feminine capacities such as nurturing and dependent feelings. Instead they feign invulnerability and behave more or less as female gladiators, which helps them adapt to male-dominated environments.

The Amazon mantra? "Do it all, do it alone, and don't ask questions." They are hard workers, go-getters, so driven to reach their goals they sometimes drive themselves into burnout and depression. A woman who insists on a "can do" attitude when confronted with any request or challenge, no matter how impossible, just to thwart any hint of incompetence, sets herself up for defeats and failures. Like an Amazon of old who cut off her right breast to be a better archer, modern-day Amazons often cut themselves off from their nurturing qualities in order to be better warriors. Is she a heroine for asserting her autonomy or a tragic figure who has adapted herself in order to fit in? Most Amazons end up a little of both, but in most cases the Amazon tactic fosters insecure people who at once deny their dependency on others yet deeply depend on others for approval because they lack self-approval.

Shape Changers, on the other hand, follow the more traditional script of the self-sacrificing woman who dissociates from masculine aspects of herself. Without a masculine balance, a Shape Changer's feminine side becomes a "negative feminine." Shape Changers will mutate and contort themselves to adapt to other people's real or imagined demands and expectations. In other words, they define themselves in terms of what others need, often at a cost to themselves and, like Amazons, deny their own needs or vulnerabilities. Overly dependent on external approval, Shape Changers seek acceptance by acquiescing, accommodating, and empathizing to a fault.

Whether an Amazon or a Shape Changer, these false selves result from the limitations women impose on themselves in order to please the dominant group and win approval. Amazons will hang out as boys to gain that approval, while Shape Changers hang out as everyone's support system to get it. Both take care of everyone but themselves.

In truth, we all need and seek approval from others just as children do. It is an endearing human frailty we share. Sensitivity to other people's reactions and expectations can lead us to behave in ways we hope will meet those expectations. But when the drive for external approval overrides our true and authentic selves, when external approval becomes a substitute for self-acceptance, and when external approval means denying our needs, then we invariably lose our balance.

As you will see in the following stories, Iron Butterflies often find themselves swinging pendulum-like from one end of the spectrum to the other, flipping between Amazon and Shape Changer in search of that elusive balance.

Finding this balance takes patience, perseverance, and courage, and often includes facing repressed rage and frustration when a woman discovers that she has colluded in a system that undermines her authentic self. When women realize how much they have compromised themselves, they may react to this self-betrayal by becoming Furies, out to exact vengeance. More important, however, connecting to the Fury can open a portal for women to reach a deeper understanding of themselves. Their fury may burn a connection to dissociated aspects of themselves, searing a path to the authentic Iron Butterfly where they shed the chrysalis of self-imposed limitations.

These stories offer cautionary tales about the dangers of becoming hardened rather than strong, a slow process that can develop undetected and can seal off women's power. They also provide testimonies to the subtle power of personal transformation: you don't need to move mountains to change your world. By bringing opposites together, taking a little here and putting it there, you can create a new balance that expands rather than limits the way you express yourself. As you read these stories, notice the common patterns of dissociation, a need for approval, and a suppression of needs and other vulnerabilities—all the ways women make themselves invisible to others and themselves. When you recognize these patterns of self-limitation, you can make wiser choices that win *your own* stamp of approval.

TAKE CARE OF YOURSELF

Before she founded her own successful company, Just Ask a Woman, Mary Lou Quinlan had worked as a leader in communications and marketing strategy for prestigious ad agencies such as Avon. Today Mary Lou's mission is to change the way American companies market to women, that is, to discover what women *really* want. To do this, she creates a more feminine environment based on collaboration, where women can relax and feel free to tell their truths. Their discussions about a subject or product become lively, and, in the end, major brands learn more than they would with a more linear approach. Mary Lou shares her insights in her books, Just *Ask a Woman: Cracking the Code of What Women Want and How They Buy* and *What She's Not Telling You: Why Women Hide the Truth and What Marketers Can Do about It.* In addition, she has written a lifestyle book, *Time off for Good Behavior: How Hardworking Women Can Take a Break and Change Their Lives.*

The relaxed, intimate, and collaborative atmosphere of Mary Lou's company is a far cry from what she experienced at Ayer, a major advertising agency she headed before she left to create Just Ask a Woman. In retrospect, she realized she had become an Amazon at her former company: "I was so wrapped up in my job role, so driven, wanting to succeed and be perfect, never letting my guard down, being the 'can do it all' woman. It was my goal to be self-sufficient by pulling up my bootstraps. If anyone asked 'Mary Lou, can you do this?' the answer was always, 'No problem.'"

For instance, one morning, while Mary Lou was riding to work in a cab, the cab crashed and left her injured. An ambulance arrived, and paramedics strapped her onto a stretcher and whisked her off to the emergency room. Lying on the gurney, what did she do? She called the office! Later in the day when she was discharged from the hospital, she had barely closed her front door before she called the office to tell her people she would be in the next day. She was more annoyed that her injuries had kept her from her day's appointments than she was that her injuries might imperil her health and well-being. "When I think about that day," Mary Lou told me, "I say to myself, 'Do you realize what happened and how out-of-bounds that was? How crazy are you?' I didn't see myself."

When Mary Lou says "I didn't see myself," we hear the words of dissociation, a blindness to all her repressed needs buried by an over-diligence in preserving an image of herself. "I thought everybody wanted me to be someone who gets it right, gets it done, and [is] always cheerful," Mary Lou admitted. "I wouldn't acknowledge when I needed help. I couldn't let myself off the hook. I never saw a reason to stop, to consider what I was doing. Without this job, I saw no light at the end of the tunnel. I feared I would fall off into nothingness. I never thought if I stopped doing that job I would have this other great job. I wish I had lightened up on myself a little."

Lightening up does not appear in the official Amazon manual. Mary Lou saw that she was not just being hard on herself; she was getting hard, and her hardness was showing up in her attitudes toward people. If someone called in sick, she reacted not with sympathy but with annoyance because, damn it, someone was not getting the job done. Single-mindedly focused on the job itself, she became oblivious to the person performing the job. Her style became harsher and more impatient: her language got rough at times, and she'd ignore her heart and make coldhearted decisions. She was, she realized, turning into someone other than the true Mary Lou.

Mary Lou had always cared deeply about people, but now even that inclination devolved into just another item on her to-do list. Time to display a good mood? Here's a smile. Need my time? It's yours. She gave people anything they wanted and ended up giving herself away. "I really needed to please everybody," Mary Lou confided. "By the end of the day, I had nothing left to give. I had overstepped some invisible line." When Mary Lou stepped over that line, she lost her balance.

Earnest to prove herself a "can do" person, Mary Lou strove to be all things to all people and ended up being no one to anyone, even herself. Her needs? Wrapped in a box and stored on a shelf. Then something happened to open her eyes. And when they did open, she turned into a Fury.

It began when Ayer's CEO left abruptly and Mary Lou found herself in the top job. If her life was wrapped up in her job before, it was totally consumed by it now. For some reason, her former boss had never introduced Mary Lou to a very important, long-term client. Now, in the wake of his departure, she found herself in the awkward position of telling a stranger that he would now be dealing with her. This disruption angered the client, who treated her with cool disdain when she said she and her team would fly to the client's office to reassure them they were in good hands. "Many times I felt like I was begging them," Mary Lou recalled. "I crawled to try to keep that account."

Mary Lou felt a little scared, but she wasn't about to reveal that fact. Instead, she donned her most confident face.

> That's where the actress thing kicks in for me. I've always loved acting, and I put on a show for them about how confident we are. I did a whole video about how much we loved them, I mean, it was unbelievable. We needed them so much and I didn't want to lose them; the uncertainty of their commitment to us was just eating away at me.

On her return, Mary Lou took a rare vacation with her husband, and although her body went on holiday, her head remained buried in her work, with the phone glued to her ear as she continually checked in on the office awaiting any word from the client. She was clad in her bathing suit, standing by the pool, when she heard that the client had bolted. All wet and with tears streaming down her face, she took the next plane out to reassure the staff that the company would get through this difficult time.

When she arrived at the office, she saw glum faces on all the people associated with the account. Having worked on the account for years, they saw their future going down the drain. In an act of motherly concern, Mary Lou arranged for a transition counselor to come in and give them a seminar to help them cope with their loss and grief.

On the day of the seminar, she was on her way to introduce the counselor in the company's theater room when someone handed her a piece of paper, an invitation to a party that the employees were throwing to celebrate their new future with the client. The client, who wanted the people on the account but not the agency, switched agencies and invited the one hundred fifty people from Ayer to continue working on the account. The new agency would gladly hire all of the Ayer people on the account, giving them the same job with the same salary. Mary Lou felt blindsided. That's when the Fury flew out.

> Something broke in me. I walked down the hall, and I never felt such rage. I walked into the room where the transition training was supposed to happen. They were all sitting there very smugly happy, you know, feeling all palsy with each other, and looking at me like, "Screw you, we have jobs." I stood in front of them and said, "We brought this person in here to have a session for you because we cared about you, because we were concerned about you. But then I was handed this invitation. Without any one of you talking to me, it seems that one hundred fifty of you from this agency are getting together to celebrate what will put a wound in this agency financially. People are going to lose their jobs because of this and you're celebrating. Here's what I think of this" and I tore up the invitation, "and here's what I think of you" and I said, "F** you all!" I stormed out and slammed the glass door so hard I almost broke the glass. I walked down the hall to my office, my body shaking, my cheeks burning red. I slammed my door like nobody's business, and then burst into these horrible tears because I was so angry and felt so abandoned. It was betrayal big time, of me, of the agency, of the other people still working here.

When the client left with all those people in tow, Mary Lou felt as if the Grinch had stolen the whole town's Christmas, without leaving a single crumb behind. The final blow fell when Jose, who worked in the mailroom and for whom Mary Lou felt affection, practically burst into tears as he broke the news to Mary Lou that the other agency had offered him a promotion, a raise, and better hours as a courier. "I want to go," he said softly. Mary Lou looked at him saddened and said, "You too, Jose?" "The sense of abandonment was horrible and it changed me. You really question how much you give and what it's worth. A skeptical part comes in, like an edge."

Amazon women who believe that the loyalty and time they have invested in others will return to them with interest can face a rude awakening, but an awakening that can rattle an Amazon into a new balance. Mary Lou's rage blazed a new path to a burning question: Am I giving too much of myself away? Feeling the pains of abandonment, she could no longer deny her vulnerability or continue a pretense of invincibility. As difficult as it was to wrestle with these feelings, they gave her an edge of skepticism about the merits of Amazon ways.

Eventually, she launched her own company with an environment that respected the whole person, one where taking care of herself and others meant as much as taking care of business. Mary Lou used all her years of experience to create a team of women who held each other in high regard and were encouraged to follow their own passions as she led them into uncharted waters in the branding business. Mary Lou discovered there was a light at the end of the tunnel, where her many talents as a leader, an author, and a speaker were fully unleashed. True to being an Iron Butterfly, she transformed a devastating moment into a new strength of conviction that marked the beginning of an amazing, now ten-year success story for her company.

GIVE YOURSELF WHATEVER YOU NEED

In the fifties and sixties (and even today, though much less frequently) young, middle-class women inherited a script from their mothers and grandmothers: get your degree (BA), get married (MRS), bear children (MA), and make sure you get a teaching certificate so you can work when all your kids are in school. For some, this script fulfilled their ambitions. For others, who felt the tug of other ambitions, this script exerted a social pressure to meet expectations that ran counter to their heart's desire. In an effort to compromise and fit in, these women would often contort themselves into the personae I call Shape Changers. These contortionists went along to get along, embracing images that were not their images; but, in the end, they merely undermined themselves and their talents.

I'm not going to talk a lot about Shape Changers because we all know them as the traditional model of the good woman: self-sacrificing and always putting others before herself. Afraid of being unloved and un-accepted, Shape Changers color themselves for whatever the occasion requires, or what they think the occasion requires. They are everybody's best friend except their own. Until one day, when they look inside, they discover nobody's home. Alison Godfrey's story captures the dilemma of the Shape Changer.

The life of Alison Godfrey has been full of waves. The CEO of Life-Waves, an organization that creates health through an unusual exercise program designed by Alison's husband, Irv Dardik, Alison was first an Amazon woman, then a Shape Changer, and finally, her authentic self.

In her early twenties, Alison worked as the worldwide director of mar-keting at Johnson & Johnson, a stunning accomplishment for a young woman, but the position carried a big price: she needed to become an Amazon. "I behaved like the typical business male in a woman's body," she confessed to me:

> Dictatorship, take no prisoners, business as aggression. The entire man-agement system was brutal. Nothing about dealing with the employees as human beings. It was doing anything you needed to do to get more pro-ductivity out of people. And it didn't matter if it was eighteen hours a day, seven days a week, on the road. You burned them out, turned them over, and started again. They would bring in young people, because you could pay them less for the same cycle. It was a very angry place. It was awful.

To succeed in this environment Alison needed to turn up her aggres-sion, something that didn't come naturally to her. "To have that ag-gressiveness, I needed to be angry all the time, be very confrontational. Part of what drove the aggressiveness was that I felt I was never enough. I had to be better, faster, badder, because deep down, I felt incompetent." Alison compensated for and camouflaged her own vulnerable feelings of inadequacy by showing up at work by seven in the morning and putting in a minimum of twelve hours a day. It didn't occur to her to question the system instead of herself. But eventually her future husband, Irv, a doctor, would kindle a nagging doubt about the wisdom of working in such an environment.

Irv, as different from his wife's corporate cohorts as you could imagine, set about rattling the cage that Alison had built for herself, calling her a drone and little more than a cog in the machine. Although his words upset her, especially since she felt so proud of her elevated status, the seed he planted in the back of her mind sprouted and began to grow. Something, she realized, was wrong with her picture of herself.

It all came to a head with downsizing. When corporate bigwigs decided they needed to get rid of an entire level of middle management men in their fifties, they assigned the task to Alison. She made it through three interviews. The first one ended when the man started to cry. The second concluded with both of them crying. By the third one, Alison burst into tears before the manager even walked in the door. With her feminine, empathic side awakened, she went to the vice president and said, "You can take your job and stick it. This is inhumane." She stormed out, leaving her Amazon self behind.

This was the acid test to see whether she would rise up the corporate ladder at Johnson & Johnson. Realizing she couldn't stomach the corporate gladiator world, she started her own business importing heart monitors, a product that complemented Irv's heart wave program. As time passed, Irv's project became bigger and bigger, and Alison became more and more of a support system for him. "I was doing whatever I had to do to get this brilliant man to where he needed to be." She might have left the Amazon behind, but she now found herself morphing into a Shape Changer dedicated to supporting someone else's dream. "I wasn't human anymore," she recalled:

> I had no needs or expressed any needs. I just did everything for him. If he needed me to listen for hours, I would stop whatever I was doing right then and there. The foundation of our relationship was whatever Irv was doing and needing. I'd gone from the worst stereotype of male leadership to being a stereotypic female support structure. I had completely abandoned myself again.

Married and with two children, Alison became everyone's caregiver: taking care of the kids, taking care of the home, caring for Irv and his work, opening their home to his clients, and building his business. "It was an easy way to not take responsibility for dealing with myself," Alison admitted, "and for how other people dealt with me. I could blend in and go away. It was about not being there for me. It was tricky for me because my personal life was so intertwined with this shared vision of Irv's work. It's what I wanted too."

At one point, Alison and Irv had invited six very sick people to share their home while the patients participated in Irv's exercise program. One day one of the women, an anorexic with obsessive-compulsive disorder, lay on the floor in the living room performing repetitive leg exercises for hours. When Alison walked in and saw her two-year-old daughter on the floor copying the woman, she hit a mental wall. Packing up her kids, she moved out.

> When we got back together, yes, it was different, but I repeated my behavior again. In retrospect I see this role had a lot of reinforcement. My mother, who called Irv her son, always stood up for him. Even though she had a career her whole life, she treated me as if I didn't work. It was so strange. I was invisible to her. If Irv and I had a fight, she would say to me, "What did you do?" And I would ask myself, "What did I do?"

Although Amazon Alison was aggressive and Shape Changer Alison was accommodating, both modes turned her into a chameleon who blended into her environment. And in both cases she abandoned an important part of herself. She tried to fit in by expressing no needs and by disconnecting from her own vulnerabilities. However, constantly changing colors gave her insight, because she finally saw that no matter what role she assumed, she was giving herself away. She and only she was making herself invisible to herself and to others. In the next chapter we will see how Alison found her way to an authentic self.

QUIET THE SELF-DOUBT

The impulse to please others may gain short-term approval for Shape Changers and Amazons, but in the long run these false selves undermine a woman's success as a leader. The urge to please clouds her assessment of situations, especially when it obscures the fact that someone is trying to make her small. When faced with criticism, Amazons and Shape Changers alike try to make everything OK by shouldering too much responsibility for what has gone wrong. As Alison did, they'll ask themselves, "What did I do wrong?" and not ask the other crucial questions: "What did Jack or Jane do wrong?" or "What is wrong with this situation itself?" Without a firm footing and an accurate sense of self, a woman leader can easily internalize someone else's doubts. She will wrack her mind and rip her hair out over real and imagined flaws or mistakes, behaviors that water the seed of self-doubt and cultivate an internal conversation of self-deprecation, further entrenching herself in the false selves of Amazons and Shape Changers.

When self-doubt develops into an internal conversation of beating ourselves up, we are collaborating with the gladiator defense because that conversation keeps us subordinate. Self-doubt so consumes us, we lose sight of our competence and wisdom. Self-doubt is how we give our power away; self-doubt encourages and justifies the dominating behavior of others. Self-doubt is listening to the monkey mind that keeps us small. Self-doubt is how we undermine ourselves.

Judith Baker, a thirty-something ace consultant in management and life sciences, told me an interesting story about how her self-doubt and her boss's manipulation of that doubt undermined her sense of competence until she connected to her inner Fury.

"I see now that what happened to me was a slow process of my boss planting seeds of self-doubt in me," Judith reflected. The first seed fell on fertile soil when her boss disclosed a conversation with a co-worker in which the two of them concluded that they should treat Judith as an analyst, rather than as a manager. Bringing her down a notch supposedly would help her develop as a manager, but instead it made Judith feel "diminished and patronized." Later she discovered from the co-worker that the conversation had not dealt with Judith's managerial competence at all. But by that point, the first seedling of self-doubt had sprouted. "Having managed women and men," Judith told me, "I could see that the minute any woman is challenged, she says to herself, 'What have I done?' A guy would say, 'What are you talking about?' I realized I was just like all these women, wondering what I had done wrong. I was diminishing *myself*."

At one point, an illness in Judith's family required her to work out of two cities. Stressed out, she shared some of her feelings with her boss, who used this information against her, thus realizing the worst fear everyone feels about disclosing vulnerability. "Instead of giving me that assignment with a new key client, he'd tell me I had too much on my plate. Again I felt diminished because I wanted to make the choice of what I could or could not handle."

It got worse. She noticed that crucial information from different departments had stopped reaching her desk, and she saw important opportunities pass her by. Her boss would try to wriggle into her client relationships. He would make it hard for her to do her job by stalling or not giving her the information she needed. Then he started raising personal issues, making comments such as "I've heard that people in the corporate area find you difficult to work with." Surprised, Judith would challenge such assertions, to which he would respond, "It's a real concern." All Judith could think was, "Oh, man, something is wrong with me. What have I done? I was mentally scouring through the past analyzing my behavior in excruciating detail. But my intuition was telling me, 'Don't trust this guy.'"

Judith's boss deployed the gladiator defense to undermine her sense of competency and self-worth. Intuitively, Judith knew not to trust this person, but like so many women, she didn't listen to herself. In hindsight we often scold ourselves when we do that, essentially saying, "I just knew that was coming!" Unfortunately, Judith gave more credence to her doubts than to her instincts. Although someone else forced vulnerability on her, she exacerbated it and colluded by doubting herself.

The turning point came the morning before Judith was to give a presentation to an important client. She found herself in the waiting room with her uninvited boss, who had decided to sit in on the meeting. On several earlier occasions, Judith had tried to engage her boss about some of his allegations, but he always sidestepped the issue. Now, with some time on her hands, Judith brought up his accusation that others found her difficult. He said, "Well, you know, we haven't come to a resolution on a particular contract and I understand that people in this specific area said you were abusive."

Judith remembered her epiphany: "At that point, it was *bong!* I got perfect clarity and got really quiet. I said, 'Really.' He said, 'I would be really worried if I were you.' At that moment it occurred to me that this person had malicious intent for me." Judith unpacked the materials for the presentation and said, "Here are the materials for the meeting. I resign. I'm sure you can handle it." She got up and walked out. Her flustered boss ran out after her as she was hailing a taxi. "You can't do this," he said to her. "You're just running away." Judith calmly replied, "No, I'm not. Everything is all set with the presentation. It'll be fine." With that, she climbed into the taxi, leaving him standing there bewildered with the materials in his hands.

When she got back to her office, Judith called several people in corporate management to tell them about her resignation, explaining that she simply couldn't work with her boss. She also confided his allegations about her "abusive behavior." The entire senior management was dumbstruck.

Judith then turned her attention to her staff, asking each person privately whether she had ever treated any of them in a demeaning or abusive way. One woman, with a heavy Boston Italian accent said, "Whaddya talkin' about? Nah, you haven't been." The allegation was an outright lie; Judith felt redeemed. In the end, the CEO, promising her a different boss, asked her to stay.

"I realized that I had been sucked into somebody else's game that had me going around and around, what's wrong with me?" How long did it take her before she reached what an outsider might consider an obvious insight? Five years. Even after her full vindication, Judith still needed people to confirm that the boss had behaved inappropriately. "I'm still learning," Judith admitted during our conversation, "because my automatic mode is to be accommodating, to give the benefit of the doubt. It's like swimming in water. When you scuba dive, you forget about the water and then at that point, oh, I'm under water. That is the conversation of self-deprecation."

Judith grew during this debacle. "My reaction to leave was my youngest, most immature reaction. I shouldn't have been that dramatic. But I couldn't help flipping into self-righteous indignation, which felt good and also led to a whole new way of being for me." After more mature reflection about how she had gotten herself mentally stuck in a box of self-doubt and how she could let herself get sucked back into it, Judith concluded that "the limitations I was experiencing with my boss were self-imposed." She could have "taken this person on," as she told me, by asking him not to attend her presentation or by creating a forum to make him accountable for his actions and words. While people who heard the story of her abandoning her boss with egg on his face cheered her on with a resounding "Go, girl!" Judith rued her behavior as an unbridled Fury.

In hindsight, she would "rather be a powerful presence, whose boundaries are clear, with edges you can't cross. Letting myself be powerful is a gift I give to myself now." The clear boundaries that she etches out for herself recognize her tendency to avoid confrontation and to readily question herself instead. "The more I can know this about myself, embrace that part of myself, then there's a chance I can keep myself from being controlled and manipulated." Judith became stronger from this experience because, rather than disowning or controlling her vulnerabilities, she embraced them, which paradoxically connected her to her power. Seeing that she gave too much benefit of the doubt to others freed her to give herself the benefit of the doubt.

Judith has taught herself to recognize when she is not fully expressing herself or silencing herself: she feels a physical pain high in her upper chest, the area that in ancient India is called the "heart chakra." When her body speaks, Judith now listens, a topic we will discuss in the next chapter. Your body, it turns out, can tell you a lot, if you only learn to listen to it.

Of course, women can fear the consequences of speaking up and challenging a situation, but anyone can learn to do as Judith does. If you don't feel safe speaking your mind, seek out women friends who can help you think through the problem. This practice has done wonders for Judith. "I've been called by my friends, 'the iron fist in a velvet glove.' I am learning to believe in myself, and when I feel some of the weight of doubt,

I realize it is nothing but a passing thought. Before the dark creeps in, I reconnect with my true self by being with an inspiring thought."

Self-doubt is a way of giving over your power, but it can also show you the path to reclaiming that power by changing an internal conversation of self-denigration into an external conversation in which you can express your vulnerability and doubts in the safe company of women. Together, women can help each other discover and rediscover that elusive balance we all need.

Although our culture may pressure us to become Amazons and Shape Changers and Furies, Iron Butterflies demonstrate that those roles may stem from people's expectations, either perceived or real. But we can just as easily arise from limitations we impose on ourselves. No one ordered Mary Lou to give herself away or Alison to abandon herself. They did it to themselves because they worried too much about what others wanted. While gladiators should pause and ask themselves "What do I feel?" as a way of reconnecting to dissociated parts of themselves, Amazons and Shape Changers and Furies might ask a different question: "What do I want?"

Chapter 9

BODIES

Listen to Inner Wisdom

One is not born a woman, one becomes a woman.

Simone de Beauvoir

We all know the hero's journey: the hero embarks on an adventure fraught with monsters and danger, learns lessons along the way, and returns home to share them. Strong women leaders do the same, not in some jungle or faraway land, but in an internal terrain. An Iron Butterfly's journey into the heart and mind and soul usually begins with a crisis, an unexpected external event that rocks her world and stops her dead in her tracks. Though stymied, she learns to forge a path out of the crisis to a new awareness or discovery of her authentic self. Unlike the journey of the hero who asserts his power over the environment, the Iron Butterfly journey is one of self-empowerment.

This internal journey is fraught with its own monsters and dangers. It is often a descent into despair, where she questions all that she has ever assumed about herself, where she examines and abandons beliefs once held dear to her heart, where she confronts hard realities once clouded and ignored. On this journey, she sheds the chrysalis of her false self and comes face to face with her denied and dissociated vulnerabilities. Shaken into going where she wouldn't go on her own, into the dark caves and crevices of her soul, she, nevertheless, finds herself on a path to healing and becoming whole; she comes home to herself.

During her descent into her shadows, she discovers the gift of vulnerability and the potential it offers to transform weaknesses into strength, self-doubt into self-confidence, worthlessness to worthiness, imbalance into harmony, uncertainty into wisdom. By accepting this gift and acknowledging what she once denied, she transforms and reinvents herself by shaking off all that is "not me," all the compromises and acrobatic gyrations and adaptations she has made along the way in order to fit in, to gain acceptance, to make everything right in her world.

Often this journey begins when the body speaks, which will be the focus of this chapter. The body, writes psychologist Carol Gilligan in her book *The Birth of Pleasure*, "is our strongest barometer of our consonance with or dissonance from the world around us." When the barometer registers dissonance with our world, whether at work or in our personal relationships, the body alerts us to toxic environments. We can talk ourselves into ignoring or minimizing toxic threats to our well-being, but the body's truth ultimately prevails.

Our bodies speak to us in many ways, and yet we often overlook these signals. We neglect to pay attention to our internal world because we have become so focused on our external world and appearances, as we discussed in chapter 7. We don't listen to what the knot in our stomach, the pain in our neck, the ache in our joints might be telling us.

These bodily ailments or stagnations, connected to our emotions and spirit, impede the realization of our full, authentic selves. As the acupuncturist, dancer, and choreographer Marcus Schulkind told me, "The path to healing is through motion, to move out of stagnation, to move through locked places in our bodies and images of ourselves." Rather than ignoring signals that telegraph these stagnations, we should pay close attention to them because that is the first step on the arduous journey of healing. Healing, a process of moving with and through these bodily stagnations, comes in its own time and requires patience and perseverance. When we heed our bodily experiences, and observe and allow sensation and feeling, we tap into the history and the wisdom and the messages for personal development the body holds. Paradoxically, our physical pains and pleasures become our spiritual guides.

LET INANNA GUIDE YOU

The Sumerian myth about the goddess Inanna and her sister Ereshkigal describes Inanna's descent into the shadows and her subsequent transformation. I like the story because it reminds me that no woman need make her own journey alone if she lets Inanna guide her.

One day when Inanna, the queen of heaven and earth, opened her ear to the moaning of her sister Ereshkigal, queen of the underworld, she decided to abandon her own realm and make the descent into the "great below." To prepare herself, she set a crown on her head, hung beads around her neck, sprinkled sparkling stones across her breast, wrapped a gold ring around her waist, and donned a royal robe. Properly attired, she set out for *kur-nu-gi-a*, the netherworld, with her faithful servant, Ninshubur, by her side. When she arrived at the outer gates of *kur-nu-gi-a*, she commanded Ninshubur to wait for three days. If Inanna didn't return by that deadline, the servant was to call upon the elder gods for help.

Inanna knocked loudly at the gates of the underworld demanding that Neti, the gatekeeper, open the door. When Neti questioned why Inanna would go down a road from which no traveler ever returned, Inanna said she came to see her older sister Erishkigal. Neti dutifully delivered the message to Erishkigal, telling her that a giant and powerful goddess, arrayed in splendor, stood at the threshold of her realm. Erishkigal told the gatekeeper to bolt the seven gates of the underworld, then, one by one, to open each gate a mere crack, forcing Inanna to remove her royal garments in order to pass through each gate. "Let the holy priestess of heaven enter bowed low," she proclaimed. As Inanna passed through the first gate, Neti removed her crown. At the second gate, he removed her beads; at the third, her sparkling stones; at the seventh and final gate, her robe. Naked and unadorned, Inanna entered the throne room of her sister. Immediately, the judges of the underworld surrounded her and condemned her. Fastening the eye of death on Inanna, Ereshkigal spoke words of wrath and struck her down. She then hung her corpse, like a piece of rotting meat, from a hook on the wall.

After three days and no sign of Inanna, Ninshubur went for help, but none of the gods would come to her aid except Enki, god of wisdom and water. Enki removed dirt from under his fingernails and created two creatures, neither male nor female, and gave them the food of life and water of life to carry to Inanna. He instructed them to enter the doors like flies, and whenever they heard Erishkigal cry out, they were to repeat her cry.

Accordingly, the creatures slipped through the cracks in the gates and into the throne room, where they came upon Ereshkigal lying naked and unkempt, moaning with the cries of a woman about to give birth:

"Oh, oh, my insides!" she moaned and the creatures moaned back, "Oh, oh, your inside!"

"Oh, oh, my belly." "Oh, oh, your belly!"
"Oh, oh, my heart!" "Oh, oh, your heart."
As she continued to moan out her agony, they named her pains back to her. Finally, the queen, feeling relief, stopped moaning and gratefully blessed the creatures, offering them any gift, any riches they desired.

They asked for Inanna's corpse, the piece of hanging meat, which Ereshkigal gave them. Sprinkling the food of life and the water of life on the corpse, they watched Inanna rise, ready to ascend from the underworld. When she returned to her realm, she saw her world through new eyes.

Inanna symbolizes the conscious world of the ego while Ereshkigal represents the unconscious mind. Inanna hears something stirring, something rejected and consigned to darkness in herself. Often we want to block out these uneasy feelings, retreat from these unpleasant truths that beg us to hear them. But at some point, like Inanna, we enter the dark cavern where revelation, not just pain, resides.

To protect herself from this unpleasant knowledge of herself, Inanna clothes herself with her weapons of power, all her status symbols. But the work of the descent requires her to strip herself of pretense until she stands completely naked, helpless, and powerless. She has to totally let go: let go of the perfect-woman image that she projects, let go of all the adornments associated with her power and prestige, let go of all the illusions of control over her life and others. Her whole queenly image with all its entitlements and privilege shatters. With her defensive armor removed, Inanna stands there authentic, in all her nakedness and vulnerability.

Exposed and defenseless, she faces her sister, her exiled shadow self. It is not a pretty sight, this miserable and moaning Ereshkigal who would like nothing better than to destroy her shining, superficially resplendent sister. She does just that, murdering her with the death eye. But wisdom restores Inanna, raising her from her rotting former self to see the world with fresh eyes. What a perfect metaphor for the transformative work strong women do to fashion themselves into leaders in the new era. In order to transform, a part of us must die to make room for rebirth.

Like the little creatures created by Enki to aid Inanna, we can name our pains back to ourselves until the pains begin to heal. By acknowledging our pains, we "embody" them. Here's what I mean. Often we say we have a bad knee or a bad back, scolding these parts like disobedient pets or petulant children. But if we pay attention to these bodily messages, let them know we hear them and kindly engage in a conversation with them, we can go into the dark depths and come back a more authentic, a more whole, healthier, happier self.

The stories ahead illustrate this descent into the "body of knowledge" and spotlight benchmark points along the journey that leads Iron Butterflies to an embodied authentic self and a sense of coming home to themselves: befriend the painful places, stop doing what doesn't work, stay open, let go of anger, heed your instincts, and empty out all that is "not me."

BEFRIEND THE PAINFUL PLACES

Angela Farmer, a master yogi, and her partner and husband, Victor van Kooten, were at one time the two leading Iyengar yoga teachers in the world. Eventually, they developed their own style of yoga, which introduced a more feminine side to their yoga practice. This feminine approach appealed not only to Angela but also to many other women who are her biggest followers. Angela's descent into her own body and her journey of personal transformation demonstrate how listening to the body can reveal the wisdom that resides there.

At age eleven, Angela's hands and feet started to turn black. Fearing an ailment that would lead to gangrene, the doctors cut through her spine at her neck, her abdomen, and sections of her sympathetic nervous system. They never warned her of the side effects she would suffer, such as never sweating again. "The reason we have sticky mats in yoga," Angela informed me, "is I needed friction because my feet would just slide away from me because I didn't sweat. All my students wanted one too, and so the yoga mat business began." The doctors also didn't tell her about pain in her hands, a loss of sensitivity, and infertility.

"Because of my condition, Angela told me, "I wanted to feel life in every part of me; it was my deepest longing." To do that, she took up modern dance and discovered yoga at a time when the word made most people imagine someone lying on a bed of nails. Her yoga teacher guided Angela to a class with her own teacher, Iyengar, who was visiting in London at the time. Since Angela had been looking deeply at the origins and essence of movement and was hungry for guidance, Iyengar took her to depths she had never imagined. In order to travel to India and study with this remarkable teacher, Angela begged, borrowed, and sold everything she owned. "Iyengar is a genius," Angela recalled:

> But he was also brutal. I got put down, hit, kicked a couple of times. The verbal abuse was the hardest to handle. He said he was breaking our egos and I just believed him. I thought I just had to get rid of my ego. But gradually I felt like I lost more and more of who I was. I had surrendered

everything except my "good friend," my intuition. One day, the abuse was so strong, I felt that the only way to survive and learn from the master was to let my intuition go and I surrendered even that. I thought if I worked harder, I would break through something. I sold out. I had to go that way in order to wake up.

Later, still searching for that elusive connection to her body and her self, Angela went back to India a second time to continue her studies with Iyengar. One day, as she came out of a back bend, her body spoke loudly and her vision was clear; although she had bent over backward in search of an authentic self, nothing inside her had changed. All these contortions, all this abuse, wasn't getting her to where she wanted to go, even though she didn't know how to get there. One truth did dawn on her, however. When she strolled down to the market and sat with the Indian women who possessed little more than a colorful sari and a pile of fruit, she felt good. "They had what I was looking for. They were in their bodies, seemed happy, and were generous."

This simple insight devastated Angela. She had given her whole life over to this current practice and enslaved herself to a teacher she had placed atop a pedestal of omnipotence. At the same time, the man she loved married somebody else. Two pillars of her life had toppled. "I felt like a cigarette scrubbed out in the ground. Everything was plumbed out of me. I was nothing. But these experiences were given to me so when I came back from my trip, my life would change."

Once she knew she needed to move on, she began a long, slow unfolding process of discovery. "There was a tiny voice inside me that actually couldn't speak, but it was there. I began to listen more to myself, to feel my body. We are given all these yoga teachings and they come down like the Ten Commandments—we have to fit ourselves into it. I wondered how did the gurus learn? They had no teachers. My practice began to change."

Angela and Victor pulled the rug from underneath all the Iyengar traditional form by asking such questions as "What's beneath the form? Who is in there? What do I really feel?" Other yoga practitioners shunned them, criticized them, or feared them. Ultimately the Iyengar community ostracized, then banished them. "I suddenly felt very naked and very small," Angela recalled, "but at least I felt real. We were little refugees; we never knew if we could survive."

Angela began to see her practice through new eyes. Yoga, she saw, can overemphasize the aspiration toward perfection. Competitive people who see someone executing a better asana try to do one better and in the process can lose sight of some other aspect of themselves they should develop. "If people overemphasize the strong parts of themselves," Angela concluded, "their more vulnerable parts get hidden or contracted to a deeper level until they become almost invisible to a person. You can become very strong and armored in yoga, and so to 'undo' becomes more and more scary."

For Angela it boiled down to recovering her self-esteem and self-worth by believing in what comes through her body rather than from what someone tells her. "The wonderful thing about yoga is that it brings you back into your body where all the memories of your life are stored. By unraveling parts of the body that have been injured or held tight or wounded, we can recover a part of your life that is missing."

It's never too late. It came to Angela later in life and it required the help of more than a single guru. "I uncovered, with the help of a skilled cranial-sacral therapist, a brutal sexual violation when I was very young. Unearthing this terrifying experience left me completely numb, 'glued' to the table it seemed, in horror that anyone could do such damage to a baby. When finally I could utter the word 'why?' the wise therapist simply said, 'People do what has been done to them.'"

At first she felt overwhelmingly sad recovering this lost part of herself; only a part of her had lived this life.

> But then a miracle happened! This moment became the biggest turning point of my life. It has opened my doors for compassion and a deep connection with other women who have suffered early abuse. It has led me to a whole new way of practicing yoga, going deep inside and slowly, gently meeting those places that were locked up in fear all those years. Amazingly, with gentleness and patience, deep relaxation and breath, these little lost parts find a voice and return, giving me a sense of fullness and wholeness that I was searching for all my life.

One of the feminine components she has added to her repertoire is a focus on the pelvis.

> That's where women for centuries have been blocked and disconnected, because it has been considered to be something dangerous and "dirty." When women get more feeling in their pelvis, they get in touch with the perineum, which increases their awareness of the first and second chakras. Women sever their sensation from this area because of shame, fear, and education, but more often, with sexual abuse. When they connect to it, it is so empowering and wonderful.

Many women can benefit from unraveling themselves back to their vulnerable places, revisiting old traumas and injuries, making friends with the pain, and recovering lost parts of themselves. As Angela advised:

> I think it's important to have a practice where you meet yourself every day. Face those places of resistance coming up in you. When the pain comes in, I know I have to stay and wait. It's the process of meeting what I am in the places that are stopping me. All of a sudden, something releases. A beautiful sense of spreading happens and I drop a little deeper into my body.

The descent into the body, especially into its secret pain and torment, can help us recover our power, our beauty, and our joy in life.

STOP DOING WHAT DOESN'T WORK

When we are misaligned and disembodied, our bodies seek equilibrium and unity by expressing physically what the mind fears to say. When we ignore those messages, the body persists and speaks even louder, sometimes in the form of physical illness and even creating a crisis that prevents us from moving forward along the usual path. Make some change, our body says, otherwise "we" aren't going anywhere.

Janiece Webb, vice president at Motorola, has undertaken many descents, as we all do, but a pivotal one occurred when her body literally stopped her in her tracks, forcing her to face the truth about herself and the Amazon's life she had created. At the time, Janiece's work required her to fly around the world, sometimes as many as seventy-five thousand miles in two weeks, back and forth to Europe, Asia, and Latin America. Preoccupied with showing everyone that she could deliver expected results, she stopped listening to her physical, emotional, or spiritual self. "I was trying to brute-force my way through things at work," Janiece told me. "It was a matter of pride, my sense of doing the right thing, not wanting to fail, not wanting to admit to a mistake, not wanting my family to see me as not strong. I was being macho. Even though I was working in a hostile environment where rocks were thrown at me, I was going to show them." Somehow Janiece managed to sustain that pace for eight years, until hepatitis struck her down. Bedridden, she faced Ereshkigal and learned something new about herself.

> The hepatitis taught me I had no control. The more I fought the disease, the worse I got. The more I said my mantra, "I can do it," which had

always worked for me, the harder I got knocked down. Being macho and being tough was absolutely the worst thing I could do. My body was telling me that I would not win this battle with that set of tools; I would need to grow new ones. I was raw emotionally, spiritually, and physically, and I had to work on all of them simultaneously. I realized if I didn't take care of these aspects of my life, that I was, in fact, killing myself.

What a blow to her macho self-image. She could not, in fact, fix everything with sheer willpower; she could not climb every mountain without paying a steep price.

I realized those ways were really an egocentric view of life. At the time I thought I was doing it for a good reason, proving I could handle myself, that I cared, but it was driven by the ego. It's not my job to make it OK for everybody. Power used to be macho, bravado, I can go through the brick wall. Power now is quiet, centered, a balance of masculinity and femininity. I have to be intellectually growing, emotionally, physically, and spiritually growing, to be fully healthy. I can't give them up anymore.

By accepting her vulnerability, she found more, not less, inner power. "I didn't need this muscling out anymore. I realized I'm not the macho man. If that's what I have to be in this work environment, I don't want it. It was a relief."

Only when her body insisted that she stop did Janiece shed her armor and her tendency to tough it out. Like Inanna, Janiece became vulnerable when she was stripped of her defenses that enabled her to stay in a gladiator culture. But by listening to and following her unconscious needs, she discovered that all she stood for, all that Amazon behavior, not only did not serve her, but, in fact, almost destroyed her.

Her body expressed in physical language what was not being said verbally, that her work environment was literally sickening. Janiece purged herself of the toxicity of a gladiator culture and found a new balance among body, mind, emotion, and spirit—a new reference point that she could not override and that would protect her more effectively than any Amazon armor.

STAY OPEN

While listening to her body led Janiece to connect to her authentic self and rethink her work life, it prompted Kathe Schaaf to rethink her marriage.

Kathe cofounded Gather the Women, a global matrix, a gathering place for women and women's organizations to share and to activate the power of women's wisdom. At a pivotal point in her life, her body sent a clear signal that she was out of balance, both literally and figuratively.

Talking with me about her former marriage, she described her ex-husband as a gentle, funny, loving, and kind person with whom she shared a bucolic life, seemingly not exactly grounds for divorce. Although they lived as a "nature" couple, living in an old stone farmhouse in the country with their golden retrievers, tending to their many gardens, canning vegetables, and cooking feasts for friends, it turned out that they weren't a natural match for each other and their personal journeys would take them down wildly divergent paths.

Kathe confided:

> In this safe and loving and protected life, I was on a quest to know more of myself, to know more about the amazing universe, to rediscover my own spirituality. When I would share my journey with my husband, he would look at me like he had no idea of what I was talking about or who I was becoming. The more my thinking and sense of myself evolved, the further apart we grew. He would tell me he wasn't interested in growing, that he was happy the way he was.

One morning Kathe woke up feeling dizzier than she had ever felt in her life, clutching at walls and tables as she tried to walk and restore her equilibrium. She hoped the symptoms might pass, but when they didn't, she finally went to see her doctor, who tentatively diagnosed her with multiple sclerosis. If he was right, MS symptoms come and go. Outside his office, Kathe looked up to the sky and with a voice of surrender said, "OK, God, I've got the message. I am out of balance. I am not living the life you brought me here to live." That epiphany changed Kathe's life forever.

"There was part of me that was happy being with my husband," Kathe told me. "But there was also a part of me that was waking up from a long sleep, and my body was just calling out to me and saying, 'It's time to wake up.'" This awakening compelled Kathe to dismantle the life she had built: she left the marriage, left her job, left her house, and left the state. Even though she had made these choices of her own free will, that did not ease the pain of separation or abate her anxiety about her uncertain future. Sleepless and depressed, Kathe lost nineteen pounds, what I call the "divorce diet," something that often happens when someone goes through a major life transition. In spite of the anguish, she told me, "I had to do it." She could not override the dictates of her body, which had become her spiritual guide.

One day wandering by the lake, tearful and fretting about where in the world she would live, she ran into a friend she hadn't seen for years. Her friend, it turned out, was also wrestling with a life-altering transition: a new job would provide her with housing in Milwaukee, leaving her with a vacant condo on her hands. "Within a day, I had a place to live that was free. It was perfect. Things like that just kept happening. I just kept putting one foot in front of the other," Kathe recalled. "Divine grace kept appearing, holding me, moving me in the right direction. I had this inarticulate knowing that I had to just stay open."

As she restructured her life, Kathe's MS symptoms periodically went away and came back. The dizziness, the numbness, the tingling on the left side of her body, became a personal barometer for Kathe, indicating to her when she was literally and figuratively out of balance.

Kathe met her current husband, and she got pregnant with her first baby three months after the wedding and bore another son four years later. Pregnancy generally exacerbates all the symptoms of MS, but to Kathe's surprise and delight, her symptoms went away for good. Her body had led her to the life she was meant to live. "It was just this huge wake-up call about creating balance in my life, to listen to my body and soul."

Uncertainty accompanies every step of the Iron Butterfly's journey, and it can lead to a period of depression, as it did for Kathe. Depression itself often walks hand in hand with fear, a fear that some adversity will annihilate the core self. Sometimes the loneliness so overwhelms us we could drown in it. But depression can also mark the beginning of healing, as psychologist Dana Crowley Jack discusses in her book *Silencing the Self: Women and Depression*, "Particularly when a woman has molded herself to fit her partner's values and preferences, she fears that the loss of the relationship means a loss of self. She does not recognize that it is within unsatisfactory forms of relationship that the self has already undergone its most serious erosion." Until Kathe's body spoke, she had not fully realized the extent to which she had molded herself to the life her ex-husband wanted. In her quest to find the life she wanted, where Kathe could live true to herself, Kathe needed to stay open, pay attention to her physical cues, and not try to impose a direction but rather let the journey unfold naturally instead.

LET GO OF THE ANGER

Remember Alison Godfrey from chapter 8, the CEO of LifeWaves who swung between being an Amazon woman and a Shape Changer and abandoned herself in both roles? Ultimately, she found part of her abandoned self by awakening to her body's history and thus opening the door to heal old wounds and become whole.

It all happened during a team project that Alison's company sponsored in Kansas City. A physical therapist named Kelly (a member of Alison's team) found out that Alison often recoiled if a stranger unexpectedly touched her. In fact, she had once slapped someone who had inadvertently startled her from behind.

Kelly asked Alison if she wanted to explore the source of that reaction and Alison thought what the hell and agreed. Kelly observed, "The person who doesn't want to be touched is someone else. Ask that someone else why she doesn't want to be touched." Alison asked the question quietly to herself. "Suddenly," Alison told me, "I blurted out, 'I was molested as a child.' The whole room was aghast. I burst into tears. And everybody is thinking, 'Too much information!' I'm thinking, 'Oh, shit. Who knew this could happen?'" She had dealt with the sexual abuse by burying it.

> I was put in situations by my mother as a child where I was sexually abused. She had a dear friend, a female alcoholic and homosexual who wanted to take a nap with me. I would be hysterical, begging my mother not to make me lie with her, and my mother would force me, ordering me to be kind to our guest. I was seven. Next, she was dating a man and his butler had me in the closet. I was twelve. I tried to tell my mother, but she didn't want to hear one word. When I was eighteen, I was attacked by my mother's friend's husband, who was a dentist, and he used gas to completely knock me out. One time my boyfriend was outside waiting and he had this psychic moment and burst into the office as I was being raped while unconscious. The dentist ended up in jail for raping women in dental chairs, and my mother testified as a character witness for him! So I grew to be someone that if you came up from behind me, I'd slap you.

When Alison first recovered these horrific memories, she shed many Iron Butterfly tears before moving into rage and outrage. Then one day she asked herself if she really wanted to live her life as an angry person. "Talk about out of control. Do I want to stay there and be a victim or be the adult I am?" Alison told me. "Then I realized that I had been victimizing myself all those years by saying all I want to do is make everybody happy."

That insight led to another revelation:

> What all this really meant was I should take care of myself. Before I only got as far as trying to change my husband's behavior, so he would take care of me. I realized it had nothing to do with him; it was all

about my behavior. I went through a phase saying, "it's about me," but that didn't mean it wasn't also about other people. It's just that before I wasn't there in those relationships. I had to count too, so that I wasn't invisible anymore.

By instinctively slapping those who startled her, Alison's body was trying to tell her something: "Descend, dear Inanna, into your dark past. Explore the place that has gone numb and then hardened."

Alison began the healing process by letting herself move through her unfolding emotions. She cried Iron Butterfly tears, sad and hurtful tears that cleansed the wounds and cleared her eyes. She cried tears of righteous anger and wisely let them go, freeing herself from the eddy of victimization. When we can let go of our anger at the injustices we have suffered, as Alison did, then our Iron Butterfly tears can wash us onto our own welcoming shores where we can again hear the rhythmic pulse of our own needs.

HEED YOUR INSTINCTS

The body speaks to us with many voices. In Candice Carpenter Olson's case, her body spoke through psychosomatic symptoms, a process through which people express emotional discomfort and conflict in a physical rather than a verbal language. The symptoms, although lacking a biological base, are not imagined or feigned. Candice's symptoms made an internal conflict so painfully felt, real, and undeniable, they initiated a journey of shedding outdated images of herself, just as Inanna did.

Candice longed to start her own business, but as a single mom, she felt she needed a job that would provide a weekly paycheck to support herself and her family. However, every time she concluded an interview, she found herself rushing to the nearest bathroom to throw up. "I told myself I wanted to sell out," Candice told me, "but this body wasn't going to let me."

Finally she listened to her body's voice and started iVillage, an online community dedicated to bringing women together. For thousands of years, women had gone down to the river with jugs on their heads and connected with other women to accumulate and share knowledge. Candice wanted to carry on this tradition by a different river, the World Wide Web. The result, iVillage, built on a spiritual and tribal base, nurturing community and a sense of family that resounded with fun and laughter.

When the company went public, it naturally evolved to a more corporate culture. "But it was a major change," Candice told me.

It became all this male energy, very alpha, and we got caught up in it. I remember my partner Nancy Evans and I having a working lunch and we caught ourselves unconsciously eating steak with our hands. Being a public company was like ritualized war. As CEO, my job flipped into a corporate job where tribal values were no longer valued, and all they were concerned with was wanting every financial quarter to look the same. Suddenly the company I loved was a very different experience for me.

At the same time as she began battling more and more at work, her role as mother demanded more feminine softness. "The rubber band, the two parts of myself, the masculine and the feminine, just got tauter and tauter," Candice recalled.

As the lines between the two worlds became more divergent, they also became more blurred. My hardness was bleeding over at home and my softness was bleeding over at work. You get hard leading in the world; it requires enormous male qualities and I was less and less willing to subjugate the feminine part of myself. For a half a decade I was the public face of a very public company. Where was the private woman inside that public face, and when would I get to represent her?

Bound up by this tension, Candice started to lose her will to lead. At the same time iVillage stock collapsed, prompting terrible feelings of guilt and sorrow for investors and employees. Stressed and exhausted, she grew deaf to her inner voices and lost her once finely tuned intuition. "I also resented the trade-offs I had been forced to make between my life and my work," Candice told me. "I was having to park myself outside the door when I showed up for work. I knew instinctively it was time for me to go, but I didn't listen."

Then she began to experience strange physical symptoms. Candice, who had never gone to doctors, visited six in six months. "My tongue started hurting so much I couldn't eat or drink anything. I thought I had some kind of cancer; I thought I was dying from something. But in reality my body was begging for relief and I wasn't listening."

Then one day she had lunch with a friend, who told her he had just walked out on his job. Hearing that, the rubber band snapped in Candice. "I said, 'That's it. I'm out of here.'" She got drunk with a girlfriend, went to the office at midnight, carted out every vestige of her past life, and never went back to that building again. She left with the title of chairman. Although she paused her professional life, however, her journey was far from over.

Then I fell and fell. It was six months before I was on my feet again, six months of spinning, of wondering, "where am I?" on drugs and alcohol. Finally, reality intervened in the form of a small child, and I said, "Enough already." The fall was very vulnerable. With vulnerability, there's a sense of exposure that can be almost physically frightening. But you are doing hard work even though it seems you are doing nothing. You're shedding an old skin, the hell you've lived inside, the old way of knowing yourself and letting others know you. Spaces between accomplishments are every bit as important as the accomplishments themselves. This was one of those spaces.

One day she released the pause button. Her interest in her nightly pileup of taped TV shows had evaporated along with the four candy bars a day. She stopped organizing and reorganizing her closet and found herself once again drawn to books. When she gave up the title of chairman, she hit the fast-forward button. "I was shocked by the freedom and energy that was released by this simple shedding of what had become largely a symbolic title. We carry weights we don't even know about until we put them down. I realized that what matters is to have your outer and inner selves in alignment and allow them to grow together."

Candice awakened to her softer, feminine side when she became a mother, as many women do. However, since her work environment didn't welcome this side, she faced a dilemma. That dilemma manifested not as a dreaded *disease*, but rather as a *dis-ease* with how she was living her life. Listening to her bodily murmurings for relief, Candice completely extricated herself from the gladiator culture in order to find a new alignment in herself where she could be the same person in all contexts. Like Inanna who was stripped of her royal garb, leaving the corporate world stripped Candice of her public CEO image and all the power associated with it. Vulnerable and without a reference point to ground her, she descended into despair, not knowing who she was. Her authentic self emerged as she recovered her intuition, which led her back to reading books, moving her through her depression and on to another journey. Candice now heads Transitions Institute where she helps other executives shed their old cocoons and reinvent themselves as she did.

EMPTY OUT ALL THAT IS NOT YOU

Connecting to your authentic self, coming home to yourself, defies description, and yet when you arrive there, you find yourself in such a calm, clear space, you wonder why it took so much time and effort to get there. Choreographer and dancer Paula Josa-Jones reached her destination by her body guiding the dancer rather than vice versa. It all started when she saw Eiko and Koma perform.

Eiko and Koma are two brilliant Japanese choreographers who have performed all over the world, moving audiences with their exquisitely slow and evocative movement. Paula found their performance breathtaking. "I first saw them perform *Grain* in New York in 1983," Paula told me. "I was riveted, it shook me to my roots. It was one of those elemental, transformative moments in performance. So when they offered their Delicious Movement Workshop at their home in the Catskills, I immediately enrolled."

Paula arrived at the workshop with her bag of dance techniques, her performer self, her toolbox of dancer's knowledge and experience. "I had just finished the Laban Movement Analysis training in New York, where I had learned to analyze movement from many perspectives, and I felt very full and fresh with that information. I learned to use space to spiral down to the floor in many ways," Paula recalled. "When I did this fluid spiraling movement one day in the workshop, Koma said, 'Stop!!! Just go down!' I was shocked. It was as if someone said, "Let go of everything you know; be naked, simple, present. It was terrifying and exhilarating in the same moment."

The workshop focused on Butoh-influenced techniques that ran completely counter to Paula's conventional training with all its controlled forms and shapes in motion. Instead, this work focused on dissolving rather than defining the body's boundaries, allowing the body to shape change rather than being composed, and opening the body to a place of receptivity. Eiko called it "trembling," a still point where movement is born. In one movement Paula recalls, Eiko bent over and lifted her arm in a way that her body became a broken branch with a dying flower at its tip. "Over time I learned to *become* a transparent, subtle flow of images, moving from the inside, from listening, rather than focusing on shaping the outer form of the movement." It was letting the body *be* the dance, rather than using the body to dance.

At the end of the workshop, the instructors expected each participant to perform an original piece. "I spent the whole day grasping for ideas. I wanted my dance to be perfect, for it to express everything I had been learning," Paula told me with a laugh. At 7:30 in the evening, when they were gathering for the performances, Paula still did not have an idea. On her way to the studio, she noticed Koma's tuxedo jacket hanging on a coat hook in the house. Instinctively her hand shot out; she grabbed the jacket and put it on.

When the time came for Paula to perform, she had no inkling of what she would do. The thought of performing in front of an audience without any plan or choreography was a terrifying thought, but she took solace in her Japanese teachers' admonishment to empty and listen inwardly. "I couldn't think about it, I had to take a leap of faith."

Paula stood on the stage clad in the tuxedo jacket with her back to the audience.

> I started to move, and this exquisite dance fell out of me whole. I went deep into myself, into the coat, Koma's spirit in that coat, into the sacred space of performance and the stillness. It was authentic. That dance became a piece that I called "Tremble." I call it that because I felt that tremble, a stepping out of and beyond myself onto a living, breathing, growing edge—dangerous and tender.

Paula had arrived at her own magical place.

> That moment was a real turning point for me. It was like somebody held me up and shook and shook me until all the spoons and the forks and pebbles and shells and debris I had collected clattered out. I got emptied out. I became willing to let all that I knew about movement fall away from me. It was exhilarating and absolutely right. The realization for me was that it wasn't about getting filled up with knowledge, or experience, or expertise, or anything else. It was about being empty. From that emptiness, I could feel my authentic self, and hear its voice through my body. From that place, anything could happen, a pirouette, a spiral, a flower blooming at the end of a broken branch—it is all available.

This is one of the greatest gifts of vulnerability, a journey of being emptied of all that is not you. And the body tells the story if we will listen for the tremble.

Chapter 10

DIVINITIES

Following the Spiritual Light

> As the Ya-Yas slept that night in the Thornton City Jail, the moon loved
> them. Not because they were beautiful, or because they were perfect, or
> because they were perky, but because they were her darling daughters.
>
> From Rebecca Wells, *Divine Secrets of the Ya-Ya Sisterhood*

Pat Mitchell, former CEO of the Public Broadcast Service and now president and CEO of the Paley Center for Media, had big dreams:
someday she would live a different life from the one she knew in her small
Georgian town of five hundred people. The first in her family to graduate
from college, she had married and taken a job teaching at a local college,
accomplishments that seemed to have fulfilled her dream. However, a nagging restlessness plagued the young teacher. Instead of feeling fulfilled, she
felt something missing in the safe and predictable life she had created and
that her family wanted for her. A few years after the birth of her son, Pat
divorced her husband and began to reassess her expectations and to revisit
her original dream.

"When I found myself on my own, having to support myself and my
child," Pat told me, "I began reevaluating if this life was what I really
wanted or was I just fitting into the circle of expectations, which is very
powerful in the South. That's when I connected to an earlier dream of
moving far away. Maybe I could live in New York and be a journalist."

To ease her family's strong opposition and fears over her moving away on her own, Pat did it incrementally, first to Virginia and finally to New York, where she landed a job as a journalist with *Look* magazine. Nine months later, when *Look* went bankrupt, Pat found herself without a job during a time when the magazine industry had gone into a steep decline. With no jobs on the horizon, Pat followed an acquaintance's advice to explore opportunities in the television industry, where women were beginning to make inroads. After knocking on the door of every television executive in town, she found herself in a frustrating limbo, either overeducated or undereducated for almost every position. "You get a lot of rejection, particularly in television, and it was hard to take it any way other than personally."

Unemployed in the Big Apple, with a five-year-old child and no savings or steady income, Pat began to question the merits of her dream to work in the media. Should she return to teaching? Go home to Georgia? Or should she stay the course? "It was a horrible time with huge amounts of doubt," Pat recalled. "I don't know how I got through it." To make ends meet, she picked up all kinds of odd jobs, and with the help of a Russian neighbor who babysat for her son, she even worked nights for a spell as a waitress. "Every day I was trying to decide: should I stay or should I go? And my mother kept urging me to forget the dreams and be practical. Come home."

She managed to keep her doubts and fears at bay until one night, after months of trying unsuccessfully to leverage odd freelance jobs into something that could pay the rent, she admitted to herself that she needed to borrow money. Reluctantly, she borrowed what she needed from her best woman friend—an amount, Pat feared, that would stretch her friend's resources. Nevertheless, Pat picked up the money in the middle of a terrible thunderstorm and took a taxi home. As she stepped into her apartment, she realized she had left her bag in the taxi. "The loan and every bit of security I had was in that bag. That was it. It was time to pack up and head home, forget the big dreams, accept the condition of fear." Just as she gave up hope, her phone rang and a voice asked, "Is this Patricia Edenfield Mitchell?" She hesitated to answer, remembering her mother's warning not to talk to strangers. Then she heard words from heaven. "This is Rabbi Goldberg," the voice said, "and I have your bag."

> Within minutes, there he was, standing in the rain giving me back everything: my friend's loan to pay the rent, my identification, my dreams. As I tried to thank him and tell him what this meant to me, he smiled and said, "Well, Patricia, everybody needs a rabbi some time, and tonight you got yours." In place of fear and insecurity, I now had a rabbi and a month's rent. I landed a television job in Boston soon after that, and the big dreams started coming true in ways I had never imagined.

From "Trust in God" to "What doesn't kill you makes you stronger," adages to keep our spirits up during dark and doubtful times abound. But it's not easy to seal off those fears that naturally descend during periods of great uncertainty. Perhaps "God doesn't give you more than you can bear," but s/he doesn't give you any less either. "Cast your bread upon the water to see it return a hundred fold." OK, but sometimes you only get back a loaf of soggy bread. Yet we keep going. More than anything, keeping fears at bay, trusting the unfolding process of life, casting your fate to the wind, and honoring your journey to your true purpose defines what I call courageous vulnerability. It's a challenge to not give up, to persevere when yet another mountain looms in your path, to exercise patience when you can no longer see any light at the end of the tunnel. Tempted to retreat to familiar comfort zones, we give up in the name of practicality or plain despair.

The Iron Butterflies I met relied on some form of religion, spiritual experience, a guiding force, or a life-altering event outside the confines of religion to lift them to a new level of consciousness and self-realization and keep them on their true path. Pat's story illustrates the challenges and the blessings we face when we follow the spiritual light of our true purpose. The encounter with the rabbi offered her just enough encouragement to get her back on track with her heart's desire and her soul's passion. Understanding that she had received a sign, Pat did not give up and her persistence was spiritual work. Overcoming her doubts and fears while holding on to her dream was spiritual work. Finding the courage to let herself evolve rather than give up and retreat to old ways was spiritual work. At the core of spiritual work women find self-esteem, a sense of self-worth, and the courage to pursue a greater destiny.

In this chapter we will encounter the signs, synergy, and moments of grace that have guided alert Iron Butterflies on their way through difficult times of doubt and disorientation. Some readers may think of such turning points as divine intervention, others may prefer more naturalistic, agnostic explanations. Whether they interpret spirituality as a manifestation of a higher life force or power, or just as a metaphor for untapped psychological resources, women are increasingly responding to talk of the Feminine Divine and concepts of the Goddess.

In the previous chapter, we discussed how the descent into the body connects a woman to her authentic self; in this chapter we will see how the ascent of the spirit (however one interprets that term) awakens her to her true path and her rightful place in the cosmic order of things.

First, we will observe women regaining what they have longed for, their spiritual equality, by seeing the feminine heart and face of divinity. In addition to calling upon God (almost always defined in male terms), some seek out the Goddess for spiritual guidance. Then we will see how the power of forgiveness enables storm-battered Iron Butterflies to shake the rain off their wings and fly again.

EMBRACE THE FEMININE DIVINE

Like many other aspects of contemporary culture, religion has felt the impact of feminism. The awakening of feminine consciousness has led women to seek new directions in religion and spirituality to accept that they, too, can embody the divine. For others, however, that's a pretty bold idea, and I find that many women have difficulty accepting it as truth. Women don't often "get it" and for a good reason: most religions have insisted that women can't embody the divine. St. Augustine, for example, argued that God first made man in his image, then created woman in man's image. Therefore, women, he concluded, cannot embody the image of God. This false argument simultaneously alienated women from their bodies and their feminine spirituality. If women can't embody the divine, then there must be something wrong with women's bodies, and those inherent flaws prevent them from being divine.

The late Mary Daly, the female theologian, killed that line of logic when she said, "If God is male, then male is God." Obviously, male is not God, even though some gladiators might wish to think so. Daly counters this ancient falsehood with a nongendered way of thinking about God, which does not objectify God as a noun, a thing, or a person. Instead she urges us to think of God as an intransitive verb (which requires no object) rather than a noun, that God is continually being and becoming and can mean something different for each individual.

When I asked Professor Azizah al-Hibri, an interpreter of the Qur'an, if God is masculine, she said this:

> God states in the Qur'an there is nothing like him, so it would be wrong to apply gender. But he has compassion and mercy, which are very feminine qualities. God is not angry or punitive. God is forgiving. He is not at all the patriarchal God we have been told He is. He is above and beyond that.

Precipitated by the effort to find a nongendered meaning of God, widespread interest in women's spirituality arose within the feminist movement in the 1970s. Female theologians began to criticize classic theology as male-centered and anti-woman, starkly evident in the exclusion of women from the clergy, the references to God as "he," and representations of God in male bodies. In the 1980s, a veritable revolution occurred in liberal mainstream churches, with the production of revised versions of hymn-books and prayers to include less male-centered language. Catholic, Protestant, and Jewish women fought valiantly to enter the ministry, suc-ceeding in some denominations (Episcopalian, for instance) more than in others (Roman Catholic, for instance). Within and outside mainstream religions, women scholars in disciplines such as history, archaeology, and anthropology delved into the question of conceptualizing divinity with female terms of referencing, the Goddess as a counterpoint to God.

Seeing the feminine in the divine opened a broad new path to women's spirituality, a phenomenon where women's search for their own spiritual power and equality occurred simultaneously with the expanding work on prepatriarchal religions and the Goddess, as we discussed in chapter 2. Although some feminists didn't think spirituality deserved a place in fem-inism and regarded it as a diversion from the more important political and social struggles, high priestess ZsuZsanna Budapest, known as the mother of the feminist spirituality movement, begged to differ. In an interview with *EnlightenNext* magazine, she insisted:

> Without the Goddess, feminism is not going to work, because you're going to burn out. You've got to have spirituality connected with your political aspiration because that's how the animal works. Feminism gives you your womanhood and an analysis of what it's like to be a woman in this time and space. Without feminism, if you think you are just like a man, that it doesn't matter what gender you are, you are in a huge denial. Because it matters every bit what gender you are in this time and space. If you can accept that and you get to be female identified, then you can start working with the Goddess in earnest. Because then you are her daughter and you can see your reflection in the divine.

The image of the Goddess holds a special power for many women, as Margot Adler of National Public Radio pointed out:

> The idea of a goddess, one that stands simply for the creative force within, or an actual deity, is a difficult concept for some women to embrace. But for others it is an idea that for the first time freed them from the vestigial prejudices they may have held about their own body. No longer were they the daughters of Eve, the sinner, a mere bone of Adam; they were part of the divine cosmos.

By reclaiming their spiritual equality, women felt empowered, as feminist poet and essayist Adrienne Rich pointed out: "Images of pre-patriarchal goddess cults did one thing: they told women that power, awesomeness, and centrality were theirs by nature, not by privilege or miracle; the female was primary."

The feminine divine has found her way into women's literature, art, and music, spawning a plethora of goddess books from such notable authors as Barbara Walker, Merlin Stone, Adrienne Rich, Marija Gimbutas, Riane Eisler, and Jean Shinoda Bolin, to name a few. The goddess influence and its popularity emerged in such bestselling novels as, *Divine Secrets of the Ya-Ya Sisterhood* by Rebecca Wells, *The Mists of Avalon* by Marion Zimmer Bradley, and *The Secret Life of Bees* by Sue Monk Kidd. And yet this quiet movement that asserts a spiritual equality for women and strives to balance the masculine divine remains largely ignored by the greater culture. Perhaps the fact that it is an interior, self-empowering movement and doesn't compete for power or demand turf is not sexy enough for the media to take notice.

Perhaps the many individual expressions of the Goddess make her elusive. But she is coming back! We see her in the pilgrimages of the black Madonna, in people's dreams, in the form of snakes, in luminous female figures, and as dark, powerful figures, emerging out of the shadows. Thank the Goddess for doing her share to usher in the Era of Women, encouraging all women to step out of the shadows and claim their power.

EXPERIENCE THE FEMININE DIVINE IN NATURE

The Goddess represents the force of life, connecting us to the energies of earth, to nature, and to the cyclical realities of birth, life, death, and regeneration. If you recognize nature as an expression of the feminine divine—after all, we do call her *Mother* Nature—then you necessarily think and act as an environmentalist, understanding that if humans do not regard our earth with reverence, we stand to lose the balance and harmony of nature and invite its destruction and the end to all human life. We are a *part of*, not *apart from*, nature. Some environmentalists regard Gaia, the Earth Goddess, as a living being in her own right, an entity that emerges from and consists of profound interconnections. Conquering the earth and exploiting new frontiers as we have done in the quest for domination not only hurts nature but human beings as well. Jean Shinoda Bolen nicely described the link between the feminine divine, women, and nature:

I think women within the current Goddess movement are exploring this idea of having a receptive body that picks up energy. But a woman has to have an affinity to the idea of earth as Goddess and then have the ability to connect her body to Mother Earth in order to experience this. My own spiritual experience before I got connected to earth energies was about transcendence. I would go out to the mountains and look at the stars, and it gave me a sense of the divinity that was out there. But it's different from feeling energies of Mother Earth, which is an embodied connection. The feminine earth Goddess is coming back with a new status that is equal to the masculine, transcendent God.

The feminine divine emerges in women's lives in many forms, as Elizabeth DeBold noted in her article "The Divine Feminine, Unveiled" in *EnlightenNext* magazine:

There are some who see the Divine Feminine in the unique life-sustaining roles that have emerged from our biological role as mothers. Others speak of a feminine principle that is a force in the human psyche and a fundamental aspect of the manifest world. And still others are engaged in reclaiming or re-creating rituals to celebrate ancient goddesses, to make this feminine divinity more visible and conscious. Common to all (or most) is the sense that the sacred is not to be found in a transcendent realm out there somewhere but that the sacred is immanent to life.

The journey of women's spirituality follows a circular route. Women connected to their bodies, and thus embodied, are more receptive to earth energies. This receptiveness also creates a feminine consciousness, a sense of the feminine divine within themselves. Ultimately, the feminine divine stems from the very earth energies that inspire women's spiritual journey. What a gorgeous micro/macro, inner/outer, grounded/transcendent spiral dance!

We can feel the feminine divine as an embodied experience, one that unifies the body and spirit rather than separates them, and one that can guide us on our Iron Butterfly journey to becoming strong, authentic women, leading in the new Era of Women.

Paula Slovenkai-Driscoll told me a remarkable story of her embodied experience of the Goddess, a descent into her body initiated by nature that propelled her ascent to a spiritual and profound cosmic sense of interconnectedness. Remember Carol Jamison's goddess group from chapter 1? Paula initiated that group.

Paula, an artist and mother of two girls, had always found solace in religion and all its beautiful rituals. Listening week after week to a male priest preach about a male God, she began to notice something missing in her Catholic church and other religions as well. And it began to bother her. "Where's the other half?" she asked herself. "You can't have life without male and female. If God is the image of man, what does this say about women? Why don't we hear anything about the women in the history of the church?" One time during mass, as the priest proclaimed, "the kingdom, the power, and the glory are yours, now and forever," something snapped in Paula. "It's like they just conquered someone else's land! I felt physically ill. I had to get out of there." That moment launched a cycle wherein Paula left the church, only to return to it and then leave it again. Although she tried different denominations, none of them satisfied her spiritual needs.

One spring day she went for a walk in the park. Watching the wind blow through the trees and the morning light dance on the budding leaves, she felt a sacred presence all around her and within her. The spiritual experience she couldn't find in a church engulfed her in a park. To her amazement, as she approached a playground, she saw a circle of stones in the middle of a ball field. She stepped into the center of the circle and stood there. "I felt this energy coming up from the ground," she recalled. "It shot out through the top of my head. I felt the spirit in me. All those fears and doubts, those feelings of being separate and alienated evaporated. The earth was my mother in a way that my own mother could never be. In that circle, I experienced that we are all one. I realized I never was separate; I felt totally connected."

As she walked home, she tried to understand her experience. She sensed a deep knowledge, that the feminine divine was coming back, not only in her life, but in the world. Feeling invigorated, alive, and fully awake, she asked herself, "What am I going to do with this energy?"

She decided she would gather some women together. One meeting led to another, which developed into a core group who met monthly to celebrate the feminine divine. Although the women in the group supported one another, it wasn't a support group focused solely on solving personal problems, although sometimes they did do that. Instead they focused on awakening the feminine divine in themselves. They would dance, drum, and chant under the full and new moon. They reveled in evenings of deep sharing; sometimes they didn't say a word. They always blessed one another and included something related to the earth and nature, such as meeting on a beach or by a river. They celebrated the fertility of the feminine with sensual candlelit feasts of food and wine, often belly dancing, and always creating a sense of celebration and spaciousness. Within the confidence of their sacred circle, they shared visions, dreams, and wishes.

"We would blow into the group from our busy lives, distracted, preoccupied, hassled," Paula told me. "But once in the group we were immediately reminded that now is our time to get centered and connect to the spirit." Their commitment to the feminine divine and to one another continued outside the group meetings. If women needed help or support between meetings they would phone each other. They called it the "Goddess hotline," a place to turn in a time of need, where together they would all pray for that group member.

Meeting regularly released a magical, transformative power that moved the women into a new consciousness and way of being. "We found ourselves thinking outside of the box," Paula observed. "We transcended cultural boundaries where we were no longer a mother, a wife, a daughter, or whatever your job title was. We were female in the purest sense, and we were free. It's an ecstasy that nobody teaches you or talks about. It's an ancient feeling that ties us to all the women who celebrated in this way before us."

The transformative power of the feminine divine left no woman untouched. Each found herself talking about things she hadn't told any other person. One woman, who had never trusted other women, began to trust these women. For Paula, the transformative power of the Goddess led her to self-acceptance. "I used to admire certain women because they were masculine, for being intellectual and go-getting people, thinking, 'When will I grow up and be responsible and do real work?' I've been letting go of that. Now I realize I have been doing real work for years."

The feminine divine left no one untouched. At first the husbands expressed some discomfort and suspicions about these women-only gatherings, but then they began to reap benefits themselves. With their wives' encouragement, they thought about their own priorities. One husband quit a high-paying but stressful job for a less lucrative job he really loved. As Paula observed, "We can all break free."

The children also felt the impact of their mother's transformation. For example, Paula runs a Goddess camp for her daughters and nieces, where she teaches the girls to feel good about themselves and their bodies by connecting them to nature and their natural cycles. When I asked Paula's seven year-old daughter, Anya, how she experienced the Goddess, she said this:

I feel the Goddess in the trees, the flowers, when the wind blows my hair. She's very powerful. When I'm feeling shy and I want to say something, she makes me feel powerful so I can say it. I feel her spirit give me strength to stand up for myself. I always feel she's inside me; even if I'm crying, she's inside me. Everybody has the Goddess inside them, but they don't know that.

From the mouths of babes.

I asked her what she did at Goddess camp. "We belly danced, got dressed up in pretty skirts. We didn't have to be taught to dance; we just knew how." The wisdom of young Anya surfaced with her unhampered connection to the feminine divine: she just knows how to belly dance.

When Iron Butterflies connect to the feminine divine, they color a world outside the conventional lines, a world where they discover a strength rooted in their feminine essence that empowers them to stand up for themselves. We don't need to pursue or search outside of ourselves to find the feminine divine; She exists in all of us. It's just a matter of unearthing her, surrendering to her, and letting her nourish us.

CONNECT TO PURE FEMALE ESSENCE

Paula mentioned that when she connects to the feminine divine, she experiences female in the purest sense, a woman beyond roles, an in-the-body and out-of-the-body experience, when all the senses are alert and receptive, yet also an experience beyond the senses. Such an experience is always within us, as young Anya said. Rumi, a thirteenth-century Persian mystic asked, "Why do you stay in prison when the door is wide open?" Certainly Nature's door stands wide open for women to discover the feminine divine, although she can also emerge in the most unexpected places. One night, my daughter Rasa and I found another door.

Rasa, an environmentalist, feminist, and loving mother and daughter, works for OxFam America. For me Rasa has served as priestess, lending her insights to my work, and partnering in the exploration of the meaning of the Goddess in our lives. This shared spiritual journey crystallized one evening several years ago. After receiving her master's degree in England, Rasa moved back home temporarily until she found a job in environmental work. She went through a frustrating transitional period in her life, working several waitressing jobs as she searched in vain for her true place in society. Our evenings together, however, provided a bit of heaven, with one night in particular standing out from the rest. As a Mother's Day gift, Rasa wrote about her experience that night. I could tell the story in my own words, but I really want you to hear my daughter's lyrical voice:

> I'm sitting in the kitchen. My hands rest on the three-hundred-year-old wooden table, smoothed by many hands and thousands of dinners. It's late. A wine bottle sits empty on the counter. I'm in yet another intense discussion with the woman seated across from me at the table. This

glorious woman is sharing the end of the evening with me. Just the two of us.

I put on one of my favorite CDs, a tune that I have really bonded with this past year while I was studying in England. The woman says to me, "I can't believe this! I have so many memories associated with this album!" We laugh at how many things we do share in common, despite the age difference.

And then the song starts to play "White Rabbit" by the Jefferson Airplane. We both get up, close our eyes, and begin to move. For me, it's the hips that move first. I feel the rhythm. . . . I feel the motion. . . . I feel my soul moved by this song. I open my eyes and this glorious woman feels the same. She moves in a different way and to a different beat, but we are the same.

I hear the lyric about Alice becoming ten feet tall, and I realize that Alice is me. She's the inner child, that visceral feeling that tells me what is right and wrong for me. Every woman has an Alice within her. I connect with this lyric because my Alice begs me to remain true to her. I am the girl that feels like she's huge and has to squeeze through a tiny door. The girl that's confused and feels like she has to understand a completely different reality, and adjust to it, and do well in the new reality. A girl who feels like she is lost and desperately needs to find her way home to a place where she is comfortable and knows who she is and what her position in life is. Yet at the same time, having the time of her life in this scary, strange, psychedelic reality.

I dance with my eyes closed. I feel the Goddess within me, flowing up and down my spine and through my soul. There is nothing in this world that I have ever experienced so organically, so electrifyingly.

I open my eyes and there she is. We hug with so much love. A journey shared. I look at the Goddess who danced with me and say, "I love you so much, Mom!" I laugh and she giggles and with sparkles in her eyes she insists, "Let's do it again!"

What an ecstatic dance for both of us! At that moment we felt the essence of female, with the Goddess swirling within us, around us, encircling us with her essence. There was one moment when we were dancing, singing along at the top of our lungs. I looked at Rasa and saw the feminine divine. She is my daughter and my friend, but in that moment, she embodied the essence of female. We had transcended all roles, joined together in our common femaleness amid the glowing presence of the feminine divine. If you doubt me, ask Alice. She'll let you know.

WATCH FOR THIRD-EYE EXPERIENCES

Does it matter whether we call the divine God or Goddess? Only if we think of them as mutually exclusive. I agree with author Charleen Proctor who wrote, "Women have been revisiting the Goddess as a symbol of empowerment. They tell me they have this image, even in conjuction with their current, traditional belief system; it takes nothing away from God." Regardless of what we name the higher power, Iron Butterflies often hear the spirit speak to them. When it does speak, we should heed it as a voice of divine intervention guiding us to where we need to go, keeping us on our true life's course. For some it arrives as a visceral experience, as it did for Paula. For others, it comes as a sign, as it did for Pat Mitchell, or as a vision, as it did for clothes designer Linda Lundström.

Though Linda refers to the divine as God, she produces a line of clothes called Goddess Gear. Linda always watches for signs from God to guide her through life's challenges. One involved a crisis in her company:

> God speaks to me through something like intuition. I call them "third-eye experiences." What happens to me is I pay attention, I get a sign, and then I do what the sign tells me. The sign is very real, practical, like a two-by-four hitting me over the head. For instance, at one point, my business was going down and we had to do all kinds of cutting back and the next thing I knew, we would have to lay off seventeen people. I felt nauseous for a month. I had built this quality work environment, a holistic place where we cared about and respected people, an ideal community where family was important. And yet I was going out of business.

On the day Linda laid off the people, she still hoped for some miracle to intervene, but in the end, she felt buried under an avalanche.

> I was trying to keep things from happening. I went home and I felt I was in an altered state. There was a beautiful snowfall with big snowflakes descending onto big snowbanks. I decided to take a walk to clear my head. I walked to the end of the sidewalk from my house and then I was afraid to step onto the street. That's how rocked my world was. So I sat down on the snowbank and said, "OK, God, I'm really needing you now. I'm afraid to step onto the street in front of my own home. There's no traffic, the streetlights are on, it's perfectly safe, and I'm afraid. Please send me a sign."

She peered into the sky but saw nothing but snowflakes. Then she glanced down the street, her eyes resting on what looked like a huge stop sign:

I had never seen it like that. It just seemed to be expanding and glowing. There I am in my red LaParka coat, in the white snowbank. The stop sign and I were mirror images. I walked into the house and asked my husband if he ever noticed how big that stop sign was down the street. Was it new? He said he didn't think so. Then I realized the sign was my sign. I had to stop trying to stop everything from happening. I had to have faith. There was something going on bigger than me, and I had to trust it, that it was taking me somewhere better. And it did. I learned so much. I lost my innocence and gained some wisdom. When I went out the next morning, the stop sign was its normal size.

Like the descent into the body, the ascent to a higher power requires a degree of surrender and profound trust. For Linda, discovering her true path meant letting go of what she knew, her status quo in life. In other words, she had to allow herself to be vulnerable and accept uncertainty. This diffused state, however, allowed Linda to open herself to what she calls "third-eye experiences," experiences guided by intuition rather than reason. By letting go, she set the stage for motion, for something organic to happen and for new possibilities to emerge. Linda's story teaches us that sometimes in our darkest hours, when the shadow of doom rests on our shoulder, the death of a caterpillar can mark the birth of a butterfly.

TAP THE POWER OF FORGIVENESS

When women descend into their bodies, they face their shadows and see their wounds, both self-inflicted and inflicted by others. Iron Butterflies rise from these depths on the wings of forgiveness that lift them to a higher self and propel them into their spiritual work. Political philosopher Hannah Arendt wrote in *Human Condition*, "Forgiving is the only reaction which does not merely react but acts anew and unexpectedly, unconditioned by the act which provoked it and therefore freeing from its consequences both the one who forgives and the one who is forgiven." Generally we think of forgiveness as an act that benefits the forgiven, but as Arendt pointed out, it also liberates the forgiver. When we forgive ourselves and others, we initiate a process of healing, of becoming whole, of moving forward and becoming our best selves. On the other hand, when we withhold forgiveness, we choose to remain a victim, confining ourselves to a limbo where we can't begin to recover from whatever harm we or someone else has done. True forgiveness requires an act of imagination, that is, to dare to imagine a different and better future.

Mahatma Gandhi said, "The weak can never forgive. Forgiveness is the attribute of the strong." The greater our capacity to forgive, the greater our resilience. The greater our ability to bounce back from injury and injustice, the greater our chances of loving ourselves and others again. Love eludes the unforgiving as much as it does the unforgiven. Of course, some wounds cannot simply be forgiven and forgotten; they need to be revisited from time to time. But neither can we move forward in life if we believe we can't get over it, sit and feel sorry for ourselves, or blame others for our woes. Resilience allows us to engage in a spiral dance of healing, where we may recall old wounds in a way that does not incapacitate us.

Patricia Smith Melton, director of Peace x Peace, produced a feature-length documentary titled *Peace-by-Peace: Women on the Frontlines*. Shown at the United Nations and aired on PBS, the film celebrated the unheralded work of women peace builders worldwide, providing a glimpse into strong, determined, compassionate women who were transforming their communities. This project profoundly affected Patricia's understanding of forgiveness. "The ability to forgive is amazing," she told me. "I know women who were hacked with machetes and left for dead, and who have gone back to their villages and now live as friendly neighbors of the people who tried to kill them! How do you forgive something of that magnitude? What I know is that I saw the women, I saw the beauty on their faces. Forgiving is self-directed because you are saying, 'I will heal myself.' As these women learned to forgive, their villages were also healing."

Can you imagine such an incredible capacity to forgive? If the women Patricia met could forgive the worst atrocities, why can't we muster the courage to find it in our own hearts? Whatever our injuries, only when we let go of them can we set foot on a path to healing and peace. During our conversation, Patricia shared her own story of forgiveness. It began when, after much indecisiveness, she decided that she should amicably end her marriage to her first husband. For five years, with her ex-husband's support, Patricia cared for their daughter, Karen.

When I separated, my world opened up. Sunshine appeared. Within one week I became an art photographer rather than a professional convention-type photographer. Within a few months I was having one-person shows. My work became a vehicle for my spiritual work. I'd use the cameras as a window into that spiritual dimension. Looking through the viewfinder, I'd wait until I "felt" perfection and then I would snap it. These were pictures guided by an internal sense. Often, I wouldn't know what the picture was about until later. Living with my little daughter and doing my work was one of the best periods in my life.

That period greatly deepened her spirituality. She became a vegetarian, practiced yoga and meditation, underwent a variety of religious experiences, and submerged herself in her art. "The spiritual search has always been the central core of my life," she told me.

Ironically, her former husband introduced Patricia to the man who would become her second husband. The two men could not have been more different—one a conservative tax lawyer who sported crisp white shirts and neatly trimmed hair; the other a long-haired man in loose clothing who lived in a religious commune in New York State, where he had become something of an elder. Patricia and her "mini-guru" fell in love and decided to start a new life together in northern California in a small town with a good school for Karen. Since the terms of her divorce stated no geographical restrictions, Patricia felt free to go wherever she wanted. After a three-week search, the couple found a likely place to start their new life on the West Coast. Patricia called Karen's father, saying she'd like him to send Karen out at Thanksgiving for her to take a look around. Karen's father refused to send her. "That was my first clue that something was wrong," Patricia recalled. Immediately, she returned to Washington, DC.

"It was an act of emotional desperation on my ex-husband's part," Patricia recalled. "If he would have said, 'Don't move so far away or I will freak out,' I would have found a place in Virginia. It could have been OK. As it was, by the time we got back, he had gone from being a dear friend to someone determined to wrestle full custody from me to himself." Patricia soon found herself slapped with a writ restricting her movement with Karen to the District of Columbia. "I thought I could hold off what was happening. But as it turned out, I couldn't." Before appearing in court, Patricia remarried, primarily because she thought it would strengthen her position in the looming custody battle.

"It became crazy," Patricia recalled. "Karen's father went from saying in front of witnesses three months prior to the suit that I was the best mother he could possibly imagine to wanting Karen to himself. Something flipped inside him when I remarried."

Although the lawyer thought Patricia performed admirably on the witness stand and said she couldn't possibly lose, Patricia told him that she felt that the judge did not like the fact that, never the prototypical soccer mom, she had traded a perfectly good lawyer husband for a long-haired, bearded hippie. True or not, after a seven-day trial, the judge awarded full custody to the father.

"I was broken," Patricia told me, "and I had to protect my seven-year-old daughter from my breakage. I had no more funds and the decision was decisive. The judge made it immensely difficult to appeal. You cannot imagine the pain and confusion I was in." Being both fragilely human and a female warrior at the same time is a tricky combination.

Then another surprise blindsided Patricia. Her vulnerable and fragile state triggered a disturbing reaction latent in her new husband. Five days after the decision, he told her it was time to stop crying and get over it. Get over it? How can a mother get over the unfathomable loss of her daughter? He hit her for the first time, the scar of which still lines the inside of Patricia's lip. The abuse continued in cycles over the next two years, though not usually so severely. In her grief-stricken state, Patricia stayed with him. "I remembered a moment in the beginning of our relationship. I was lying in a daisy field under the sun and I realized that there were only two things I was afraid of. One was of being beaten and the other was losing my child. I said to myself, 'It's OK. Neither one of them will ever happen.' Within a year, both had come true."

The couple built a little wooden house in a beautiful Tennessee valley, where Patricia was nourished by the nature surrounding her, but their home provided her with no security or stability. "I was trying to hold on to the light deep inside me, next to the empty hole that came with the judge's decision. I was trying to heal, to make sense of my life, even though I was surrounded by this abusive threat."

Her husband's violent behavior continued in confusing cycles.

Do I question not walking out the first time it happened? Of course, but I was broken, and he was all I had, and I loved him very much. I never questioned that he loved me. That was not the question. The question was, "What was in him that was violent and that couldn't cope? And did I, given the condition I was in, have the ability to mend him and mend myself?"

I wasn't beaten as some women are, or I would have been out of there. Or if he had ever done anything to Karen or to me in front of Karen. Those were my breaking points and he knew that. But the thing is that when the slapping or kicking stops for a while, it's easy to convince yourself the abuse is over. I was living in a beautiful valley with a man who had been abused as a child. People thought he was great. He was a minor-league guru, who hadn't taken care of his own internal work.

Patricia spent a lot of time in nature. Nature responded. One early spring morning, looking at little drooping Boston lettuces that a downpour had knocked over, she heard the spirit speak to her.

I took such care of this garden, and as I was propping up these little lettuces, I heard a very clear voice say, "You, who care for the lettuces, of how much more importance are you?" I said, "He will kill himself if I leave." The voice said, "Not your first concern." It was a little annoyed like, "Do I have to explain this to you?"

The message was clear. "If I have created you, you have a responsibility to take care of this creation." It was an order to care for myself. Then I knew that I was to heal, and that I would be strong enough to leave my husband. I became alive again.

Patricia went public and told people of the abuse. Some people didn't believe her, but others paid attention. Some women believe telling people will only exacerbate the violence. It had the opposite affect for Patricia. Afraid for his reputation, her husband immediately tempered his violent reactions. A few months later, Patricia left her husband and moved back to DC to be near Karen and to see her as much as she could. Her first husband turned out to be more generous than the judge would have been in letting her be with her daughter.

When the spirit spoke to Patricia in the garden, she grasped that her healing could only follow on the heels of forgiveness. She needed to forgive herself for any actions that led to losing her daughter. She needed to forgive both her former husbands. She needed to forgive herself for not finding the wherewithal to heal her "mini-guru." And she needed to forgive herself for breaking down. Forgiveness set Patricia free to take care of herself, and to move on to a better place and a better life.

Linda Lundström, whom we met earlier in this chapter, tells her experience of forgiveness and shows that when we diminish others, in reality, we diminish ourselves.

Linda grew up in a small gold mining community in northern Ontario, Canada, where winters are bitterly cold. People were poor, so everything from soap to clothes had to be made from scratch. From these humble beginnings, and at an early age, Linda found her passion in designing clothes, a passion that would lead her to be a leading women's clothes designer in Canada with a trademark parka jacket called "LaParka." Quite unexpectedly, Linda found herself facing a hidden, inner shadow that instigated a journey of healing and forgiveness she didn't even realize she needed.

When she was in her midthirties, she found herself one day sitting in front of the television after a day's work, nursing her baby girl. She was idly flipping channels when quite suddenly she found herself looking at what she found was a shocking image: a Canadian journalist was interviewing a Native Canadian. "Why is he talking to *that* guy?" she instinctively asked herself, referring to the Native Canadian.

That intuitive reaction triggered a childhood memory about a Native person who had gotten beaten up one weekend and ended up in the hospital, unconscious.

> I remembered going to school on Monday and people were whispering in the hall about whether he was going to make it. We called them Indians, a term of disrespect. We were used to Indian boys getting beaten up on Saturday night. It was considered a form of entertainment. So when I saw this First Nations person, that's what they prefer to be called, that night on television, I was awakened to my own racism. I grew up in a racist home. My mother wasn't racist, but my Dad was constantly deriding them. I felt that God spoke to me that night, and created a situation that I had to confront.
>
> As I watched this interview, I started hearing the voices of the women in the Women's Auxiliary back in Red Lake where I grew up, talking about how they had stopped Native women from breast-feeding publicly in church. These First Nations women had to walk a quarter mile and more with their babies in order to get to church. Stopping them from nursing in church meant that they wouldn't be able to go to church, because there were no separate rooms where they could breast-feed in private. Remembering that, as I nursed my own baby, was a moment in time that changed my life, because at that moment I realized I had shame and guilt. It was a true shock of recognition. I hadn't stood up to the Women's Auxiliary, because I was a child. I hadn't denounced the person who beat up the guy, because half the time it was the police. Who would you tell? But I had participated through my silence. I started sobbing right there in front of the TV. The floodgates opened and I was being shaken up. I knew I had to deal with it.

The man being interviewed on television was John Kim Bell, a Mohawk who started the Canadian Native Arts Foundation, a foundation set up to assist aspiring Native artists because they didn't have the opportunity or economic wherewithal on the reservation. "I remembered that the First Nations kids I had gone to school with were really good artists. One boy in my class could draw anything. Once, someone asked him to draw a cowboy and he asked, 'What's a cowboy?' but he drew it anyway." Linda called John Kim Bell, wanting to make a contribution to his organization. To her great surprise, he invited her to join him for lunch.

This was Linda's very first time of socializing with a First Nations person. "He was a lovely man. I told him that I wanted to do something to help, but, being a clothes designer, I didn't know what I could do." From their conversation, Linda decided to invite Native artists to participate in a competition and submit drawings. The winning drawings would be embroidered on her LaParka line, because, as Linda told me, "LaParkas were always decorated." With John's help, she got art from all over Canada.

> My goal was to honor the art. I wanted to make amends to a people who were terribly abused and discriminated against. They produced beautiful drawings with mystical names like "water carriers" and "sister wind." Each picture came with a story, wonderful stories. All the images were feminine in some way, and I think that's very special.
>
> My Dad disapproved of my interest in Native people. I wanted his approval, but it didn't stop me that he didn't give it. I don't hold a grudge toward him because I believe that my creator chose my parents for me and they have given me gifts. Experiencing racism was a gift, experiencing the shame was a gift, because look what it gave me! It healed me.

Initially the adorned parkas sold slowly. "It was a matter of faith. I was compelled to stay with it. I was being instructed that this is how I was going to heal. Every time I connected with a Native person I felt a little more healed." Eventually, Linda's faith paid off, and the decorated LaParkas became a big hit.

Linda remembered as a child seeing Native women doing wonderful beading, so she hired them to create beaded accessories she sold through her company. She sent the women fabric and beads, and they would make their own patterns to coordinate with LaParka. For years the beaded items sold well, but the cost of sending the beads and getting the finished items back was huge.

> And then my company went through a hard time and almost closed. I had to let the beading go. I told the coordinator of the beaders that I felt really badly. She said, "Don't worry. Mission accomplished." I said, "What do you mean?" "Charlotte has a job at the post office now. She got that job because of beading. When Charlotte started getting a bit of money for beading, she could put food on her table that winter and still have a little money left over. And we noticed she started walking differently. She was walking proudly." So maybe it wasn't about the beading itself.

One day Elijah Harper called Linda and asked to meet with her. Elijah Harper was a prominent member of Parliament and a much-respected Native leader who single-handedly defeated a federal government bill that did not recognize First Nations people's rights in the Canadian constitution. Linda decided she would use this opportunity to ask him for forgiveness, believing he could free her from the shame and guilt she carried from her childhood.

> When we met, he was a man of few words. I said, "One of the reasons I said yes to your invitation is that I have to make amends. I guess I'm looking for forgiveness." He took my hand and said softly, "We forgive you." After that my role as an advocate for First Nations people was no longer motivated by guilt but by a sense of calling.

Earlier, in chapter 2, we heard Janice Mirikitani's story of abusive relationships. Did she forgive her abusers? She is on the path of forgiving, largely because the spirit spoke to her through Cecil, the man who would eventually become her soul mate and husband. Together they would build the Glide Foundation, a human service program, into a vital agency of eighty-nine programs that helps the disenfranchised.

During the 1960s, Jan was working her way through graduate school, getting beaten up every day by her boyfriend, drinking too much, popping some pills. She was pretty much a mess at that point. She needed a job, so her girlfriend, who worked at Glide, suggested she apply there for work. "I would never have walked into that church if I didn't need to pay my rent. I am always surprised at my life. I think that destiny had something to do with it because it was there that I met Cecil."

Cecil Williams, the appointed minister of a very conservative United Methodist church with thirty-five church members, all white and all over sixty, was a youthful African American with somewhat radical ideas. He took down the cross, removed the altar, played jazz, and opened up the space to a menagerie of people. Runaway teenagers, hookers, gay and lesbian groups, Native Americans, Black Panthers, hippies—all found a place at Cecil's church. "The walls became dirty. Fingerprints everywhere," Jan recalled.

> It was truly metaphoric, truly like the church being born. The place was exuding life. I saw all this activity and it was like life slapping me in my face. "Hey, wake up. There's an existence outside your own navel and your own self-pity." It was like somebody shook me and woke me up.
>
> And there was Cecil. We talked a lot about the emptiness, the loneliness, the pain that we experienced in our lives. I remember this one moment, when he said, "I love you unconditionally." It completely shook me. I thought he must be after my body. What else could it be? But he

said, "No, I accept you for who you are." And that shocked me. As a woman who has been abused, you believe that there is nothing worthy beyond the physical extent of your flesh. He spoke to my soul and that was a turning point for me. I felt I had a cause, I never left the place.

When Jan began to feel herself worth fighting for, she began to find her voice in poetry. "It was like that special effect in the movies, where the invisible man becomes more and more visible," she told me with some amusement. "My voice was small, but it grew and grew."

Glide Foundation started a circle of recovery for abused women of every ethnic background. "Hearing their brutal honesty saved my life," she said. Their brutal honesty told her that she was not alone. Their brutal honesty enabled her to speak her own truth, and be validated for it. This truth telling reaches far beyond the individual. As Adrianne Rich wrote:

Women have often felt insane when cleaving to the truth of their experience. Our future depends on the sanity of each of us, and we have a profound stake beyond the personal, in the project of describing our reality as fully as we can to each other. When a woman tells the truth she is creating the possibility for more truth around her.

Through listening to those telling their realities, Jan learned that they all shared a lack of self-worth. "You are so unworthy as a woman of color in this society. Going into recovery was a humbling experience. I realized that hanging on to the hatred, hanging on to being the victim, kept me oppressed. Victims have a really hard time forgiving because that means they have to give up being victims.

"Forgiveness is a huge act of love. Forgiveness is an act of giving for another. That's what for-giveness is about. I haven't achieved it." Jan tried forgiving her stepfather for abusing her. When he was dying in the hospital, she went to see him to have a moment alone with him. By his bedside, she told him she wanted to bury all her anger, to forgive him and let him go. That same day, the sewage backed up in her mother's house. "Shit was bubbling in the bathtub. I screamed and I laughed, when I saw this, and I said, 'He ain't letting me go!'"

The people I work with are the poor, the homeless, the wretched of the earth. I love these people, what my friend calls spoiled fruit, the ones who have been bruised, mishandled, and damaged. They truly are the sweetest fruit, because they have gone through the pain of struggle, which makes them more empathic. They live in the pulse of struggle where spirit is to be experienced.

The struggle of recreating yourself is a constant struggle to change, and we can never be complacent. I don't believe we change voluntarily. We change because we must. I believe with change comes pain. We change kicking and screaming. We burn to find a different self.

And like the mythical phoenix, Iron Butterflies rise from their own ashes, afloat on the power of forgiveness.

Chapter 11

TILT

Accepting the Gift of Injustice

> Feminine consciousness accepts, tolerates, transforms. Feminine embraces the aggressive impulse of the outgoing masculine energy and transforms it into a higher order of creativity.
>
> Debashis Chatterjee,
> "Leading Consciously: A Pilgrimage Toward Self-Mastery"

Imagine a giant seesaw formed by a two-foot-wide, sixteen-foot-long, wooden plank balanced on a steel base in the middle of a bare stage. This seesaw, called a levitron, not only goes up and down, it also swivels around. Now imagine two people grasping each end of the plank and randomly moving it up, down, and around, at varying speeds and heights, while two women dancers move on the plank, navigating all the unpredictable tilts and spins. They grip their toes to keep their balance; they creatively adapt to the changes by moving with the flow of motion rather than resisting it. At times the dancers find themselves engaged in a spontaneous improvisational dance, moving with the tilt and with each other.

This levitron dance is part of a video project called "TILT," choreographed by Paula Josa-Jones in collaboration with videographer Ellen Sebring. It explores how sudden and unexpected change challenges the fragility of balance, exposing the tenuousness of normalcy. Thrown off balance by the force of change, the dancers symbolically and literally search for both an inner and an outer equilibrium while adapting to and moving with unpredictable external events. To me, the challenge posed by the levitron conjured up the way women deal with injustice, discovering an inner balance while moving with the unpredictable tilt of injustice.

Throughout this book, we have seen courageously vulnerable women retain their integrity, standing strong when humiliated, fighting for their rights, and demanding justice. Here we will study the alchemy of courageous vulnerability where Iron Butterflies transform injustice into empowering experiences, turning all the negative words and actions intended to injure and diminish them into opportunities that enhance them.

The idea of viewing injustice as a gift may shock you, but can you imagine spending your life wrapped in a cocoon, insulated from injustice? Wouldn't that prevent you from ever realizing the strength of your convictions, from better understanding yourself and all the other people in your life and gaining an appreciation of how the world really works? I'm not promoting injustice; I'm suggesting we stand firm and meet it head-on whenever it occurs. Even injustice can contain a silver lining if we use it to achieve a presence of mind and a sense of humility that enable us to adapt and align ourselves with unfolding situations, no matter how hurtful. Unjust situations may throw us off balance, but they also propel us to search for creative solutions to restore balance in ourselves and in the situation, thereby discovering new strengths and resources within ourselves. Like the dancers on the tilt, we can sometimes engage in an improvisational dance with the aggressors themselves that can restore needed balance to unjust situations.

The gift of injustice teaches us how to be a "heart warrior," a courageous woman who fights for herself and for others by speaking from deep inside herself. As we will soon see, the blade of truth and the power of vulnerability can help us deal with aggression and injustice, offering an alternative to becoming aggressive when faced with aggression—a kiss rather than a fist.

The Norse myth of the mistletoe captures it nicely. The sweet tradition of kissing someone whenever we pass beneath the sprig of green leaves and white berries emerged from a tragic injustice. Frigga, goddess of love and beauty, wanted to make sure that no harm would come to her beloved son Balder, the best-loved Norse God. She persuaded the four elements—water, air, earth, and fire—to promise not to harm him. But in her efforts to protect him from danger, she overlooked the mistletoe. Loki, the god of Mischief, learned of this oversight and fashioned an arrow from mistletoe, which he gave to Balder's blind brother. With Loki directing the brother's hand, the arrow pierced Balder's heart and killed him instantly. In response to this injustice, Frigga didn't damn the mistletoe but adorned it with her tears, which became the plant's white berries. Instead of revenge, she honored her son by transforming the mistletoe into a symbol of love. Aggressive acts more often than not rouse us to revenge. However, Iron Butterflies, like modern-day Friggas, model an alternative to fighting fire with fire. They invite peace rather than war.

SEEK JUSTICE BY RESTORING BALANCE

Traditionally justice has been meted out through punitive methods and retribution, but if we think of justice in terms of balance, then justice requires restoring the balance that the tilt of injustice has created.

Azizah al-Hibri, law professor and author, writes about the Islamic concept of Adalah, which views justice as restoring balance. "Adalah," Azizah told me, "is justice based not on a formalistic legal understanding of reality but on harmony, balance, and reconciliation. It is reflected in the individual life, in society, in the universe. Adalah can supersede an authoritarian system of punishment in its capacity to forgive. Through restoration rather than retribution we can repair society, make it whole." In other words, an eye for an eye doesn't repair anything; we just end up with two miserable, blind people. "If you have repented," Azizah continued, "what good does it do for me to take your eye? What we need to do is sit together and talk, to find ways to soothe the hurt in me, and make sure you won't do it again." Restorative justice heals, rather than duplicates, the harm.

Restorative justice also adopts a larger view wherein an injustice does not just affect two people but recognizes that some greater imbalance in society itself may have produced the harm. From this perspective, injustice exposes the flaws in the system that must be repaired before the injustice will halt. As Susan Sharpe, author of *Restorative Justice: A Vision for Healing and Change*, observes, "It is justice that puts energy into the future, not into the past. It focuses on what needs to be healed, what needs to be repaid, what needs to be learned in the wake of the crime." When faced with injustice, Iron Butterflies focus on restoring the lost balance in themselves and others. Rather than doling out punishments, they assume the role of tilter themselves, shifting the emphasis away from aggression and toward equilibrium.

I asked Azizah if she considered injustice a gift. After a thoughtful pause, she said:

Yes, properly understood, it can be. As a woman, as a Lebanese of third world origin, as an Arab American Muslim in the United States, I have faced difficulties, and I have often wondered why God put me in these trying circumstances. At the same time, I have always felt that God put me here for a reason. So I thought about it a great deal, and then I realized the reason: I was to suffer through the multifaceted forms of injustices so that I could think about it and write about them for other similarly situated women, with the hope that they would benefit from my experience. And that is exactly what happened. Once I understood injustice in that way, I was no longer upset and stopped asking God why he created me this way. The way to look at it is to see it as an opportunity. But you can only look at it as an opportunity if you transcend the injustice; then you can make lemonade out of lemons.

TRANSCEND INJUSTICE

One way to transcend injustice without letting it engulf you hinges on knowing the difference between a *reaction* and a *response*. When we *react* to injustice, we usually do so emotionally with a knee-jerk reaction without reflection: we feel outrage, we lash out, we seek revenge. Don't get me wrong; there is a time for outrage. But violence, as we have discussed, will do little to overcome the injustice that prompted your anger. I'm talking about transforming injustice from a problem into an opportunity.

Responding to injustice requires that you step back for a moment and create a space, a crucible, wherein you can get a hold of yourself and assess the event. When you enter the crucible, you enter a heat-resistant space, where, rather than reacting to the heat of the events and negative energy, you become a participant observer, calmly and coolly observing and reflecting before you act. That way, when you do respond, you can do so with positive and constructive energy. *Responding* rather than *reacting* helps Iron Butterflies keep their internal balance when on the tilt. When their response tilts the event in a different direction, they reject victimhood, take control of their lives, and master the force of injustice so it works for them rather than against them.

Congresswoman Eddie Bernice Johnson has faced many injustices in her life, and, compelled by these experiences, she has devoted much of her career to restoring justice in the lives of others. Eddie Bernice, an African American woman representing Texas in the US Congress, won election to a sixth term. A gracious and poised woman, she enjoys her reputation as the "gentlewoman from Texas." Always a trailblazer, she has provided a model for African American women and for all women to use their power as leaders in the service of restoring harmony and balance to our society by transcending the injustice of discrimination.

> When I first moved to Dallas in the '60s, black women couldn't try on clothes or shoes in stores. I organized a group of professional black women in Dallas—we called ourselves the Fifty Sensitive Black Women—and we boycotted stores downtown. Neiman Marcus was the first store to open to black women; some remained closed. I did question what I was doing; a lot of people around me questioned it. But I did not want to live in a world where the color of your skin was an issue, and a very superficial one.

She began with an intensely personal experience of the injustice:

> My great-grandmother was pure Scotch Irish, and she could go anywhere, college was open to her. But her husband, a black man, father to my grandmother, did not have the same opportunities. More doors started to shut as each generation became darker. My grandmother would take us places where they would let her in, but they didn't want to let her grandchildren in. I just thought it was ludicrous for the color of the skin to make that much difference. Why were people so afraid to allow black people equal opportunities? I was interested in tearing down barriers.

Rather than resorting to anger, Eddie Bernice sought to understand why white people feared her race. After all, we all bleed red blood and our bodies function the same; beneath the skin we share the same humanity. She decided that others might see the color of her skin as a problem, but she would not.

Instead of taking racism personally or acting out, she embraces the aggressor/racist by looking deeper for the source of injustice. Seeking the answer to the question "What drives the fear?" led her to break down barriers because she responds not to the visible aggression but to the invisible vulnerability of fear that causes it. As writer Cyn Connolly said, "We hate what we fear, and where hate is, fear is lurking." When we experience aggression or injustice, we tend to see the power and the threat. But if we look a little closer, see the fear that drives the aggression, and address the fear, we stand a much better chance of defusing the aggression.

ACT "IN SPITE" OF YOUR FEAR

A domination culture maintains control through threats, coercion, intimidation, hurting others, and, in general, by just outright frightening people. We saw how gladiators try to make others feel insecure in order to hide their own insecurities; here we see gladiators trying to frighten others as a way of masking their own fear. Of course, just understanding the scare tactic doesn't make it any less scary. I admire theologian Paul Tillich's "courage to be" concept: affirm yourself "in spite of" fear. The power of being, expressing one's essence, holding one's truth, does much to displace and transcend fear, he observed, but it does not remove it.

Fear can cripple a person, but Iron Butterflies courageously act in spite of their fear to recover their balance in the tilt. Like the dancers, when Patricia Smith Melton courageously faced a dangerous aggressor who threatened her life, she gripped the ground with her toes and swayed with the tilt. As a result, she found herself transforming an attack into an improvisational dance with her aggressors. I do not mean to say you can always do it. It's just a possibility you should weigh.

Patricia was filming in war-traumatized Sarajevo for her documentary *Peace by Peace: Women on the Frontlines*. The footage for the project, however, would lead her into a situation where she would come face-to-face with the fire-breathing dragon of aggression.

Through a bizarre series of events and misguided information to the documentary's director, a Sarajevian woman with hidden wounds from the time of siege and shooting ended up possessing four of Patricia's master tapes, including footage of a project the woman directed. It became clear that she did not intend to return the tapes without having major portions of them erased. Some time later Patricia would learn that there were possible legal issues for the woman in showing the footage.

> After several days of telephone conversations, she came to the lobby of our hotel where we tried to negotiate with her. If we were to have a chance of getting the tapes back, it was clear we would have to agree, for whatever unknown reasons, to erase some parts and, ultimately, we agreed we would. But she still would not give us the tapes because she didn't understand our method of erasing. In the span of two hours, she backed out of three different agreements. It became clear she was fundamentally hysterical and was going to walk out with our tapes.

At this point, the documentary producer grabbed the bag containing the tapes that had been sitting within reach the whole time. A push-and-pull tussle broke out between the producer and the woman until the producer thought, "What am I doing!" and let go. Immediately the woman hit her cell phone and called her husband, screaming that she had been attacked. He arrived within two minutes, at six foot five and nearly three hundred pounds, and ready to fight, as was their grown son who arrived with him. The woman threw the tape bag to her husband. Patricia recalled the scene vividly. "At this point, our cinematographer arrived. We were all thinking, 'Hello, those are OUR tapes, OUR work, OUR documentary.'"

The husband faced Patricia and yelled that he would beat her and her crew senseless. In spite of the threat, the cinematographer and the producer, both strong women, closed in on him from both sides, with Patricia facing him. Including the son, five of them were shoulder to shoulder in the empty hotel lobby when the woman faked a fainting spell on the floor. The husband, now completely pissed off, tried tossing the women off, while still clinging to the tapes. Everyone seemed to have their hands on the tapes or prying someone else's fingers off the tapes.

The son looked at Patricia, his face inches away from hers, and said icily, "I was here during the war. I'll have no trouble killing you." Patricia watched him reach for his pocket, where she saw an object the size a gun.

I started stroking the husband's shoulders, speaking gently like a lover would, "You don't have to do this. We've agreed to erase it." His eyes were rolling wildly like a caged animal, but I kept repeating, "You don't have to do this. We've agreed. We've agreed to erase the tapes." Amid all the shouting, he finally seemed to realize that I was talking to him and he looked into my eyes. I could see him trying to understand what I was saying. When he got it, he roared, "Everyone, sit down!"

Instead of sitting down when the others did, Patricia went over to the son who stood a bit to the side.

I put my hands out to him, in a supplicating way. I had picked up his name in the scuffle and said, "Sasha, I can't do this alone. I need your help. We've agreed to erase some of the tapes, but your mother isn't hearing us. You are the only person who can resolve this situation." I kept speaking slowly and very personally, telling him it was a really bad situation, telling him it was up to him and me, implying that we were the sane ones. I kept saying "I can't do it alone." Without saying a word to me, he suddenly went to his mother and started talking to her. He became the bridge. It turned out that he worked in television and could assure his mother that we could make the erasures right there in a hotel room.

I surprised myself, I realized later, but at the time it all felt automatic and the obvious thing to do. My tone loosened the knots tightening around us. I gave the father and the son ways to regain their sense of composure and responsibility. Violent energy begets violent energy until someone chooses to change it. The last thing I said to Sasha was, "Take care of your mom." He sheepishly said, "yah." We erased almost everything, but we had enough. And the gun turned out to be a large cell phone.

Sherlock Holmes once said, "Doctor Watson, you see but you don't observe." Patricia created a space, a crucible, for Sasha to observe, to respond rather than react. By putting herself and him outside the immediate situation, she allied herself with him as the problem solvers rather than the problem. Her courage to be vulnerable in spite of her fear shifted the situation. The tussle had erupted because someone addressed aggression with aggression. When Patricia assuaged any vulnerability Sasha might have felt by establishing his importance and worth, she adroitly removed his need to prove it. By making herself vulnerable, by admitting her need for Sasha's aid, she revealed herself as nonthreatening, an important gesture toward a person traumatized by war. Patricia's admission of need forged an opening where she could master the force of aggression and quiet the dragon, transforming a need to protect a personal interest to working together toward a shared interest.

Like the dancers, Patricia moved with the aggressors on the tilt, but she also acted as a tilter when she redirected the tone and tempo of the scene. By counterbalancing their hardness with her softness, by slowing things down, she enabled everyone to win and transformed the thrust of aggression into a dance of cooperation and mutual respect.

STOP EMOTIONAL VIOLENCE

Aggressors use emotional violence to diminish and undermine someone. At its worst, violence shreds the soul, dehumanizing a person by stripping and tearing away at their integrity and sense of worth. We noted this behavior when we discussed the ways in which gladiators try to humiliate Iron Butterflies. Here we will see an Iron Butterfly do more than endure it with dignity; she transforms an emotionally abusive relationship into a respectful partnership.

Before Ricky Burges became CEO of the Western Australia Local Government Association, she worked at an organization as the sole female director among all male directors, a distinction that subjected her to her share of injustice, from fighting for a company car that the other directors automatically received to arguing for equal pay. But the biggest challenge occurred with one director who was hell-bent on sabotaging her success. He tried to prevent her from recommending creative initiatives by insisting she stay strictly within the limits of her role. Lies and dishonest behaviors surrounded her. In some cases, withheld information prevented her from doing her job, while, in others, too much information overwhelmed her and made it impossible for her to determine what she really needed to know. Her antagonist didn't even bother to conceal his efforts to block her and throw obstacles in her path. Some of the other directors found the spectacle amusing and, like spectators at a sporting event, sat in the stands, idly watching to see how it would all end. This pattern of emotional abuse continued for several years. "It was nauseating," Ricky told me, "and I was exhausted with the whole thing, thinking, 'What can I do?'"

What Ricky finally did about it came impulsively and as a complete surprise to her. One day, as she headed for a project meeting with the other directors, she knew from experience that one way or another the director would exert the usual emotional abuse. "I went into the kitchen and there was this huge carving knife on the counter. I picked it up," Ricky told me. "I saw a box of tissues, and I picked that up too. I don't know why I did that; I just did it instinctively. I went into the meeting and put the tissues and knife on the table and said, 'I'm sick of this. If I have to use these tissues, then I'm surely going to have to use this knife.' I don't know where I got this idea." Shocked by Ricky's statement, the bully director rose from his seat and walked out of the room. The next day he approached Ricky, insisting on a private conversation. "This guy who had been bullying me for three years," Ricky said with some humor and lingering amazement, "shut the door, sat in my chair, and just about cried. He said, 'I don't understand why you hate me.' We had this great heart-to-heart conversation. That was the day our relationship changed and we began to work well together."

In her showdown with her adversary, Ricky experienced what gladiators feel. By creating the choice between a knife and tissues, she said, in effect, "Look, if you make me feel too vulnerable again, I will match violence with violence." She adopted the classic posture gladiators assume to restore their threatened manhood. When Ricky threw the gladiator defense back in the director's face, she took a step beyond what we saw in chapter 5. By admitting her vulnerability (the tissues), while saying she would not take any more abuse (the knife), she leapt off the tilt and became the tilter herself, shifting the dynamics of control. Like an alchemist, Ricky turned up the heat to forge change and force the bully, who couldn't take the heat, to think hard about his own behavior. The moral: when you confront a bully, you often unmask the frightened little boy inside.

The *fear* of feeling vulnerable can be worse than actually feeling vulnerable. Once the director exposed his fear of being hated, it was detoxifying. By tilting the dynamic so that the vulnerability rested where it belonged, Ricky, the heart warrior, transformed aggression into mutual respect. Her ownership of her own vulnerability freed the aggressor to do the same. She may have threatened to use the fist, but she accomplished so much more with a handshake.

MASTER EMOTIONAL RECYCLING

A witty Southern gentlewoman, the internationally bestselling novelist Barbara Kingsolver fiercely maintains her privacy but has, paradoxically, opened her life to the world. More comfortable observing the world from the outside than sitting in the spotlight herself, she has found herself in a position to speak for and to millions of people. As she told me, "This giant megaphone got dumped down in my house, not by invitation, but it's there all the time. It's there to use judiciously. So when I feel the moment comes that I need to use it, I use it and then put it down."

She chose to use her megaphone when invited to write several editorial pieces shortly after the 9/11 terrorist attack. It was a time when the nation was traumatized, emotionally tormented, frightened, and vulnerable. Attacked, the whole country felt the tilt of injustice. Swung wildly out of balance, Americans struggled to regain their footing. They looked to their leaders to take charge and in return promised them absolute loyalty. But the need for certainty in a world suddenly rendered uncertain can also impair judgment and impede critical thinking and much-needed reflection before taking any action. As the carpenter likes to say, "Measure twice, cut once."

Enter Barbara Kingsolver and other notable thinkers who were invited to write something for their Sunday editorial page to counter the beat of war drums. While most begged off, Barbara courageously said what others feared to say but deeply felt.

> I had this inchoate sense of responsibility. I've got to say something. I can't live with myself if I don't stand up against this out loud. It was a sense of moral obligation and, as I told my kids, these are the times when you get to learn how important your values are. It's easy to be a pacifist in peacetime. If we can stand up for what we believe in now, when it is very difficult, we will always know what kind of people we are. And I did

think of it in terms of a mother. I have to do this for my kids and for everybody else's kids.

Barbara wrote a number of commentaries about the events surrounding 9/11: how our country was responding to terrorism, how we could use this horrible tragedy as a way of taking a moment to evaluate our mode of leadership in the world, and how we as a nation related to the world. She wrote about all those attributes we claim to revere as Americans: liberty, diversity, tolerance, compassion, and freedom of speech. This excerpt, from an editorial titled "And Our Flag Was Still There," appeared in the *San Francisco Chronicle* on September 25, 2001:

> Patriotism seems to be falling to whoever claims it loudest, and we're left struggling to find a definition in a clamor of reaction. . . . Does the American flag stand for intimidation, censorship, violence, bigotry, sexism, homophobia, and shoving the Constitution through a paper shredder? . . . Outsiders can destroy airplanes and buildings, but it is only we, the people, who have the power to demolish our ideals. It occurs to me that my patriotic duty is to recapture my flag from the men now waving it in the name of jingoism and censorship. This isn't easy for me.

The response to these strong words? Perhaps Oscar Wilde was right when he said that patriotism is the last refuge for scoundrels, because that's who came out in response to Barbara's editorials. Her editorials brought forth an unexpected barrage of unbridled aggression. However, from this tilt came an unexpected lesson: how to recycle aggression in a way that enlarges rather than diminishes you.

"I didn't think I was saying anything outrageous," Barbara insisted. "There were plenty of men saying these things, and some of them were saying it in Congress. But the women who said these things, like Susan Sontag, Alice Walker, how to put it? It felt as if we were tarred and feathered and dragged in front of the nation. I was publicly ridiculed, reviled, and taken to task. I watched the press as closely as I could bear, but the names that were used in ugly, hateful ways were always toward women. I think it was useful that I was a woman."

In reaction to her perspective, a number of periodicals, such as the *New York Times* and the *Wall Street Journal*, attacked her and wrote articles in which they would take something she had written completely out of context, turn it on its head, and revile her as un-American. One writer used the *Wall Street Journal* as a forum to call for banning her books nationally, and, predictably, right-wing commentator Rush Limbaugh lumbered in with his condemnation. "I didn't think I was important enough for him to hate me!" Barbara told me with a laugh. "I felt like I had driven this tiny little tack into some big thing full of air that exploded in my face."

Then the hate mail started arriving from people who had never read any of her work and didn't know anything about her, urged on by the *Wall Street Journal* writer and Rush to express their hatred and send her a one-way ticket out of the country. Gratifyingly, she also got her share of support from her fans and readers. In fact, in the six weeks after the *Wall Street Journal* called for a national boycott of her books, the boycott completely backfired, with more copies of her books flying off bookstore shelves than in any previous six-week period, except for the week Oprah held up *Poisonwood Bible* and told her audience, "Buy this book."

"That was very encouraging to me," Barbara confided, "because you start to think, 'What did I really say?' I had thought I was saying rather patriotic things. Instead there was this horrific reaction, and I thought, 'Am I being misunderstood?' You worry if you are not being clear." People familiar with her work, however, responded loud and clear. In fact, some fans sent her an American flag that they had raised over the Capitol in honor of her honest patriotism. A lot of people wrote to thank her for a display of courage at a time when the media cowered and abdicated any critical thinking. This intensely private heart warrior could have kept quiet, but she chose to speak out, in spite of the risk of public outcry.

That doesn't mean it was easy for Barbara:

> I was really upset. It was a horrible time. I went back and reread everything I wrote, looking for what it was that I had said that elicited this response. I had a very visceral reaction to these horrible threats that were so ugly. My first response was, "What will happen to my children?" Things happened that made me fear for my children. We had to implement some extraordinary measures for dealing with the mail that came to the house, but things are fine now. The wonderful thing about those jerks is they have really short memories. They've moved on to the next target by now.

She saw the global picture more clearly than most other observers, asking:

> What will become of us as a country? If I'm this frightened, then how are our Muslim friends feeling? We had a hate crime in Phoenix. I have a lot of Sikh friends because my older daughter went to a preschool run by Sikhs. I was astonished to see how people who are so extremely devoted

to peaceful coexistence (I mean, they won't even eat a ham sandwich!) were perceived by some people as a threat. It made me sad for the prevailing ignorance that this fear brought out.

In her worst moment, she remembered the book *The Art of War* by Sun Tzu:

> It's very masculine, and so is the language. But he said something that was very unmacho. "You can conquer your enemy when you have grown large enough to encompass your enemy." I kept thinking about that, and I knew that it was my answer. I thought these men who were attacking me were also teaching me something. Some revelations are so slow, but this one was very quick.

It happened all in one day, as Barbara talked herself through the predicament, step by step: how can I become large enough to encompass my enemy? She came to realize that when your worldview enlarges sufficiently to include your enemies, they cease to be your enemies. By seeing the world from the aggressor's point of view well enough to understand and respond to it, rather than reacting to it with hostile confrontation, Barbara could put the hate mail in perspective.

> It made me feel so strong that I was owning this experience. I feel much wiser than I did before. I had a kind of naiveté that led me gleefully to write those things, thinking that everybody was going to agree with this. What this experience challenged in me is the goodness and the wisdom of sticking my neck out for what I think people really do believe in and want to be reminded of. I assumed it would be valued in a time of crisis. What I learned was that when enough people are frightened, many need to hurt something, and they will choose wildly inappropriate targets. I think that's what happened to me. When people are scared enough, they want to whack something. They didn't want to be their best selves at that moment, and they were too angry at the messenger. I don't think they would have been so angry if they hadn't known I was right. You ignore fools.

After careful examination, Barbara stood by every word she felt compelled to write. "Whatever this was going to mean for my family, it was necessary. In the postgame analysis, I couldn't *not* have done what I did. I still don't think I was brave. I had to do it. I didn't see any alternative."

Then Barbara did what the best writers do, use the hurtful experience in her art. She started saving the hate mail to inform her new novel, *Lacuna*. With a certain sense of triumph, Barbara said:

I'm going to write the best novel I've ever written! I'm going to write about how in moments of fear, political forces steal language. Having gained some insights, I will now write a book that I could not have written without this experience with the hate mail. I've learned that the risks of speaking out are great, but the risk of silence is greater. I developed this mantra long ago to get through these kind of times and I said it over and over to myself during this period, "The best revenge is a happy life."

Despite her courage to speak when others kept silent, she felt extremely vulnerable and consumed with confusion, fear, and self-doubt— all the feelings that aggression and injustice intend to ignite. "Fear," wrote Aldous Huxley, "cannot be gotten rid of by personal effort, but only by the ego's absorption in a cause greater than its own self-interest." Barbara transcended aggression by committing herself to a greater calling, to the need to speak her truth, not just for herself, but for her children and her country. The fear of speaking from her heart became less dangerous than the greater risks of silence: she stood by her words "in spite of" fear.

Psychologist Carl Jung said the vision will become clear when you look into your heart. Through a soul searching and an examination of what could have triggered such a nasty response to her writing, Barbara entered the world of the attackers, understood their point of view, and saw their fear. By responding rather than reacting, she could redefine their reaction and use it as guidance toward a new solution and a harmonious relationship between herself and her aggressors. As with an aikido movement, instead of letting their force cause her to fall, she used it to move forward and emotionally recycled aggression into something positive. As a friend once advised me, "When energy isn't lost to friction or opposition, all our attention is free to generate solutions and positive actions." Nonresistance allows you to sway in concert with the tilt.

Iron Butterflies know that behind aggression lurks the shadow of fear, a knowledge that empowers them to act in spite of their fear. As a common human frailty, fear can bind the aggressor and the target of aggression together, enabling Iron Butterflies to respond from the heart and act as heart warriors. They master the force of aggression without becoming aggressive. Appreciating vulnerability in the seemingly invulnerable gives us a worldview large enough to include the aggressor's reality. Many aggressors have themselves suffered the wounds of aggression, as we saw with Sasha, and, like a wounded animal, to respond to aggression with aggression is an escalating war. Anger fuels aggression, but, unlike love, anger cannot sustain itself without another's energy and fear. Without a fearful response, threats often become meaningless. Iron Butterflies wield the power of love with an iron will and a butterfly's gentle touch. They move softly, softly with determination. And just as water wears away rock, gentleness eventually prevails over aggression, softness over hardness, compassion over fear, and truth over injustice. *Gutta cavat lapidum*: the water drop hollows out the stone.

Chapter 12

RELATIONSHIPS

Letting the Heart Fall Open

When Janet Whitla first began work as a research assistant at the Education Development Center (EDC) in 1964, little did she know that she would soon find herself applying for and landing the top job. The first woman president of EDC would not retire until twenty-five years later at a young seventy-plus years of age. She described the culture in the early days of EDC as a "freewheeling federation of a few but very large projects on education research, dominated by well-known men, guru types from Harvard and MIT, all competing for attention and funding." Goal-oriented, entrepreneurial, bright, and creative, the organization's culture provided an open, inquisitive environment where big ideas and often bigger egos ruled the day.

Janet described herself as someone who "likes to listen deeply to people, has very few ideologies, and sees many sides to things; there are many ways of getting to an end point." This rare talent enabled her to serve as a mediator in this innovative environment, helping people dissolve potentially paralyzing deadlocks. She became the "go-to" person everyone called to resolve heated arguments, and her responsibilities grew, until she finally found herself heading the organization. During her tenure, the international, nongovernmental EDC achieved unprecedented growth, becoming one of the world's largest and most respected health and research organizations, including spectacular expansion in international work. Her leadership helped a once hierarchical and individualistic environment evolve into a collaborative community of ambitious and competitive people. "We always valued people for what they were good at, but there wasn't a great deal of listening in any deep way. I valued who people really were and what they were trying to accomplish as well as their ideas," Janet told me. "Peter Drucker wrote an article about how executives need to learn to say 'No.' I think what executives need to learn to do is say 'Yes!' The more you say yes, the more people will flourish, reward themselves and the organization."

Consequently, under her leadership, people felt safe, supported, and empowered to spread their wings and take risks. "It's creating an environment [in which] people can be their best selves, to feel the courage of their convictions. I work very hard to safeguard and protect the staff no matter what our financial situation is; downsizing is not my first option. People aren't disposable. It takes a long time to build a community that is interdependent, with shared values and principles."

Deep listening, interdependence, best selves: these themes will reoccur in this chapter as we explore the role vulnerability plays in creating the collaborative environments that characterize the New Era of Women. Rod Lehman, the board chair of the Fetzer Institute, defined collaboration this way: "The inner life of collaboration is about states of mind and spirit that are open: open to self-examination, open to growth, open to trust, and open to mutual action. The relationships that arise from such radical openness become vehicles for co-creation." The practices of true collaboration are those practices of awareness, listening, and speaking that bring us into openness and receptivity. I call it "letting the heart fall open." Letting the heart fall open is a key toward social transformation. As the ancient Christian maxim tells us, "action follows being."

True collaboration, which represents the future for organizations in the Era of Women, traces its roots to the participatory approach to management pioneered by Mary Parker Follet, who focused on interpersonal relations for management and education. Unfortunately, her ideas about people-centered leadership faded after her death in 1933.

While Tom Peters and Robert Waterman, authors of the bestselling book *In Search for Excellence*, popularized the concept in the 1980s, scholars Pauline Graham, Margaret Karsten, and Joyce Fletcher remind us that Mary Parker Follet gave birth to a humanistic approach to management fifty years earlier and so reclaimed her legacy.

In true collaborations, those involved let their hearts fall open by speaking *care-fully* and listening deeply, remaining constantly aware of the open heart's sensitivity to every small gesture, word, and tone—sometimes for the better, sometimes for the worse. For the worse, this sensitivity can shut down communication; for the better, it sets the stage for an unprecedented depth of connection. Having an open heart is about accepting vulnerability, valuing it, and harnessing its positive power. With open hearts, women leaders set the foundation for true collaboration, encouraging self-examination, developing trust, nurturing growth, establishing mutuality, and cultivating receptivity.

Iron Butterflies welcome emotions and honor relationships. In fact, their capacity to handle relationships and emotional issues sets them apart from leaders in previous eras. They have developed a high degree of what I call relational intelligence (a phrase independently coined by Joyce Fletcher, Judith Jordan, and Jean Baker Miller) and emotional strength. People with highly developed relational intelligence and emotional strength allow, accept, and address vulnerability in the workplace, their own and others'. They lift the ban on vulnerability, an essential step toward true collaborations.

HONE YOUR RELATIONAL INTELLIGENCE

When I talked with Ricky Burges, CEO of the Western Australian Local Government Association, a state government agency, she described herself as a leader who is "sensitive to how I interact with someone, so that I can weave a greater sense of connectedness with people. It's like a tapestry, where I weave in and out of relationships in this organization. Organizations, where no weaving happens, collapse and become dysfunctional. Without a sense of connectedness between people, an organization is heartless and devoid of any spiritual element."

Her finely honed relational intelligence makes Ricky a masterful weaver who listens to the spoken and the unspoken and spins it all into a collective web, a clear story of what people are really saying and meaning. With its creation, everyone can genuinely connect to it, to each other, and to their work together.

For example, when Ricky took on the challenge of amalgamating two associations into one, a task no one else had accomplished despite thirty years of trying, she got it done in a mere eighteen months. How did she do it? First, she brought together representatives from opposing groups to the table, a diverse group that ranged from sophisticated, metropolitan councilors to less worldly, country ones. The country people completely distrusted and denigrated the metropolitan people, and vice versa, a "we versus them" divide that existed seemingly forever. "I was given an unusual freedom in that group," Ricky told me, "to be an interventionist, to give perspective and help them along."

The first meeting looked like a sniping contest between the Hatfields and the McCoys. Someone from the big city would make a critical comment about the country people, and the country people would fire an equally snide remark right back. "To see the change that took place within this group was phenomenal," Ricky recalled. "A group that could hardly speak to each other eventually were working in such a holistic way, with such spirit and willingness to work together."

Ricky described the small but powerful step she took to turn this group around. "What I did was express the unexpressed. They were saying one thing, but not really expressing what was really on their minds. It was risky, but I thought the worst thing that could happen was that someone would say I was wrong." Knowing everyone felt hesitant to step into the risky waters of truth, Ricky led the group to shore by acting as a translator of the unspoken subtext. "I'd say," Ricky told me, "'Just a moment. Are you actually saying that you don't trust Tom, and are afraid that you're not going to be represented fairly?' He'd respond, 'Well, that's right.' Then Tom would say, 'What makes you think that?' Then they'd be able to talk about it, whereas if I didn't bring it up, they'd still be throwing jibes at each other rather than talking about what really mattered."

One of the country people, strongly outspoken and opposed to the project and to Ricky's involvement in it, would always begin his comments by saying, "Well, you know I don't support this project, but concerning this subject, I think that's a good way to go." Ricky would nevertheless incorporate his advice, a strategy of inclusion and deep listening that won him over so much that he became a champion of the project. "He came up to me several times," Ricky recalled with a laugh, "and said, 'Something's wrong. I'm actually enjoying myself!'"

Honing your relational intelligence requires that you focus on the process rather than the outcome. When you do that, people behaving differently and moving together toward a desired goal defines progress. Ricky's talent for clarifying issues, perspectives, and intentions created a context where people could genuinely connect with one another and engage in true collaboration.

Some hard-nosed businesspeople might view these acts of self-disclosure, of attention to tone and subtext, of letting the heart fall open, as unbusinesslike and inappropriate in the work environment. I asked one of the people in Ricky's group, John Philips, what he thought of Ricky and her style. He had never before worked for a woman leader:

> Ricky's style is honest, open, inclusive. She will tell you very quickly the problems she is facing and her need for support, and she expects the same from me. That's very different for someone who comes from a very left-brain organization of engineers and lawyers with very male traits of being action-oriented: you turn up, you have an agenda, you state the facts, make a decision, and go on with it. You accept what your boss tells you, and you do it, even if it's stupid. There's a lot of cover-up. You don't admit to weaknesses, failings, uncertainties; a guy thing.

How does Ricky's style differ from that approach?

> She asks how I feel about doing something in a certain way, contextual-izes things, get things on the table, and before you know it, you're blurting out you think it's stupid. She appreciates that, invites you to work with her to improve it, and move on. She builds the relationship. Her style allows you a lot more flexibility and freedom in reaching your own potential. That was very different from the autocratic, hierarchical set of relationships I was used to.

At first, this way of working frustrated John because he felt impatient with this slower, more touchy-feely process. Why should he share his innermost thoughts? "I came to realize that it was not necessarily a more *efficient* way of working but ultimately more *effective*," John told me. "You can be extremely efficient and get things done, but miss things along the way, or you can be effective and take longer at it. Is her style busi-nesslike? I would say it is very professional."

At one point, when John was promoted to a different department, he found himself back in the old kind of organization. "It was like walking back into a strait jacket!" John exclaimed. "I came back here because I see Ricky as somebody whose example is worth following. I'm happy to adopt her style; in fact, it's not adopting it, because it's already there. It's been allowed to come out."

Ricky's relational intelligence makes navigating relationships and emo-tions look easy, but this complex work requires enormous skill and insight. Relationships may strike many as a soft topic, surrounded by subjective and emotional opinions, but science can help explain what every woman knows in her heart about their importance.

Complexity science, in a nutshell, states that in complex systems (organizations, for instance) relationships matter more than anything. How we interact with one another gives an organization its texture and feel, its culture. Secretive and suspicious interactions breed weak connections between people and a lack of cultural cohesion. Trusting and open interactions engender strong connections and a robust, adaptive culture. If as a leader you want to create an organizational culture characterized by creativity, adaptability, effectiveness, and sustainability, then emphasize the quality of relationships that make all those traits possible.

In all complex systems, small changes can produce a big effect, although we can never really predict which small change will do that. It seems counterintuitive; you would think that big changes make the biggest difference. However, a seemingly small thing—such as the everyday conversations we conduct—can affect such a big thing as whether an organization's people can adapt to fast-changing and difficult times in an effective and fulfilling way.

The quality and nature of complex systems also depends on how the agents in the system (i.e., humans in organizations) relate to one another in terms of power. Old-fashioned, military-style hierarchies foster command-and-control structures, with less and less power in the hands of those further down the chain of command. The New Era structures replace that chain with a collaborative circle in which everyone can exercise power and take on a leadership role to get the job done. No one plays dictator, and no one accepts a role as slave. In other words, the collaborative model puts relational intelligence to work by emphasizing equality, interdependence, and mutuality. Many Iron Butterflies hold high positions in their organizations, but even if they wield tremendous power, they still create relationships based on mutuality: mutual interest, mutual need, and mutual respect.

It should come as no surprise by now that I think women possess the innate relational intelligence needed to create more humane, fulfilling, profitable, and sustainable work environments based on true collaboration. Women, after all, do the work of building and maintaining relationships for society as a whole. On average, women tend to be more relationally savvy for sociological, psychological, and biological reasons.

Sociologically, people who possess less power need to relate to the powerful for survival. Throughout history, women have held a second-rate-citizen status, so we naturally developed more relational skills. By the same token, if you wield all the power, you don't need to relate to people. You just tell them what to do. Subordinates become deep listeners in order to progress; they read emotional cues, discern desires, and anticipate the needs of those in control.

Psychologically, as girls grow up, they don't need to separate from their mothers to establish their identity. Boys do. A girl's identity develops in relationship to the mother, not separate from her, and a girl grows to know herself in relation to others. Relational intelligence comes naturally. These relational skills, developed due to having a lower status, are also, as psychologist Carol Gilligan wrote, "rooted not just in social subordination, but also in the substance of their moral concern, in their valuing connectedness," which brings us into the psychological realm.

Biologically, Shelley Taylor, in her book *The Tending Instinct*, argues that women seem more hardwired for a relational perspective. Through numerous studies, Taylor found that oxytocin, a hormone associated with calm, nurturant, affiliative behavior, declines in men but not in women during times of stress. Instead of "fight or flight," women tend to respond to stress with "tend and befriend." Taylor points out that "the difference between women's and men's inclination to turn to a social group in times of stress ranks with 'giving birth' as among the most reliable sex differences there are." She goes on to say: "Throughout life women seek more close friends than men do. Girls develop more intimate friendships than boys do and create larger social networks. Groups of women share more secrets, disclose more details about their lives, and express more empathy and affection than members of men's groups. They sit closer together and touch one another more than men in groups do."

Again, some businesspeople dismiss the relational, people-orientation in business as lightweight. However, many studies have shown that people-oriented management leads to improved results in *all* traditional measures of business success: return on investment, shareholder value, employee retention, and so on. Moreover, people in these organizations say they feel happier and more fulfilled in their work than employees in more traditional management environments. Relationally intelligent leaders are good for business, good for people, good for the bottom line, and good for the soul. Everybody wins!

Although some might denigrate the feminine attributes of nurturing as too soft and warm and fuzzy, they are, in fact, hard to put into practice. The relational intelligence that emphasizes the inclusion of others and accepts and addresses human vulnerability does not appear in the business school curriculum. When it finally does, when the inculcation of the old culture of aggression and a myopic focus solely on the financial bottom line declines, the heart will fall open in business environments.

EXERCISE EMOTIONAL STRENGTH

Swanee Hunt's organization, then known as Women Waging Peace, had plunged into the task of helping the women of Srebrenica commemorate the massacre of eight thousand men. Swanee felt horrible about this disaster. "I don't use the word disaster often," she told me, "I tell my staff to say, 'We are having a crisis.' I've seen crises; this was a disaster." She laid much of the blame for the disaster on the international community, which did nothing to stop the massacre even though everyone, even the United Nations, saw it coming. Afterward, few in the international community came forward to help the survivors. "The women weren't even allowed to go to the place the massacre happened, even though the peace agreement supposedly gave them freedom of movement," Swanee said with restrained outrage. "The Serbs wouldn't let them in. So there was this horrible realization that the bodies of their precious sons, husbands, brothers, were lying on the ground, being devoured by animals. It was just awful, awful, awful."

All these thoughts ran through Swanee's mind as she met with the women of Srebrenica to plan the commemoration. Why should they trust her? After all, as US ambassador to Austria, she represented the international community that had all but turned its back on them.

As she sat talking with the women, she noted that one woman, apparently a leader in the group, was scrutinizing Swanee with a wary eye. This woman, she knew, had lost three sons, her husband, and a brother to the massacre. Feeling compelled to speak to her, Swanee sat down beside her and looked into her eyes. "I will never understand what you have gone through," she said to her. "I will never understand what you have experienced. Please don't think that I would dare imagine that. But I do know what it is like to go to sleep at night, not knowing if I can keep my daughter, who has a life-threatening condition, alive. I've been on the edge of this precipice several times."

Hearing this, the woman's eyes welled up with tears, not for herself. "How is your daughter now?" she asked. Swanee was astonished. Together, like old friends, they sat quietly, gently wiping away tears. "We connected at a deep personal level," Swanee recalled.

> It's empathy. I could see inside of her, and what I saw looked like me. And the same for her. We spoke the same language. Ironically, all this was done through a translator because we didn't actually speak the same language. But that didn't matter because I wasn't connecting at the language level, I was much more aware of her eyes. I heard her words, but what I really remember was her face and tone of voice. After that moment, we could

work together. We could do anything. As we planned the conference, they trusted me. I realized the wisdom of one of my important mentors, Holocaust survivor Victor Frankel. He said to me, "You know, Ambassador Hunt, sometimes it's only through ruins that you can see the sky."

This powerful moment between two women could not have occurred without emotional strength. Like most women, Iron Butterflies possess antennae finely tuned to emotional nuances such as tone of voice, body language, and energy levels. They tune in viscerally to the context in which emotions are expressed, sometimes not even needing spoken words to form a deep connection. Swanee's wide emotional range creates an empathic capacity to hold deep and vulnerable feelings, her own and others, that cuts to the core of our humanity where we all share the same basic hopes and fears, where we are more alike than different. Swanee's story illustrates the gift of vulnerability, that is, as Norwegian theologian Sturla Strasett and his colleagues defined it: "the unique capacity for receptivity and empathy which allows human beings to acknowledge and care for their ethical responsibility for each other, for the community and their environment."

In the business world, emotional strength gives Iron Butterflies an edge. Like all good businesspeople, they effectively engage in strategy, execution, delivery, and bottom-line issues, but their emotional strength enables them to go further and deeper. They ask people how they feel, not just what they think. They notice if people work hard and get results, but they also wonder whether they feel fulfilled by their work. Can they take suggestions or do they get defensive? Are they happy, frustrated, engaged, or bored? Do they enjoy their interactions with their fellow workers or do they feel isolated and ignored? Are they team players or do they bring so much negative energy to the environment that they drain everyone's time and patience? In gladiator environments, as long as you get results, you can act pretty much as arrogantly and rudely as you want. Not so in the cultures fashioned by Iron Butterflies, who care deeply about how people emotionally impact one another. They do not tolerate rudeness and arrogance or any other negative behaviors that reflect negative feelings. While dealing with complex feelings takes time and effort, Iron Butterflies make it a top priority because they know that clearing the emotional air opens the way to more effective and creative work.

Researchers have found that emotions play a vital part in decision making. When neuroscientist Antonio Damasio examined the ventromedial part of the prefrontal cortex in certain brain-damaged patients, he found them to be normal in every way except their decision-making ability.

Given that this part of the brain was related to emotions, Damasio concluded that those who had lost this connection to their emotions could not make decisions because they could not place a value on the intellectual options before them. Reason generates a list of possibilities; emotions choose from the list. Without emotions, we can't act. That was Descartes' error. Rather than "I think, therefore I am," we should rephrase his conclusion as, "I think *and feel*, therefore I am." That's why a culture that deals with feelings as well as ideas will make better decisions.

Iron Butterflies do all they can to humanize the world, to invite people into that sacred place inside themselves where the heart falls open, where they not only think but also *feel*. In that place of absolute nakedness, stripped of all but that soft, sweet response, in that place of stillness and awe and reverence and passion and poignancy, we find a holy sanctuary, a place worth going to.

Each of the following stories opens a door to true cooperation using relational intelligence and emotional strength. Within each story watch for the three A's that encourage the heart to fall open: Allow, Address, and Accept vulnerabilites. These small but complex actions enable us all to lead more effectively in the New Era.

CREATE SAFE HAVENS

Iron Butterflies create safe havens where people can feel vulnerable without being diminished because they willingly let their own hearts fall open. When a leader displays her vulnerability, she gives others permission to do the same. It involves integrity, of course, because you can't ask others to do what you yourself can't or won't do.

Linda Rusch, vice president at Hunderton Medical Center, told me a story that displays her emotional strength. Like many healthcare executives in today's troubled environment, Linda found herself needing to slash one million dollars from her budget, a cut that would greatly affect the nurses and the services they could provide. Slicing off that much money felt like amputating an arm without sedation. She could have sat down and done it herself, but she decided to do it differently. Linda called all her heads of departments together to break the devastating news. Knowing the difficulties this would create for the nurses, she had tears in her eyes as she said, "Guys, it's not looking good. We have to figure out what we're going to cut. And we have to do it together. I need you. Help me. I can't do this by myself."

The twenty-five nurses took out their budgets, and within an hour and a half they did what they had to do. The group came together for Linda because she let her heart fall open, admitting her need and asking for help. As Linda told me:

> Leadership isn't about them just needing me. I need them too. It's mutual. There is something humbling when you put yourself out there as not all-knowing and willing to admit that you need other people in order to be successful. When you can admit that, there is greater robustness and diversity because you're not doing it alone; you are doing it together. There is something so powerful when I say, "I need you." It's not saying I can't do it but rather, "Look how important you are." If people say to me, "I need you to help me with this," I would never look at it as a weakness. I would say, "Great. I feel privileged to help." Mutual need, very powerful.

What a difference admitting need makes! Instead of disgruntled nurses balking all the way, they rallied together and did the hard work of true collaboration. It's not easy for leaders to admit they need people, especially if they have learned to rely on the old, once pervasive "answer-man" model of leadership. However, when they make themselves emotionally strong enough to reveal their own vulnerability, as Linda did, their need leads them to rely on people and becomes an invitation for people to participate, collectively empowering them to work together to overcome limitations. Mutual need strengthens relationships because it stresses interdependence, a building block of true collaboration. When people can accept their vulnerability as Linda could, they will more often pursue true collaboration to solve problems.

EMBRACE VULNERABILITIES AS LEARNING EXPERIENCES

Janie Burks, the chief financial officer of Volunteers of America in Kentucky, an organization that provides affordable housing and healthcare, specializes in helping people help themselves to overcome poverty. She told me how the people she works with willingly open up to her. The heart falling open in the accounting department? Intrigued, I asked her to share the magic tricks she used to make that possible:

> Treating people well, listening to people well, being interested in them, attuned to them, are fundamentals of relationships. Good relationships

have a lot to do with productivity. I set a tone at work by being an example. You can't just ask people to be more open; you have to be willing to share something of yourself too. I do that. I'll poke fun at myself, and it opens the group up. That might not be viewed as professional, but I think it's important. If someone brings a problem to me and I let them know that I can identify with that personally, that fosters trust. It's just being very honest. It takes time to sit down with people, but that adds a richness to our experience of working together.

Janie went on to tell me that she dealt with emotions all day and every day, and not just as a consulting tactic. Her diligence has paid off in unexpected ways because people not only expressed their emotions to her but became, in turn, more sensitive to the emotional well-being of the people around them. If they saw someone stressing out, they'd go to Janie and outline the situation, knowing she would address it. In this way, dealing with emotions became part of the organization's cultural norm.

To illustrate her point, Janie told me about an incident in which her staff had grown upset with someone from another department, a smart and competent woman who worked hard but also operated within very narrow boundaries. Any tasks or responsibilities outside those narrow lines, she delegated to someone else. "There wasn't any reaching and stretching and flexibility that I think is important in working with other people," Janie told me. The woman's approach was "it stops here and now it's your job."

Janie decided to talk candidly with this person. "These are the kinds of conversations that it's all too tempting to put off for a very long time," Janie told me with a laugh. "When you start these conversations, you also have to be willing to have them come back at you and listen to what they think; that's not always easy." At the end of their conversation, the woman apologized for her behavior. Then Janie realized that she needed to apologize too:

> I needed to recognize that there are things that may be going on that are my problem or my staff's problem, that maybe I could have done something differently here. I apologized because I was making an issue of her behavior and not recognizing her intent. It's knowing yourself and knowing you're not perfect and being true to your values. I got a smile from her. I felt we had settled some things and established a better understanding of how we could work together.

When Janie let her heart fall open and apologized as well, she placed herself on mutual ground. Their exchange had moved them both to new places and toward a true collaboration.

Janie, like other Iron Butterflies, addresses issues immediately, wasting no time before confronting people. Confrontation? Doesn't that word suggest an adversarial, even hostile or violent, encounter? In the hands of a gladiator, it often becomes just that. But in the hands of an Iron Butterfly, it can mean a coming together on mutual ground. This sort of positive face-to-face encounter starts with an inquiry driven by a curiosity to understand behaviors rather than to attack and judge them. Iron Butterflies confront people by asking genuine rather than rhetorical or leading questions, an approach that can open the door to that sacred inner world.

Janie also views mistakes as learning opportunities, as emotionally strengthening experiences, as relationship-building moments, and as an avenue for greater transparency. She herself publicly admits to her mistakes, as we saw above, setting an example that it's not the end of the world to err—after all, to err is human. When someone makes a mistake, Janie makes it abundantly clear that the person not only will not receive punishment but will win accolades for his or her courage to admit a mistake.

For example, she once discovered that Volunteers of America had paid a full annuity to a recipient rather than in typical quarterly installments. Despite the relatively small amount of money involved, Janie felt the organization must respect donor relations with an up-front admission of the mistake. The staff accountant who made the mistake immediately admitted it and offered to call the donor and confess the error.

"I really appreciated that," Janie said proudly. "We very publicly let our staff know that this was a wonderful way to deal with this situation, taking away the threat associated with making mistakes. Instead, we celebrated his taking the responsibility for doing it and going that extra mile and calling the donor. When people do something like that, they get to be my favorite. That probably sounds maternalistic of me, but I do it anyway."

When people feel compelled to hide their mistakes or fear asking questions about problems that arise, even small, undetected errors can accumulate until their collective weight demolishes the culture. Owning mistakes and learning from them keeps the culture strong.

SHOW GENUINE APPRECIATION

Justina Trott, the director of the Santa Fe National Community Center of Excellence in Women's Health in New Mexico, and chair of the New Mexico Governor's Women's Health Advisory Council in Santa Fe, describes herself as "a facilitator of processes to get people together and see how we, together, can make things work better." She found her emotional strength and relational intelligence particularly challenged during a meeting about a controversial financial proposal the CFO had presented. As so often occurs when talk turns to the topic of money, people began haggling over inconsequential items, getting testy with each other and muttering increasingly hurtful resentments. Justina could see the tension escalating as the voices grew louder, so in the middle of the discussion she pulled back her chair and said, "Wait a minute. Something else is going on here."

In a flash of intuitive insight, Justina recognized that the staff was feeling overwhelmed, overworked, and stressed. She said, "In writing this proposal, I was trying to meet some of the needs people had. And I'm hearing from you, Jan, that it isn't working for you. I want you to know that I really appreciate all the work you put into this." Jan lowered her head and fought back tears. Justina turned to Alice, acknowledging the difficulties the budget posed for her, and Alice, too, found herself at the brink of tears. When Jan turned to the CFO to recognize that he probably felt attacked, given the fact that he had created the budget and people viewed him as a moneygrubber, he heaved a sigh of relief.

Seeing these hearts fall open, Justina switched from talking about the topic at hand to processing her co-workers' feelings. Sometimes people confuse personal value with budgetary issues. People don't tell their bosses that they feel devalued because their projects have been cut. By taking the time to appreciate people, Justina broke that link. And yes, they were feeling stressed, and they appreciated that someone bothered to recognize it. "I told them how much they meant to me," Justina recalled, "because I couldn't be doing this work without them."

After spending a good half hour on the budget without getting anywhere, the group spent an hour dealing with the emotions in the room. Then in the last ten minutes of the meeting, they smoothly resolved all the budgetary problems. Justina speculated:

> If we had continued in the same negative vein and not addressed the underlying feelings, we would have solved nothing. People would have been angry, and the same topic would have been brought up in the next meeting. Although dealing with emotions is messy and takes time, in the end it is a more effective way of achieving your goals. And this process works both ways. There have been times when I have gotten hot under the collar, and they have helped me deal with it.

Justina demonstrates the power of reflection before action. By stepping back to see the deeper feelings behind the expressed resentments, and then acting on the undercurrent of emotions, she helped the group move forward as a well-knit team rather than as a divided band being pushed forward for the sake of moving on. Dealing with relationships and emotions takes time, as Justina pointed out, but ultimately it sweeps away obstacles that litter the road to the organization's goals. It's like Chinese cooking, where you may spend an hour in the preparation, dicing, slicing, chopping, and marinating, but then cook the whole dish in minutes. Similarly, spending an hour on emotions can save ten hours of grief and get you to a good result in ten minutes or less.

More than anything else, however, Justina's example reveals the power of appreciation and how this small action can play a big role in healing the tired soul and letting the heart fall open. That people's softness rises so quickly with words of appreciation speaks to just how little we show that we care for each other, and just how little it takes to feel cared about. Companies spend a lot of money trying to motivate people, but does money itself do the trick? In one study of what motivates people working in the information technology sector, the subjects cited personal thanks as number one, written thanks as number two, and public thanks as number three. Money? Number twelve. The most effective motivation doesn't cost a dime! Psychologist William James said, "The deepest principle of human nature is the craving to be appreciated." When we appreciate people, we invite the heart to fall open and set the stage for true collaboration. "Next to excellence," wrote William Thackery, "is the appreciation of it."

SPEAK TO THE HIGHEST SELF

Cynthia Trudell, a senior vice president with PepsiCo, once worked for General Motors as head of the Saturn division, the only woman at the time to attain that level of authority in the male-dominated world of manufacturing. Her skill at allowing vulnerability in herself and others made her a relationally savvy leader.

In describing herself, Cynthia said:

I'm the kind of person who will tell her people, "I'm not totally sure where we're going, ladies and gentlemen, but I think we can go in that direction, over that hill. I am just as scared as you are, but, by golly, I want to go there badly. Will you come with me?" And they will follow me. If they never know that you have a vulnerable side to you, they can't deal with their own vulnerability. I've always believed that expressing your own vulnerability and getting people in touch with theirs goes a long way.

I particularly liked one story she told me about the time she headed an auto plant in England that had significant build-quality issues. Cynthia felt compelled to confront the executives and union people working on this car, but as a foreigner she also recognized she needed to tread softly. Regardless of cultural differences, Cynthia knew one thing for sure. "I care about these people," she told me, "and I knew in their hearts that they wanted to win." Cynthia went before the workers and invited them to go through the vehicle with her and see what they liked and what they didn't like about it." The first reaction was, "Well, we think it's OK." To that Cynthia responded, "Well, I don't, and I'm the customer."

When the team conducted a second evaluation, people began to see problems they had overlooked on the first round. Cynthia seized the moment to speak to their highest self, saying, "I want to tell you something. You are better than this, and you are going to prove it to me, but you are going to prove it to yourselves first. I can't believe that you don't want to be the best that you can be." They just stared at her, looking a little shocked and hurt. She then said, "You tell me what you want me to do. I will do whatever it is you want me to do, but I'm not going to be part of an organization that isn't passionate about quality and customers."

The next day the team gathered to confess, "We *are* better than this, and we *are* going to be better than this, but we're not sure how." Together the team and Cynthia set down some guidelines and then set about the arduous task of improving the car. Cynthia recalled:

> They began to see that I believed in them and wanted them to be better, that I was seeing something in them that they didn't see in themselves. And I wasn't even beating them up! For them it was a relief that somebody believed in them. It was very gratifying to see them do something every day to improve the quality of that product, and they themselves felt a whole lot better. There was a sense of pride with the results.

By speaking directly to the workers' feelings of vulnerability, because they had participated in producing a poor product, Cynthia allowed an opportunity for new strengths to emerge. Instead of diminishing the team, or telling them what they needed to do, she made herself vulnerable by hinging her success as a leader on their ability to tell her what they needed from her. Mutually vulnerable, she and they engaged their highest selves by creating a space, a crucible, where they could forge stronger selves.

Trust people, optimistically expect them to rise to any challenge, and honor their deepest feelings and highest selves, and you can release an irresistible force to do well.

BUILD DIAMOND BRIDGES

Relationships built on trust are like diamond bridges; they are durable, sustainable, and can span even the greatest divide. Merle Lefkoff is an international mediator who has mediated in Ireland, Bosnia, and the Middle East, and she is and the cofounder of the Madrona Institute, an organization that applies the science of complexity to diplomacy and peacemaking. Merle knows just how challenging building diamond bridges can be.

In an undisclosed location in the United States and away from the conflict zone of the Middle East, Merle helped Arab, Iraqi, Lebanese, and Israeli engineers negotiate a vital issue of the area: how to distribute water, a precious commodity, in an equitable way. Merle, who believed the success of the negotiation rested on building trust, devoted time to teach them techniques for building trusting relationships. That they all shared a common language of engineering also made negotiating a fair agreement possible.

As they discussed different ways of approaching the problem, one Arab man said, "It's just like building a house. We just have to start fresh. Let's start in the basement." An Israeli delegate leapt up, shaking his fist, and in a heavy Yiddish accent said, "We can't start in the basement because the basement is full of blood." And then he sat down.

Merle's first thought was "Oh no, the Holocaust story." At first Merle said nothing; she just looked at the men who sat silently and visibly uncomfortable. How to span this divide? "We all have to think about what was said here," she began, "and respond appropriately to it. If you leave here and haven't formed trusting relationships, then I haven't succeeded, and this process has failed. We are all Semitic people and therefore emotional. We share that characteristic, and that's all right. I trust you guys, you are smart, and you'll figure it out." By allowing and accepting the emotions that gripped the room, by reminding them of the importance of building trusting relationship, and by setting an example in trusting them and respecting their ability to overcome obstacles, Merle set the conditions for the negotiation to move forward. Back on track, she could see the group let out a collective sigh and, although an intense conversation ensued, it was also productive. Merle succeeded in building diamond bridges between the men, apparent because well after the negotiations were over, they continued to stay in touch.

Merle told me:

I miss women's voices in these kind of negotiations. Women understand that we are all connected. They recognize that the possibility for a connection is already there; it's just beneath the surface. It's a matter of finding a way to bring that connection out from undercover to the fore-front. Women will do whatever it takes to nurture that thread that is holding them together. I think we could go much more quickly and deeper in relationship building if more women were at the negotiating table.

I've heard this many times. If only more women were at the negoti-ating table, we could build trusting relationships faster that would lead us to a shared agreement. For instance, in 2000, Swanee Hunt hosted a dinner at her home for the Democratic Congressional Caucus. President Clinton walked in, after failing, forty-eight hours previously, to come to a peace agreement in the Middle East, at Camp David. "I said, 'Hello, Mr. President,'" Swanee recalled. "He didn't even say 'Hello.' He said, 'If I'd had women at Camp David, I'd have had a peace agreement.'"

Ada Aharoni, author, professor, and founder of the International Forum for the Literature and Culture of Peace (IFLAC) in Israel, shows us that we can build diamond bridges that span over divides as wide as the Israeli/Palestinian conflict. Ada, who we met in chapter 3, builds diamond bridges between Israeli and Palestinian women. Every month Jewish and Arab women come together and read poems, folk tales, and stories relating to peace in English, Arabic, and Hebrew. Ada told me:

The idea is that the main difference between human beings is culture. How do we bridge that difference? Only through knowledge of each other. Religion is part of culture, but we don't address religion because that brings us back to war. We talk about manifestations of peace in cul-ture. Peace is not only the absence of war. It is a river of activities of loving the other, knowing the other, understanding the other, educating ourselves by understanding each other's culture through literature.

Elie Wiesel, a Nobel Peace Prize laureate wrote, "We find out who we are by the stories we tell and are told." Ada and her Arab and Israeli women friends tell stories of peace, and together they build diamond bridges that connect them to their shared humanity, showing us all another path to collaboration.

LET LOVE IN

When we let the heart fall open, we invite love into the workplace. Some might define work and love as mutually exclusive terms, but who does not want to say at the end of the day, "I love my job! And I love all the people

I work with!" All the women leaders I have met care deeply about people, take great pride in mentoring and inspiring others, elicit from them their highest capabilities, guide them to transform their vulnerabilities into strengths, and work tirelessly to make the workplace a mutually rewarding environment.

Gallup polls show that most workers rate having a caring boss even higher than money or fringe benefits. In interviews with two million employees in seven hundred companies, Gallup found the relationship with a person's immediate boss most greatly influences that person's productivity and eagerness to stay with the company.

Cynthia Trudell talked to me about love in the workplace:

> When I see a person's potential and I work to actualize that potential, this is love. When you love people, you see goodness in every person. If a person is behaving in a certain way that is not goodness, they are a product of their environment. I've said to so many male managers, "Look, you were brought up so that you weren't supposed to show your emotions, not supposed to show you are scared, and men have let organizations go right into ruin for those reasons. But let's take a look here. What can we learn?"
>
> When I am with a new group of people, at the first meeting I begin with, "So, how are you feeling today?" The men look at me like, "What did she have for breakfast?" They look uncomfortable, look down at their shoes. It usually takes about three meetings before they feel they can tell me how they feel. You can't improve performance if people can't say how they feel, can't get that anger or fear expressed, can't say "I'm not sure I can do this." If you are truly interested in how somebody feels, you have that capacity to love. Love says, "I trust you, respect you, I need you." You can't love anybody if you don't laugh and learn. Laughing and learning together enriches both of our lives and love goes around all these things. Live, love, laugh, and learn—that's my slogan. That's my mission in life. It helps me stay grounded in life.

Imagine all leaders living by such a creed!

When we take the risk and let the heart fall open, we may fear that someone will harm or diminish or abandon us, but if we let fear prevent us from taking that risk, we will never increase our emotional strength, we will never hone our relational intelligence. When we interact with open hearts, we invite a depth of connection to others that is not otherwise possible. We revel in a communion with others where the ring of love echoes endlessly.

Chapter 13

LEADERSHIP

Cultivating Feminine Presence

You cannot conceive the many without the one

R. S. Brumbaugh, "Plato on the One"

A man spent years and years searching for the perfect spiritual master. After decades of fruitless wandering, he heard a rumor that just such a master resided in a particular cave in the ancient mountains. Getting there involved an arduous journey across rocky hillsides and up sheer cliffs. Finally, after pulling himself over one last ice-slick ledge, he entered a dark crevice, at the end of which sat a figure cloaked in a hooded garment.

The seeker approached expectantly. A few feet from the figure he stopped, gasped, and stumbled backward with surprise.

"Why . . . why . . . you're a woman," he stammered.

"Yes," came the quiet, strong reply.

"Well . . . I didn't know that a woman could be . . . could be a great spiritual teacher . . . could be enlightened."

"Oh, my son," came the sympathetic reply. "That just shows me how unenlightened you are."

The moral of this allegory? Women's mastery often remains unseen, like the teacher in a cave, a world of hidden arts.

Throughout this book we have uncovered some of the hidden arts that Iron Butterflies employ to master the challenges before them—talents that transform their environment and define their style of leadership. In my search for just the right words to express the emphasis Iron Butterflies place on their feminine skills, I eventually settled on the phrase "feminine presence." The phrase encompasses a woman's preference for a holistic perspective over a compartmentalized one, for collaboration over self-interest, and for inclusion over exclusion. As Pat Mitchell, former CEO of the Public Broadcasting Services, put it, "If women are truly connecting to their experiences as wives, daughters, mothers, citizens in a certain community, we will see decision making, power, and leadership through a different lens." In other words, a woman who wishes to develop her leadership skills should not only rely on the male traits so often associated with conventional leadership but should, instead, draw power from her natural feminine presence. In this chapter, I want to talk about ways women can draw those arts out into the open and release the full power of feminine presence. Before we meet five Iron Butterflies who have done precisely that, let's take a look at what I consider the five essential characteristics of feminine presence: (1) the paradox of vulnerability, (2) mastering and nurturing, (3) holistic thinking, (4) the one and the many, and (5) rooted and wandering.

THE PARADOX OF VULNERABILITY

Women often achieve mastery in their lives when a challenge arises, a challenge they greet as an opportunity for growth rather than as a problem to fix. Allowing for growth and evolution is a natural feminine tendency, one that contrasts sharply with the masculine tendency to fix a problem and impose an order. A feminine approach provides fertile ground for the emergence of unexpected, but highly desirable, solutions. That approach, however, flirts with uncertainty and the unknown and invites feelings of vulnerability.

When Iron Butterflies feel stretched and daunted, they recognize their feelings of vulnerability as a sign that they can seize this opportunity to do something important. The Chinese symbol of crisis means both challenge and opportunity. The same applies to vulnerability and strength; they are inextricably entwined. Our weaknesses are our teachers, pointing the way to developing potential new strengths. If you approach challenges with curiosity rather than fear, you create a context for learning and are able to bring much more resourcefulness to the situation. Often this natural and organic approach to challenges creates alternative, novel environments that counter the entrenched domination culture and challenge the status quo.

How you master your environment, how you deal with the unexpected and unknown, those unavoidable vulnerable moments of uncertainty, defines your character. It also characterizes your leadership, be it in business, in politics, or in any other type of social organization or context.

The traditional masculine style of leadership deals with vulnerability and the challenges it poses in a *singular* way, emphasizing autonomy, control, and glorifying the leader himself. It values and implements a mechanistic, goal-directed, hierarchical approach that engages linear thinking to fix problems and compartmentalizes people into specific slots with specific labels. It's all about certainty in an uncertain world. In contrast, a feminine style of leadership adopts a *holistic* approach that sees both the one and the many. It nurtures the whole person within a larger context, engages collective power to overcome obstacles, and adopts a more organic, open-ended, learn-as-you-go, nonlinear approach for achieving objectives.

Because the feminine style differs dramatically from the entrenched masculine or "gladiator" style of leadership, women's mastery continues to remain unseen and unrecognized, just like the female teacher hidden in the cave. These Iron Butterflies not only make a difference in the world, they make feminine presence visible and accessible.

MASTERING AND NURTURING

When you meet feminine presence, as the seeker did, you encounter a calm authority that nurtures freedom and possibilities. Unlike a gladiator presence, which evokes "shock and awe," the feminine presence does not call attention to itself. Rather than proclaiming, "Follow me, I have the answer, do as I say," feminine presence sets ego aside and says, "Come with me, we can find the answer together." It evokes and celebrates what *others* do. Rather than subjugate and control, feminine presence empowers and encourages. Iron Butterflies invite others to follow their example as passionate, compassionate, flesh-and-blood creatures. Their feminine presence, with its preference for collaboration, compassion, and cooperation, helps everyone discover and develop viable alternatives to traditional hierarchies of self-interest, personal power, and competition.

Feminine presence inhabits the individual, but it also informs the collective consciousness. The Iron Butterflies you'll meet in this chapter use these talents to enhance all women's capabilities, to elevate individual women who have not yet enjoyed their share of freedom, opportunities, and power. When women support and nurture other women in mastering new skills and developing new strengths, they are performing a radical act because they're breaking a long, historical cycle of women in competition with one another. Historically, patriarchy divided women by positioning them to compete for men, for jobs, and for resources. Think about it. As recently as a hundred-plus years ago, women couldn't own property. By limiting women's access to power and resources, women were limited in their opportunities to realize their full potential. While women naturally tend to support one another emotionally, they too often sublimated that tendency in the workplace. As Phyllis Chesler wrote in *Women's Inhumanity to Women*, "While the war against women rages openly, visibly, another quieter war against women is in progress, one that demoralizes women and makes it difficult for them to bond or to fight back."

Unlike the gladiators, women often haven't learned to cover each other's backs in the workplace. That's changing. With so many young women participating today in team sports, women are learning the value of a group effort and mutual support. Today more and more women are participating in thousands of organizations whose sole purpose is to support women professionally, such as the Women Presidents' Organization, eWomenNetwork, Downtown Women's Club, and Women to Women International. When women work together to develop themselves and each other in a nurturing, supportive environment, when they collaborate in joint ventures, their combined feminine presence can accomplish more positive social change than any mechanistic problem solver ever could. In the New Era, women will realize that feminine power is a collective power and fulfill Bella Abzug's prediction: "In the 21st century, women will change the nature of power instead of power changing the nature of women."

HOLISTIC THINKING

Deborah Rosado Shaw is a single mom with three sons. But she is no ordinary mom. By dint of grit and determination, she wrested herself from poverty and social hopelessness to become CEO of Umbrella Plus, a multi-million-dollar corporation that supplies fashion and sun products. She has won many accolades for her accomplishments, especially in the Hispanic community. She attributes much of her success to her holistic perspective, not an easy thing to do in a world where many men and women too unconsciously try to impose a compartmentalized, linear view of the world.

Having achieved success as a businesswoman, Deborah was often invited to sit on corporate boards, one of which consisted solely of women. One day this particular company decided the board would benefit from a series of leadership exercises. One of these involved assuming different roles and deciding which one worked best in a given situation. The exercises were created by men and led by men. Deborah balked.

"These guys," Deborah told me, "simply didn't realize that it is impossible for women to walk in the world with only one identity. When I walk into an environment, I am all those things. I am an entrepreneur, an office manager, a mother, all at the same time. I said to them, 'You are forcing your worldview on us. You don't understand how we work. You don't understand what has made us successful.'" The other women on the board agreed and they rebelled against this ridiculous compartmentalizing exercise. They sent the men back to the drawing board to create a different, more realistic exercise.

It happens all the time. People try to mold their image of women leaders on the male model. They ignore, or cannot see, how women *actually* practice leadership: affirming the whole person and rejecting a hierarchical approach that limits people to their titles and ranking. Rather than focusing on definitions and stereotypes that keep all round pegs in round holes, they pay attention to the broader context. Deborah's story illustrates the subtle and often unconscious ways we are indoctrinated into thinking of ourselves as a box of parts, rather than as a whole person. It also shows us that when women hold on to their own perspective and stand together as this board did, we can resist those who put us into stereotypical boxes. How does Deborah's own holistic perspective contribute to her success? For one thing, it takes her to a place where business is *personal.*

> When I am with women, I am aware of the other people in their lives. That perspective allows us to have an expanded conversation, to see different points of view. It brings speedy solutions because we can see challenges as well as opportunities that sometimes take longer or don't even surface in conversations when you are only working with one role. Bringing different roles into the room allows an intimacy to exist. If your care and concern for loved ones is as present as your desire to sell widgets, people feel that and connect to that. I find this connection missing in "bottom line only" environments.

Deborah validates what we women often know in our hearts, that one of the biggest secrets to our success is our ability to create intimacy. And we do this by embracing the whole person, which makes for a stronger, more connected relationship. In a gladiator world, however, women feel compelled to hide this art because so many people dismiss it as unbusinesslike, when, in reality, it's good for business. Women will camouflage certain skills because they think their display will hurt them in the business environment.

"We can use them privately, but not publicly," Deborah observed. "I play along with the rules of engagement when it serves my purpose, but then I will go beyond that and we, as women, do this silently. We as women don't share with each other that this is part of how we become successful."

So what would happen if women shared with each other how they create strong connections and invite intimacy in their relationships? What if women spoke in mixed company as they do in an all-women's meeting? As Deborah observed, doing so can change the conversation: "The more women we can have in a room to change the quality of the conversation, to include the personal, the greater chance we have for expanding a male world and its view of leadership and success."

THE ONE AND THE MANY

A holistic perspective not only respects the whole person but also looks at the context in which people live and work: it includes the tree and the forest, the individual and the community, and all their intricate relationships. A holistic perspective strengthens an individual's ability to maintain sight of the big picture and to inspire others to commit to the overall mission.

Why do I classify a holistic perspective as a feminine art? Dr. Beatrice Bruteau, author and pioneer at integrating science, mathematics, philosophy, and religion, puts it nicely: "The feminine is a dynamic union of the one and the many, a process in which the one ever becomes many, and the many are ever reunited with the one. This process constitutes wholeness, and it is this wholeness that is the root meaning of femininity." CAT scan studies graphically illustrate this fact, revealing that many parts of a woman's brain light up when a researcher asks her a question, while the same question lights up one or a very few areas of a man's brain. Men focus narrowly on the question, while women make many connections around it.

Why this difference? Physiologically, the female nervous system contains a larger corpus callosum, a group of nerve fibers that connects the left and right hemispheres of the brain. This difference in anatomy makes women faster at transferring data between the computational, verbal left brain and the intuitive, visual right brain. As a rule, men tend to rely more heavily on the left brain, women more heavily on the right brain.

Rutgers University anthropologist Helen Fisher, author of *The First Sex: The Natural Talents of Women and How They Are Changing the*

World, has written extensively on gender differences in the brain and behavior. "Women integrate more details faster and arrange these bits of data in more complex patterns. As they make decisions, women tend to weigh more variables, consider more options, and see a wider array of possible solutions to the problem. Women tend to generalize, to synthesize, to take a broader, more holistic, more contextual perspective of any issue. They tend to think in webs of factors, not straight lines." Fisher coined a term for this broad, contextual, feminine way of reasoning: web thinking. Web thinking equals holistic thinking.

On a practical level, you can observe the difference between a holistic and a linear approach by observing any mixed-gender business meeting. Men and women do things differently at meetings. Janiece Webb, senior vice president and the highest-ranking woman at Motorola, sees it all the time, but it took her a long time to figure it out:

> Women come in and say, "We are all here to solve problems." Men come in thinking, and it is an unspoken message, "OK, Frank. You get yours today and we'll support it. And I expect you to support mine next week." Men only talk about one issue. It's either their issue or their colleague's issue that they want over the goal line. Women walk in with no sense of that. And men look at women like they are flakes, thinking, "Why is she trying to solve everything? Why doesn't she shut up? I want an efficient meeting."

More often than not, our culture reinforces and rewards the linear way of thinking. In her book *Unlocking the Clubhouse: Women in Computing*, Jane Margolis explains why so few women work in the field of computer science. When asked about their interest in computer science, 44 percent of female students tied it to social issues, a holistic perspective that contextualized computing: they were interested in how they could apply their computing skills for social good. Only 9 percent of males described their interest in this way. Instead, the majority of male students offered a more linear response: they focused on coding. Many female computer students eventually experienced a crisis of confidence in their work because the preference for linear thinking undercut their wider view. When Carnegie Mellon included social purpose in its admission process to computer science, the number of women in the program increased from 7 percent in 1995 to 40 percent in 2006.

Can we shift the reward system to emphasize the more holistic perspective needed to grasp our interconnected, global world? Not only can we, but we must. In his book *A Whole New Mind*, Daniel Pink argues that linear thinking may have reached its limits. "We are moving from an economy and society built on the logical, linear, computer-like capabilities of the Information Age to an economy and society built on the inventive, empathic, big-picture capabilities of what's rising in its place—the Conceptual Age."

Our world has grown too complex to be limited to linear thinking solutions. It cries out for a feminine presence and her holistic perspective.

ROOTED AND WANDERING

Unlike a masculine and linear style of leadership that goes for the goal, feminine presence engages in a nonlinear journey of twists and turns. This journey toward personal and social transformation takes Iron Butterflies into unknown and unfamiliar territory. Entering an uncharted world, they find themselves paradoxically rooted and wandering, rooted in their resourcefulness, in the clarity of their boundaries and values, and in their vulnerability as they confront the status quo, yet wandering in the sense that their quest never ends. Unlike gladiators, Iron Butterflies will admit to uncertainty as they enter new territory, even as they feel confident they will come closer to their destination. This knowing and not knowing bestows on them a deep sense of humility and an iron-willed determination.

Of course, men, too, can adopt a humble, caring, and determined style of leading. Gandhi, Jesus, Rumi, and Buddha—these great men exuded the compassionate authority of feminine presence. Recently, business author Jim Collins described the most successful leaders, those he labeled "Level 5 Leaders," in his bestselling book *Good to Great*. These leaders he pointed out possess a paradoxical combination of deep personal humility and intense professional determination, a variation on feminine presence that strengthens rather than weakens their influence. This style of leadership comes more naturally to women, who feel comfortable with both an iron will and a gentle touch.

Although rooted, feminine presence wanders on an associative and intuitive path that draws on a reservoir of inner flexibility. Women learn as they go, adapting at every step. Adaptability, however, is a double-edged sword. When we adapt in a way that compromises our integrity or true self, that can turn us into Amazons or Shape Changers, as we saw in chapter 8. But when we adapt without abandoning our authentic selves and hold fast to our values, we can gain valuable lessons and broader skills. When we encounter setbacks, we can pause to reorganize or improvise and find other paths that take us in the same direction and toward better outcomes. Gladiators typically dismiss this adaptability as indecision or flip-flopping. Iron Butterflies call it creativity.

According to Dr. Eileen Hoffman, a specialist in women's health, adaptability is hardwired in women:

> What makes females different from males is that the female has to be able to biologically adapt to her pregnancy. In order to do that, there has to be a lot of plasticity in the system, where every system has to have a wide range of responses. Women have more variability in all systems throughout life. For instance, their heart rate variability remains higher for longer, a very positive attribute in physiological health. And they are hardier: more female fetuses survive than males; more elderly females survive than males. I believe that it's built into the software, a great capacity to adapt and respond to variation and stress.

In other words, women do not deserve dismissal as "the weaker sex" after all. Yes, they may lack the brute strength of men, but they enjoy a subtler, at times more powerful, strength: resilience and tenacity. Feminine presence may not win the hundred-yard dash, but it will win the marathon.

In the balance of this chapter I will introduce to you five Iron Butterflies, ordinary women doing extraordinary things, and who I think epitomize fem-

> **Five Guides for Enhancing Feminine Presence**
>
> Nurture the collaborative spirit.
> Dream big.
> Wed vulnerability to collective power.
> Discover the spirituality of hospitality.
> Initiate the cascading power of care.

inine presence. Their stories and their voices provide five guides any woman can follow to enhance her own feminine presence and apply its power to lead in the New Era.

NURTURE THE COLLABORATIVE SPIRIT

Iron Butterflies view participation in any undertaking as a joint effort with others, not as an isolated, autonomous task. As they learn to master their own challenges, they always encourage others to do the same. When women work together to nurture a collaborative learning environment, they amplify a feminine presence that can change their world. Iron Butterflies create environments where women thrive by supporting each other in collaborative spaces that generate opportunities and stimulate all women to actualize themselves, to master skills, and to connect to their feminine presence. Feminine presence also stems from women's greatest weakness, their long exile from positions of authority inside mainstream institutions. Iron Butterflies discover that their outer status is an asset, leaving them free to act outside institutional lines and to create alternative realities whose mere existence often challenges the status quo.

Few women demonstrate this possibility more beautifully than Wangari Maathai, the Kenyan woman who won the 2004 Nobel Peace Prize. Wangari created the Green Belt movement, a project designed to counter the deforestation in her native Kenya, where a corrupt government had allowed environmental destruction to go unchecked for decades. To date, women participating in the Green Belt movement have planted more than thirty million trees. Affectionately called "tree woman," Wangari works right alongside her sisters, her head draped in a turquoise turban resplendent with African patterns, her smile as broad as the savanna. Wangari, a well-educated and intelligent woman, won a Kennedy scholarship to the United States, studied at the University of Pittsburgh, and earned her master's in biological science. She was the first woman in eastern and central Africa to earn a PhD in veterinary medicine from the University of Nairobi.

She started this movement in the simplest way, by responding to the needs of rural women for firewood, animal feed, and building materials. A small action produced a powerful outcome, a hallmark of feminine presence. She shows us that we can all make a difference by simply listening and responding to the need for change in our own worlds.

Wangari invited women to solve a big problem collaboratively, engaging their natural intelligence and common sense. As she has said, "African women in general need to know that it is OK for them to be the way they are—to see the way they are as a strength, and to be liberated from fear and from silence." This, I believe, applies to all women. Fostering the innate wisdom of feminine presence that is in all of us connects us to our often unrealized strength and power.

Understanding the innate wisdom of the women around her, Wangari planted a seed in fertile ground. She educated the women about broken social structures and bad governance and their rights as women, particularly in instances of rape and child abuse. Although the solution to these social issues would take time, the women realized they could do something right away. They could stop environmental degradation. They could start planting trees, which would serve their own immediate needs while healing Mother Nature.

Of course, Wangari faced the resistance of authoritarian powers, leaders who didn't hold themselves accountable to the Kenyan people. Kenya's former president Daniel Arap Moi called her a "madwoman" and a "threat to the order and security of the country." If love and care are insanity and corruption is sanity, let us all be madwomen every day of our lives!

Wangari had heard all that before. When her husband filed for divorce because he could not control her iron will, the judge in their case agreed with her husband. Over the ensuing years she was arrested several times, imprisoned, and beaten up by hired thugs. Relentlessly, she stayed the course, nurturing women's power and mastery, and employing her own and a collective feminine presence, not only to prevail, but also to win global acknowledgment for her work. Wangari had not just planted seedlings; she had sown the seeds of change.

Wangari's story offers both a literal and a metaphorical example of the power of feminine presence. Like Wangari, Iron Butterflies continually fly into the stone walls of domination. Sometimes they seize a hammer and smash it down, as a gladiator would, but more often they choose a less adversarial path to deeper-rooted social change. Near the wall of domination, they plant a tree, the tree of women supporting women as they unite for change. The tree takes root, and as it grows its roots spread *under* the wall, their strength eventually eroding and toppling it. Like the roots of a tree, women, grounded in themselves, connected to each other, and joined together in grassroots efforts, spread the roots of feminine presence that can undo the thickest walls.

DREAM BIG

Iron Butterflies accomplish amazing things by dreaming big, but they don't dream alone. To actualize their dreams, they create networks where none existed before. Remember Deborah Rosado Shaw, whom we met earlier in this chapter? That's what she did. It took time, but she ultimately connected to her own feminine presence and cultivated a collective one.

In 1996 Deborah stood at the podium in a banquet hall at the Waldorf-Astoria gazing out at fourteen hundred high-powered businesspeople. "Today I share with you a sweet moment," she began. "Mine is the journey that speaks to the power of the human spirit and what can be done when we dare." Deborah had come to the Waldorf to receive that year's Avon Women of Enterprise Award, in recognition of her remarkable achievements. In this very same hotel years before, Deborah's grandmother had scraped out a meager living, scrubbing the floors.

To arrive at this sweet moment, Deborah had conquered adversities that would have knocked most of us to the ground. Born into poverty in the South Bronx, she grew up next to the church, now a ruined shell, where her minister father preached. She recalled the neighborhood as being a place "where children lived an unimaginable human existence," where it was entirely possible for a student to be stabbed during a school bathroom break or a child could die asleep in his or her own bed from stray bullets. Determined to get out and bright enough to do it, Deborah won a scholarship to Wellesley College, where she ran smack into a wall of racial and social prejudice. After a year, unable to bear the humiliation any longer, she dropped out and returned to the miserable home environment she had fled, where she found that the only difference she felt now that she was back home was that she no longer had a plausible reason for hope.

But Deborah didn't give up. As she grappled her way into the world of business, she faced the same kinds of prejudices she had encountered at Wellesley, with added prejudice against her gender. Undeterred, she scored commercial success and proved herself to be a woman the world must take seriously. Eventually, Deborah presided over her own multimillion-dollar business, Umbrellas Plus. She dressed like a man; she behaved like a man; she played the prototypical Amazon woman. She did it pretty much by herself, wearing a sort of "camouflage" she deemed crucial to success in a male world.

Succeed she did. She bought a big house in a fancy New Jersey suburb, as far away from the dismal South Bronx as she could imagine. She had money in the bank, nice jewelry, and all the adornments women supposedly crave. Despite her apparent success, however, Deborah sank into a deep depression, into what she later called a "soul crisis." Just months before the Avon celebration, she could barely crawl out of bed each day. All she could do was listen to motivational tapes. She felt hopeless, lost, and like a failure, which made her question whether being the "umbrella girl" was what it was all about, what she really wanted out of life. It was while preparing a short speech for the Avon event that Deborah took a hard look at her past, present, and future life, a process where she began to recapture her true values. She came to the conclusion that she had become so focused on escaping poverty that she had lost sight of the defiant, streetwise girl she once was, who knew what really mattered and who was only interested in her own version of success.

As she told her story to the audience at the Avon event, the "neatly compartmentalized" pieces of her life began to meld together, and "with every word I recovered another piece of myself." Things in her past, once sources of shame, became sources of power in the present. This insight restored her wings and changed her life completely. "I had become myself again. I reconnected to the feminine Deborah that had been lost for so long, the Deborah who doesn't want to do it alone."

That day in New York an Iron Butterfly emerged from her chrysalis as all the cells of her life came together as a whole story. She regained her own feminine presence and a desire to connect to others. Rather than pursuing someone else's meaning of success, she would discover her own version.

Deborah went on to write *Dream Big!* a book that gave her a platform for sharing her experiences with others. As she toured the country, she heard amazing stories from other women and realized that "success depended on being part of very powerful networks." Powerful networks. We all hear about the importance of networking, but creating *powerful* networks goes far beyond sharing business calling cards and e-mail addresses to something much more personal and meaningful. Deborah reveals another secret to successful women leaders. Because we are so inundated with masculine-infused leadership, we sometimes feel we have to do it alone in order to succeed. But women connected to their feminine presence don't go it alone. They cultivate powerful networks and use these networks to create other powerful networks as Deborah does. "I decided I wanted to create a powerful network for Latina women, a national online community. I thought, if we can influence the mothers who sit at the kitchen table, we will be more effective at getting to the real issues." Feminine presence sits at the kitchen table. Deborah had found a new mission, to surface the intelligence and the assets of women and encourage them to share their gifts with others. Whether she is the "umbrella girl" or a woman nuclear physicist, she can show other girls and women a new universe of possibilities.

Deborah's holistic perspective serves the whole community by helping individual Latina women dream big and realize their potential. When one fulfilled dream joins with another and another, pretty soon you have formed a community of strong, successful women with powerful networks of support.

Most women already enjoy a network of friends and family, but do they consciously strive for a powerful network? Ask yourself if you talk about your dreams with others? Do you explore how you can help one another to actualize those dreams? Do you commit yourself to action on behalf of yourself and others? Engaging in this conversation with your book group, with your "girls' night out," with your online buddies, brings your network to a deeper level, a spiritual level, where women together realize their individual and collective potential.

Deborah told me about a time she spoke at a conference about successful women where all the women presenters were described as playing big in the world. Deborah stood up and said, "Wait a minute. We are playing too small. In the Hispanic community, we have the highest teenage pregnancy rate, highest high school dropout rate, highest illiteracy rate, and the fastest growing population in the United States. Clearly, we are not fully expressing our values and skills, because if we were, there is no way this could exist." Women should, insists Deborah, bring values to the forefront, pay them more than lip service, and act on them with courage and passion; in short, they should be a feminine presence in their communities.

By applying her skills and resources to contribute to the greater good of her community, by nourishing the whole woman and the whole community, Deborah helps transform vulnerabilities, such as limited education and resources, into new strengths and new possibilities for the one and the many. She has planted a tree beside the status quo system that can ultimately spread its branches and roots to transform the Hispanic world, one person at a time.

Like Deborah, many women have achieved success in traditional, bottom-line terms, via a traditional, masculine approach. But, like Deborah, for many that success feels a little hollow. When she finally embraced feminine presence in her leadership, not only did Deborah achieve success in traditional bottom-line terms, she extended her influence to improve other people's lives.

WED VULNERABILITY TO COLLECTIVE POWER

You might dream big, you might develop strong networks of support, but you still might feel vulnerable, wondering how you can actually achieve your dream with your supportive network. Donatella Cinelli Colombini's story shows how she transformed her personal insecurities and self-doubts by inviting others to participate in the fulfillment of her dream, a successful wine-making operation in Tuscany run solely by women.

A hundred kilometers south of Florence, the Fattoria del Colle owned by Donatella's father, and the Fattoria del Barbi owned by Donatella's mother overlook the splendor of the Tuscan countryside. Both fattorias (farms) produce wine, truffles, olive oil, prosciutto, and cereals. For four centuries, these estates, owned by Donatella's ancestors, were passed down from father to son. In 1989, Donatella's parents decided to divide their properties. They gave the main winery of the family, the Fattoria del Barbi, to Donatella's brother while Donatella received a small property in Montalcino called Casato and the Fattoria del Colle in Trequanda. In truth, Il Colle was more than a little run-down and hardly a coveted prize, and all that remained of Casato was the ruin of an old farmhouse surrounded by an old vineyard. Under Donatella's care, however, the estates flourished, much to the surprise of her mother, who would have preferred Donatella's brother to manage all the land. Just as the morning mist bedews the vines on the Tuscan hills, Donatella has gently infused a feminine presence at her two properties, something quite radical in the male-dominated world of Italian wine making. It took a lot of iron will to do it.

Today Donatella has a reputation as a powerful leader and visionary, though it wasn't always like that. Friends recall a timid, soft-spoken woman kept securely in her place by her mother, Francesca, a formidable woman. The "Lady of Brunello," as Francesca is known in the Italian wine-making business, could scarcely have been anything else. For a woman of her generation, establishing a strong stature in a man's world of wine took a certain unrelenting insistence to be recognized. However, for a woman of her daughter's generation, a new possibility beckoned for Donatella.

A major turning point for Donatella's confidence came when she started the wine tourism movement in Chianti, by introducing Wine Day, a festival at which wine producers open their cellars for tastings. The Wine Day event is not only a system to increase wine tourism in Italy, but it has also evolved into an international event that includes countries from all over the world. Donatella made it happen, not with her mother's style of doing it alone, but with collaboration and inclusion, an approach she applied to developing Fattoria del Colle and the the Casato property.

Developing the two estates was no small task. The vineyard at Il Colle had no practical facility for making wine, and Donatella's brother wanted her to give up the notion of running a winery and leave the family winery to him. Indeed, her mother and brother kept telling her that her brother should manage everything because he was competent and she was not. "I realized," Donatella confided in me, "that I had to be independent from my family. It was very difficult for me." It was difficult because Donatella had worked on the public relations side of the business for her mother, but had never been involved in the wine making and the economics of the business. "Everyone said I wouldn't be able to do it," Donatella recalled. "Now I can tell them that I am able to do it. There are new vineyards and two new wineries on both of my estates. I sell my wine in twenty-six countries and have been awarded several prizes. I am less afraid. I understand that it is better to make a mistake than not to decide at all. I am now willing to take risks."

And risks she did take as she confronted the wall of a masculine wine tradition. Instead of taking a sledgehammer to it, however, she planted a vine at its base. Learning slowly, day by day, she mastered her environment and created a new reality. Adept at holistic thinking, she established teams of equals at the fattoria, eliminating the middle managerial structure that traditionally told everybody what to do. Donatella explained the big picture to the staff and expected everyone from the field workers to the office help and the cleaning people to participate in the whole process—from tasting the wine, to knowing the different wines, to understanding the process of making wine. Those who disliked this new approach left or were gently encouraged to leave.

Donatella began to create conditions where women on the vineyard could not only learn but also combine their knowledge and actualize their power. For instance, when Donatella took over Fattoria del Colle, she opened a restaurant. She wanted it to be of the earth, of the place. To this end, she spent a summer gathering local recipes from the old women in a nearby village, recipes that had been handed down from mother to daughter for centuries. These recipes made up the core of the menu, such as zuppa di Trequanda (bread soup with vegetables) and Pici con sugo di nana (handmade pasta with duck sauce). I have dined there, and I can tell you it celebrates the very essence of Tuscan food: simple, rich, deep, and sublime, prepared by women of the earth, of the place, who know how to create a bit of heaven.

Donatella's most radical act to date is the Prime Donne project. The crowning achievement of Donatella's stewardship at Casato in Montalcino is a Brunello (the prized varietal wine of Tuscany) that Donatella has labeled Prime Donne or "first woman." This femina wine is produced completely by women, including Donatella's assistants in marketing and promotion, the label designer, and the cellar master. Casato is the first Italian winery with an entirely female staff, and for this reason Donatella changed its name to Casato Prime Donne.

The label bears Donatella's family crescent, except for one change. The traditional crescent displays four doves, representing the members in her family. The Prime Donne crescent depicts one of the four doves flying outside the crescent, soaring to freedom. Like the dove in the label, Donatella has broken away from Italian tradition and has learned to fly freely on her own, and with her own flock.

One of Donatella's cohorts, Barbara Magnani, works at both wineries as the enologist, the wine maker, a rare position for a woman. While Barbara had previously worked at three wineries, she had never served as the enologist since prestigious wineries prefer men as wine makers. Finally, at Casato Prime Donne, Barbara realized her dream of making a fine Brunello.

Barbara had heard a lot about Donatella as a woman of accomplishment, but when she met her, she was surprised. She found Donatella to be down to earth, very pleasant, someone who tried to make her comfortable. She showed the project, explained her plans for the future, and asked Barbara for her opinion, a novelty. "In my previous jobs," Barbara told me, "I was simply told the decisions, and then had to execute them. With Donatella, we talked together and we decided together. I was part of the project. It makes you work more willingly. Her leadership comes from her ideas, but also from her ability to engage people as equals. She changed my life."

Donatella consistently lays out the big picture and invites people to contribute, affording everyone the freedom to accomplish great goals. Rather than governing from the top down, she practices a grassroots approach in service of the whole on a level playing field.

In a world where a male palate decides the qualities of wine, Donatella relies on four women—an international panel that comes from Italy, Great Britain, Germany, and the United States—to oversee the various phases of aging. In this way, Donatella hopes to create a wine that suits a woman's palate. Two of the women tasters agree with Donatella that a woman's palate differs from a man's; two disagree. This divergence of opinion generates some lively conversations, and has led, eventually, to a new wine-tasting process.

In place of a strict list of criteria, Casato Prime Donne conducts a more holistic evaluation. Donatella wanted the panel to give a top-of-their-head response to the wine, thus letting the elements of the wine come together as a whole and allowing the tasters to gather an overall impression of it. Maureen Ashley, one of the tasters, describes the process this way: "If you taste using the criteria list, it pushes you into categories that create an enologist's wine. We chucked the form all together. All we do is taste the wine and jot down our impressions. The whole process is much more fluid. It allows us to taste in a much more constructive way because we're thinking, 'Do I like it, or do I not?'"

Daniela Scrobogna, who serves as the Italian wine taster on the panel, wanted to join Donatella in her challenge, and she liked that Donatella stressed doing tastings instinctively. "She looks for the likeability, the pleasure side of wine," said Daniela.

Donatella invites women to connect to their pleasure, an associative process, rather than to adhere to a preordained set of dissociated variables. At Fattoria del Colle and Casato Prime Donne wine making replaces rigid hierarchy with fluid simplicity and swaps a time-honored male approach for one imbued with feminine presence. And it works. Nevertheless, the male world of wine presents a challenge to the women, as Daniela noted: "You have to be twice as good, and you're always being tested."

Donatella has profoundly influenced women who work with her, as her friend and cohort Sylvie Haniez of Podere Terreno attests. "Being involved with Donatella's work has become part of my life. It is a very important experience because this isn't just about wine. It's a movement."

How Donatella creates a sense of community that permeates the culture at Il Colle became clear when I talked with Donatella's incoming tourist manager, Alexandra Fisher.

> Donatella has shared her family struggles with us and we share ours. We are all sensitive to each other's moods. I can see immediately if she is having a hard time, just from her eyes. I ask what's wrong, and we talk. Donatella really cares about people. She saw my ceramic work and said at some point, when things settle down a little, I should have more free time to do my ceramics. A lot of leaders don't think like that. She cares about a balance in people's lives.

That's why Alexandra thinks of Donatella not as a boss, but as her friend. Donatella isn't a traditional boss, and at first that was confusing for the staff. They weren't accustomed to mutuality. Early on, Donatella organized a short course with a psychologist so the women could better understand the benefits of working together in a collective fashion. Of course, Donatella participated too. "We came to realize," said Alexandra with a smile, "that her way is better for us and for Il Colle."

All the women I interviewed at Il Colle seemed perfectly attuned to each other; what affects Donatella affects them in a personal way, and vice versa. Antonella Marconi, another staff person, talked about this connection in terms of a sense of community they share on the vineyard: "Like a chain, we are all connected to each other. Everybody is able to contribute to the vision and benefit from that vision. Donatella hopes that others will copy what she has created here, that is, giving women more possibilities. She holds the power in a soft way. She doesn't use the power for herself, but for the vision."

Donatella's "soft way" has succeeded beyond her wildest imagination. The Prime Donne wine, even as a newcomer on the scene, has won several important awards. How does her mother feel about her daughter's enormous success? Donatella explained:

> It is not an easy period for my mother. She used to work a lot but now she has nothing to do on her estate. Instead she has devoted herself to writing books. Our adventure, which my mother and my brother have been part of, is a good adventure. The funny thing is that being forced to break away on my own turned out to be exactly what I needed to do. I have big luck!

When Donatella ran into a wall of resistance, she did what Iron Butterflies do. She planted a vine. The vine grew. It bore fruit. And as its roots crawled under the wall, the wall weakened and fell. By wedding her vulnerability to collective power, she cultivated a force more powerful than a hammer: the gentle persistence of feminine presence.

DISCOVER THE SPIRITUALITY OF HOSPITALITY

Nancy Schwoyer achieves feminine presence with an extraordinary form of hospitality. One of the founders of Wellspring House, a safe haven for homeless mothers and their children, Nancy demonstrates just how profoundly one woman can extend her feminine presence to protect and affect the many. Being hospitable to the rejected, she changes the relationship between the haves and have nots, thereby changing lives.

Growing up in a blue-collar family in Pennsylvania, where one grandfather worked as a coal miner and the other as a steel worker, Nancy Schwoyer may not have known material wealth, but she did enjoy the comfort of community. As a youth, Nancy was good at everything, especially sports. Now seventy-two years old, she recalls the pivotal moments that shaped her worldview and guided her to her life's work:

> A baseball little league was starting in the coal mine town, where I was spending the summer. I tried out for it. I got rejected because I was a girl. When I told my Pappy [grandfather], he took me by the hand, and we went back to the little league. He went up to the coaches and said, "I'll put her up against any of your players. If she can't play ball, that's OK. But you have no right to reject her because she's a girl."

This was a radical act in 1946. When the boys threw her their best stuff, she knocked them into the outfield. She could catch anything they threw at her. She got on the team.

Her grandfather's act of support and belief in her taught Nancy an enduring lesson. One person, with right on her side, could challenge and even change the establishment. "That became a paradigm for me, standing up for people who are left out for whatever reason, no matter who they are—women, black, poor. I have given my life to it."

Another defining moment occurred when Nancy's mother fell victim to breast cancer and, after a radical mastectomy, could not perform some household chores. The family, living in North Carolina, hired a black woman, Inez, to help out one day a week. When Inez first came to the Schwoyers' home, Nancy went to the front door to let her in, but to her surprise Inez said, "Honey, open the back door." Nancy's mother intervened, insisting that the newest member of the Schwoyer "family" use the same door everyone else did. Inez balked, explaining that in North Carolina, if neighbors saw a black woman entering the front door of a white person's house, she might suffer bitter consequences. "That was a pivotal experience. So many people in our society have to go in by the back door; I wanted everyone to be able to use the front door."

Not long after that, Nancy's mother died. Now a seventeen-year-old girl, a night school senior in an all-girls school run by nuns, Nancy joined the convent. Almost immediately she questioned her decision. In retrospect, she realized that she was looking for some kind of family and security in the wake of her mother's death. "The first day, I was in this funny black and white outfit, running up the stairs in the convent, and at the top of the stairs, the superior looked at me and said, 'You're not allowed to run.' I thought, 'What have I done!'"

Nevertheless Nancy stayed the course, taking her final vows seven years later. For the next twenty years she pursued her calling as a nun, which involved, among other things, becoming active in the civil rights movement in the South. Eventually, however, she tired of the rigidity of the church. With the nun's life making less and less sense to her, she had a spiritual crisis, became depressed, and finally, in 1981, asked to be released from her vows. She and six others, five women and one man, ages eighteen to fifty-six, had been talking about building a new life together in a place where they could create an alternative community. When they found a beautiful, seventeenth-century farmhouse in Gloucester, Massachusetts, they took it over and incorporated it as Wellspring House.

"There was a well in the front yard," Nancy explains, "and it was a perfect metaphor for our mission. Wellspring is an endless source of nourishment, and a place where people gather for refreshment for their journey. We decided we would participate in social change by practicing hospitality; it would be our spirituality. Hospitality is a way of being open; it is a criterion for social change." They wanted a house big enough to accommodate others who needed a home for a while. They forged a community where they made decisions by consensus, dedicating themselves to mutual learning and no formal hierarchy. They put down roots literally: they grew organic vegetables, respected the land, and were sensitive to how they used the environment's resources. It was immediately attractive to people, and they started to come for help. "I believe," Nancy told me, "if people can imagine that they can do it, the act of imagination unleashes something, the resources that you need come forth, and what is imagined gets carried forward. What is often lacking in our country is imagination."

Opening their home to the homeless and living with the disenfranchised took more than imagination; it took courage, hard work, sacrifice, and passion. When I asked Nancy how she could take on such a mission, she said, "I don't know how people can work in partnership with homeless families unless you actually live with them. I can't imagine not doing this work. The disenfranchised teach us so much if we are willing to listen. It's what keeps me passionate." Nancy gives hospitality a whole new meaning.

To date, Nancy has lived with over five hundred families and provided shelter for over a thousand homeless women and children. Wellspring House has alleviated poverty for many families, providing not only temporary housing but also longer-term solutions to their poverty. Nancy and her allies have focused on the solutions to poverty by helping homeless women and their children obtain homes, education, jobs and job training, parental support, counseling, and a stable family life in a safe environment. Nancy's hospitality is no Band-Aid treatment. Enveloped by Wellspring's hospitality, homeless women can find a place in society, transforming their vulnerabilities into strengths.

"We are not just a social service organization," Nancy insists. "We are a social change organization, which means relationship change and transformation. We help people who are victims of injustice change their relationship to unjust systems and that in itself changes the system."

The power of Nancy's holistic view, attending to one family at a time while addressing the many contributing causes of poverty and literally providing roots for wandering souls, has planted a tree of feminine presence beside the system. That tree and its unstoppable roots, fed by a wellspring and nourished by women and men joined together to help others, offer a pure symbol of sacred work, forged in a crucible of hospitality.

Each of us engages in some form of hospitality, but we tend not to realize its tremendous power. This, too, is one of women's secrets to success. As Nancy's story illustrates, you can enhance your feminine presence with an act as simple and as profound as opening a closed door with a welcoming smile.

INITIATE THE CASCADING POWER OF CARE

Care is such a gentle word, but like the roots of Donatella's vine and the hospitality of Nancy's well, it can exert tremendous power. Let's return to the story of Linda Rusch, whom we first met in chapter 1. As vice president of Patient Care Services at Hunterdon Medical Center in Flemington, New Jersey, Linda planted her tree of feminine presence, not beside but within the healthcare system. As it continues to grow, it may change more than Hunterdon; it may help alter the very nature of healthcare. Under Linda's leadership, Hunterdon Medical Center, a 176-bed facility, has consistently excelled, scoring in the high ninetieth percentile for patient satisfaction and quality outcome.

Linda is a petite dynamo of enthusiasm and positive energy who has won many awards for her leadership and thinks of herself as a cultivator of people. A skillful cultivator she is; she evokes and engages feminine presence in her nurses. When she looks you in the eye, you believe she sincerely wants to know who you are and how you feel. At Hunterdon, where women make up 85 percent of the hospital staff, Linda has fashioned a culture imbued with care and a palpable connection among the nurses. They, like Donatella's staff, work in perfect harmony, highly attuned to one another.

Although compassionate and caring, Linda is also a fierce protector of her nurses. She takes care of the caretakers by bringing them pizza when they are working overtime, providing educational opportunities, and keeping her office door open at all times. In a world where most healthcare institutions suffer a shortage of nurses and a high turnover, and where most nurses feel overworked, overwhelmed, and undervalued, Hunterdon boasts a retention rate of 97.5 percent. In addition to caring for her colleagues, Linda also cares for the community. She has inspired her tireless staff, despite their hard work and shortage of spare time, to give to the community outside of work, creating a large volunteer effort in Hunterdon.

Linda simply asked the nurses, "How do you care about the community?" In response, nurses initiated ongoing and evolving projects in their free time. "We're not making anyone do community work," Linda insists.

"You can't *make* people volunteer." The nurses do it because they *want* to, because their own hearts urge them to do it. Their earnestness is infectious, provoking others to think of new projects they might launch themselves. These volunteer projects generally focus on helping women in the community. It's wise to focus on women because study after study shows that investing in women has the highest return. If you take care of women's poverty and education, the population growth and small-scale rural economic growth will largely take care of themselves.

At Hunterdon, the maternity unit set up a domestic violence program and a baby fair to teach potential and new mothers about childcare. Others collected money for women's shelters at Christmastime. Linda's feminine presence cascades like a waterfall: she takes care of the nurses, and the nurses in turn take care of their patients and the community. They put true care back into healthcare. The nurses feel fulfilled. But this way of being, this feminine presence, also contributes to the bottom line. While most hospitals languish in the red, Hunterdon turns a profit. CEO Bob Wise attributes it to the Center's feminine presence:

> Healthcare has always been dominated by women because of their compassion and commitment to care. Since the fifties, the masculine side has been in charge, a testosterone-driven model that generated hierarchy and kept men at the top and in positions of leadership. It's the feminine power of healthcare, the sensitivity, the compassion and its expression, the personal relationships, that we value here. I believe those hospitals that value the feminine side and support it will be the hospitals that succeed.

Bob Wise's own leadership has benefited from the power of feminine presence. "It keeps me young!" Bob told me with a laugh. "I've learned to lean on others. We lean on each other. People here can handle demands, and that takes pressure off me and lightens my load. Rather than seeing barriers and limits, what I see are people coming up with solutions, sharing ideas, offering time and energy."

Hunterdon's nurses devise solutions because they actively imagine and implement new possibilities, largely because Linda offers them great freedom coupled with tremendous responsibility. Hunterdon has long governed itself with a democratic system of shared power, which allows each staff nurse to involve herself in the creation, design, and implementation of systems that most directly affect the patients. Carrol Fiorino, the nurse manager of a ward they call the Wild West, describes how freedom and responsibility has given her a new sense of personal power:

We're rough around the edges; we're kind of loud and laugh a lot. And when chaos comes, and it's always rearing its head, we know we can get through it. We are not the same people since Linda took over. She has given us freedom to pursue what matters to us and holds us accountable. I was a homebody before. Now, with this freedom, comes this mouth. The sweet, shy girl my husband married doesn't exist any more!

The Hunterdon way encourages boldness, creativity, self-direction, and integrity, but it also demands accountability for mistakes. Mistakes, however, invite rethinking, not punishment. As Carrol points out:

The expectation here is to get out there. It's OK to make a mistake, but you have to recognize what you did and determine what you could have done better. The fear that an idea won't be accepted is taken out of the equation, so it makes us very bold. Women are untapped as a resource, I think. I just feel that we can be more. A lot of times people put their thumbs on women, and it's a question of whether we allow it to happen. I feel very free here. And I encourage it in others. Before, I was pressured to be somebody other than myself, to be on this cow path, and stay exactly in line. Now I can do what feels right to me. Now I'm so far out there, there's no way back.

Once women connect to their feminine presence, there is no turning back. Women who cannot walk off the straight and narrow cow path are carefully pruned from the culture. As Linda told me:

People have to be on board with our values. If you're not a team player, which means caring, compassionate, helping co-workers, kind to patients, you won't be here very long. Either you leave or we'll ask you to leave. We don't rescue.

Pruning is very important. When we see dead branches on a tree, we cut them off so that it doesn't take the nutrients out of the whole tree. It's the same with organizations. People who drain rather than contribute to the whole are pruned. Some managers have difficulty pruning, but it's easier when you think of what benefits the whole.

In her commitment to care for the caretakers, Linda tries to ensure that the nurses fulfill not only their professional needs but also their spiritual needs. To that end, she launched a course on healing for all three hundred nurses at Hunterdon. The healing was directed toward the nurses themselves, toward helping them become centered in their spirituality as healers and toward their wholeness. And this care of the caretakers cascaded down to the patients. Nurses not only tended to patients' physical needs, they also inquired into tending to their spiritual needs.

Care lies at the heart of feminine presence and the leadership it engenders. Care may not be a power word, but it drives a powerful action. When we care deeply, we enhance our innate feminine presence. Connecting to feminine presence is like an embrace. Embrace your holistic thinking, which respects the one and the many. Embrace your rooted and wandering journey and know it is an organic, rich path. Embrace a collaborative spirit and feel the comfort of walking hand in hand. Embrace hospitality in a world that begs to be held. Embrace other women's dreams and find your own fulfilled. Embrace the unimaginable and see forces gather in support. Those embraces will bring you in the company of Wangari and Deborah and Donatella and Nancy and Linda and enable you to do what they have done: change the world with the power of feminine presence.

I'd like to end with one last story, a story that captures the simple brilliance and beauty of feminine presence. It's a story that Linda tells her new nurses to introduce them to the care that drives the Hunterdon culture. And it's a story she retells to established nurses to remind them why they are there. They call it "The Endless Journey."

THE ENDLESS JOURNEY

Shortly after a patient named Dorothy celebrated her seventieth birthday, doctors diagnosed her with terminal cancer, which resulted in several visits to Hunterdon Medical Center for treatment. Lying in her narrow bed during her fourth visit, Dorothy realized it would be her last. Even though she had called her family in England to say her good-byes, and although the nurses on the Three West ward had become an adopted family for her, Dorothy felt lonely. That's when head nurse Carrol Fiorino and her sisterhood of caregivers brought the transforming powers of feminine presence to the "English patient."

As Carrol and her team of nurses hovered around her bed, they marveled at Dorothy's courage and faith as she shared with them her anticipation of what she called "an endless journey." Carrol asked how the nurses could ease her passage. After a few moments of quiet, Dorothy looked up into Carrol's eyes. "I don't want to die alone," she whispered. "I want to be held."

The nurses joined in a silent, collective vigil to fulfill that wish. One by one they quietly went back to their stations, except Carrol, who lingered behind. Pushing aside how silly she might look to anyone who saw her, she lifted the bed covers and crawled into the bed to hold the English patient in her arms. Dorothy was shaking, because, despite her courage, she feared death. Nestled in Carrol's arms, her shaking gradually subsided, until she fell asleep. After a while, Carrol heard her call bell ring. As she began to climb out of the bed, a nurse appeared at the bedside, leaned over, and whispered into Carrol's ear, "Move over. I'll take your place. I love her too." So began a round-the-clock vigil among caring sisters and their dying friend. Nurses stayed late to hold her, others came in early. At the end of two days, they could feel Dorothy's spirit leave them. They had fulfilled their promise; she was never alone. She began her "endless journey" held by each and every one of them.

Feminine presence.

EPILOGUE

You were born with potential.
You were born with goodness and trust.
You were born with ideals and dreams.
You were born with wings.
You are not meant for crawling, so don't.
You have wings.
Learn to use them and fly.

Rumi

REFERENCES

CHAPTER 1: WEBS: EARNING MY WINGS

David Gergen, "Women Leading in the Twenty-first Century," in *Enlightened Power: How Women Are Transforming the Practice of Leadership*, eds. Linda Coughlin, Ellen Wingard, and Keith Hollihan (San Francisco: Jossey-Bass, 2005), p. xxix.

Roger Lewin and Birute Regine, *The Soul at Work: Embracing Complexity Science for Business Success* (New York: Simon & Schuster, 2000).

Janice Mirikitani, *Love Works* (San Francisco: City Lights Foundation, 2001), p. 91.

Daniel Pink, *A Whole New Mind: Moving from the Information Age to the Conceptual Age* (New York: Riverhead Books, 2005), p. 1.

Gloria Steinem, *Outrageous Acts and Everyday Rebellions* (New York: McMillan, 1995), p. 385.

Richard Tarnas, *The Passion of the Western Mind* (New York: Balantine Books, 1993), p. 444.

CHAPTER 2: REMEMBER: TRAINING HERSTORY

Michael Albert and Noam Chomsky, *Stop the Killing Train* (Boston: South End Press, 1999).

Karen Andrews, "Women in Theravada Buddhism," paper for Institute of Buddhist Studies, Berkeley, CA, p. 7.

Anne Baring and Jules Cashford, *The Myth of the Goddess: Evolution of an Image* (New York: Penguin Books, 1993).

Rich Barlow, "Caucus on Religion Thumbs the Past," *Boston Globe*, August 6, 2005, p. 191.

Sandra Billington and Miranda Green, eds., *The Concept of the Goddess* (New York: Routledge, 1999).

Chronic Poverty Research Centre, Chronic Poverty Report 2004–2005, UNDP, Human Development Report 2005.

Richard Covington, "A Long Miscast Outcast," *U.S. Newsweek & World Report*, April 25, 2008, p. 72.

Eve Ensler, interview at iVillage.co.uk, 2002, p. 2.

Marija Gimbutas, *Civilization of the Goddess* (San Francisco: HarperCollins, 1991).

Lucy Goodison and Christine Morris, eds., *Ancient Goddesses* (Madison: University of Wisconsin Press, 1998).

Bob Herbert, "Politics and Misogyny," *New York Times*, op-ed, January 15, 2008.

Karen King, *The Gospel of Mary of Magdala: Jesus and the First Woman Apostle* (Santa Rosa, CA: Polebridge Press, 2003).

Cara Krulewitch, Marie Lydie Pierre-Louis, Regina de Leon-Gomez, Richard Guy, and Richard Green, "Hidden from View: The Violent Death among Pregnant Women in the District of Columbia, 1988–1996," *Journal of Midwifery and Women's Health* 46, no. 1 (2001): 4–10.

Indira Lakshmanan, "Unresolved Killings Terrorize Women in Guatemala," *Boston Globe*, March 30, 2006, p. 1.

Brian Lavack, *The Witch Hunt in Early Modern Europe* (New York: Longman, 1995).

Caitlin Matthews, *The Elements of the Goddess* (Shaftesbury, UK: Element Books Limited, 1989).

Rosalind Miles, *The Woman's History of the World* (London: Michael Joseph, 1986), p. 16.

"Not a Minute More: Ending Violence against Women," World Health Organization fact sheet no. 239, 2003.

One in Three Women, http://www.oneinthreewomen.com.

Office on Violence against Women, United States Department of Justice, http://www.ovw.usdoj.gov/.

Elaine Pagels, *Adam, Eve, and the Serpent* (New York: Vintage Books, 1988).

American Rape Statistics, http://www.paralumun.com/issuesrapestats.htm.

Edward Peters, *Inquisition* (New York: Free Press, 1988).

Heather Pringle, "New Woman of the Ice Age," *Discover*, April 1998, pp. 1–11.

Cokie Roberts, *Founding Mothers: The Women Who Raised Our Nation* (New York: Harper Perennial, 2005).

Pat Robertson, *Bring It On* (Nashville, TN: Thomas Nelson, 2008).

Naomi Harris Rosenblatt, "Daughter's of Eve," *U.S. Newsweek & World Report*, April 25, 2006, p. 6.

Gayle Rubin, "The Traffic in Women," in *Toward an Anthropology of Women* (New York: Monthly Review Press, 1979).

Leonard Schlain, *The Alphabet and the Goddess* (New York: Penguin Group, 1998), pp. 82, 202.

Merlin Stone, *When God Was a Woman* (Orlando, FL: Harcourt Brace & Co, 1976).

Sharon Tiffany and Kathleen Adams, "Anthropologies 'Fierce' Yanomami: Narratives of Sexual Politics in the Amazon," *National Women's Studies Association Journal* 6, no. 2 (Summer 1994): 169–96.

Laurel Thatcher Ulrich, *Well-Behaved Women Seldom Make History* (New York: Alfred Knopf, 2007).

Adrienne Zihlman and Nancy Tanner, "Gathering and Hominid Adaptation," in *Female Hierarchies*, eds. Lionel Tiger and Heather Fowler (Chicago: Beresford, 1978).

CHAPTER 3: CATERPILLARS: CLOSE THE GENDER GAP

"Another Wall Street Settlement," *New York Times*, August 15, 2004, p. A22.

Lisa Belkin, "Diversity Isn't Rocket Science, Is It?" *New York Times*, May 15, 2008, p. E2.

———, "The Opt-Out Revolution," *New York Times Magazine*, November 26, 2003, p. 11.

Aaron Bernstein, "Women's Pay: Why the Gap Remains a Chasm," *BusinessWeek*, June 14, 2004, pp. 58–59.

Kimberly Blanton, "Few Women Reach Top at Law Firms," *Boston Globe*, October 24, 2003.

Amy Caiazza, April Shaw, and Misha Werschkul, "Women's Economic Status in the States: Wide Disparities by Race, Ethnicity, and Region," Institute for Women's Policy Research, Washington, DC.

"Case against Wal-Mart Widens," *Boston Globe*, June 23, 2004, p. C2.

Riane Eisler, *The Chalice and the Blade: Our History, Our Future* (Gloucester, MA: Peter Smith Publishing, 1994).

"Ending Poverty Begins with Women," WOW! Work of Women, http://www.workofwomen.org, March 2009.

Elsa Ermer, Leda Cosmides, and John Tooby, "Relative Status Regulates Risky Decision Making about Resources in Men: Evidence for the Co-evolution of Motivation and Cognition," *Journal of Evolution and Human Behavior* 29 (2008): 106–18.

"Feminism 2.0," *Utne Reader* 146 (March–April 2008): 32.

Ken Gewertz, "Faludi Fears Feminism Trivialized," *Harvard Gazette*, April 28, 2005, http://www.harvard.edu/gazette/2005/04.28/13-faludi.html.

Ellen Goodman, "Harvard's Political Correctness Has Come Full Circle," *Deseret News*, Salt Lake City, Utah, February 25, 2005, http://findarticles.com/p/articles/mi_qn4188/is_20050225/ai_n11825045/.

Lena Graber and John Miller, "Wages for Housework: The Movement and the Numbers," *Dollars and Sense Newsletter*, Boston, MA: Economic Affairs Bureau, September 2002, pp. 45–47.

Steven Greenhouse, "Woman Sues Costco, Claiming Sex Bias in Promotions," *Boston Globe*, August 18, 2004, p. C3.

Teresa Heinz, "The Retirement Gap," *Boston Globe*, October 8, 2005, p. A15.

Bob Herbert, "Words as Weapons," *New York Times*, op-ed, April 23, 2007, http://select.nytimes.com/2007/04/23/opinion/23herbert.html?_r=1.

Lisa Jervis, "The End of Feminism's Third Wave," *Ms.*, Winter 2004, http://www.msmagazine.com/winter2004/thirdwave.asp.

Sarah Kliff, "Sorry, Hillary, but Girls Already Rule," *Newsweek*, March 17, 2008, p. 32.

Mary Liepold, "Power, Sex, Money, and the Partnership Way: A Conversation with Riane Eisler," Peace Times, http://www.peaceXpeace.org/resources/Eisler1.asp.

"National Survey on Retention and Promotion of Women in Law Firms," National Association of Women Lawyers (NAWL), November 2007.

Sasha Pfeiffer, "Many Female Lawyers Dropping off Path to Partnership," *Boston Globe*, May 2, 2007, p. A1.

Anna Quindlen, "We're Missing Some Senators," *Newsweek*, March 2005, http://www.newsweek.com/id/49219.

Deborah Rhode, "Women, Leadership and Stanford School of Law," *Stanford Lawyer* 63 (Summer 2002).

CHAPTER 4: CHOICES: PURUSE YOUR PASSION

William R. Allen et al., "Examining the Impact of Ethics Training on Business Student Values," *Education and Training* 47, no. 3 (2005): 170–82.

Erik Brady, "Girls Coach at Center of Critical Title IX Clash," *USA Today*, November 5–7, 2004, p. 1.

Martha Burk, "The 40-Percent Rule," *Ms.*, Summer 2006, p. 57.

Victoria Burnett, "Women's Role Divides Afghan Gathering," *Boston Globe*, December 30, 2003, p. 4.

Center of Women's Business Research, 2006 Fact Sheet on Women-Owned Businesses in the United States.

———, "Success Strategies for Women Business Owners Selling to Large Corporations and the Corporations Seeking to Buy Them," March 2, 2003, http://www.nfwbo.org/SuccessStrategies.htm.

Eleanor Clift, *Founding Sisters and the Nineteenth Amendment* (New York: Wiley, 2003).

Patricia Cohen, "Signs of Detente in the Battle between Venus and Mars," *New York Times*, May 31, 2007, p. A13.

Jared Diamond, *Collapse: How Societies Choose to Fail or Succeed* (New York: Penguin, 2000), p. 485.

David Dollar, Raymond Fisman, and Roberta Gatti, "Are Women Really the 'Fairer' Sex?" Policy Research Report on Gender and Development, Working Paper Series no. 4, 1999, http://www.worldbank.org/gender/prr.

"Election Workers Killed in Afghanistan," http://www.CBCnews.ca/world/story/2004/06/26/afghanistan040626.html.

Carol Gilligan, *In a Different Voice* (Cambridge, MA: Harvard University Press, 1994).

Edie Hilliard, "Radio and Women: A Report on the Status of Women in the Radio Industry 2006–2007," May 2007, http://www.radiomiw.com/pdfs/WOMEN ANDRADIO-2007.pdf.

Karen MacPherson, "Careers Dominated by Women See Shortages," *Blade* (online newspaper) April 14, 2002, p. 2.

Jackie McMullan, "Once Silent, She's Now a Strong Voice," *Boston Globe*, March 31, 2005, p. C8.

Susan Pinker, *The Sexual Paradox: Men, Women, and the Real Gender Gap* (New York: Scribner, 2009).

Anna Quindlen, "To Hell with Well Behaved," *Newsweek*, June 28, 2004, p. 66.

Rhona Rapoport, Lotte Bailyn, Joyce Fletcher, and Bettye Pruit, *Beyond Work-Family Balance* (Hoboken, NJ: Jossey-Bass, 2002).

Patricia Wen, "The Gen X Dad," *Boston Globe Magazine*, January 16, 2005, pp. 23, 30–32.

Marie Wilson, *Closing the Leadership Gap* (New York: Viking, 2004).

"Who's Talking: An Analysis of Sunday Morning Talk Shows," White House Project, 2001, http://www.thewhitehouseproject.org/culture/researchandpolls/WhosTalking01.php.

CHAPTER 5: GLADIATORS: DEALING WITH MUCHO MACHO

Belinda Board, "The Tipping Point," *New York Times*, May 11, 2005, p. 11.

Joseph Campbell, *The Power of Myth* (New York: Anchor Books, 1991), p. 2.

Jim Collins, *Good to Great: Why Some Companies Make the Leap and Others Don't* (New York: HarperCollins, 2001).

Kelly DiNardo, "Marriage Rates Rise for Educated Women," *Women's eNews*, April 6, 2004.

Helen Fisher, *The Natural Talents of Women and How They Are Changing the World* (New York: Random House, 1999).

Don Fost, "Mergers a Rite of Passage for U.S. Companies," *San Francisco Chronicle*, December 19, 2004, p. A1.

Deborah Gruenfeld, Dacha Ketner, and Cameron Anderson, "The Effects of

Power on Those Who Possess It: Social Structure Can Affect Social Cognition," in *Foundations of Social Cognition*, eds. Galen von Bodenhausen and Alan Lambert (New York: Lawrence Erlbaum, 2003).

Mark Hulbert, "Measuring C.E.O. on the Hubris Index," *New York Times*, May 22, 2005, http://www.nytimes.com/2005/05/22/business/yourmoney/22stra.html.

Judith Jordon, "Valuing Vulnerability: New Definitions in Courage," Stone Center Working Paper no. 102, 2003, p. 3.

Dacher Ketner, Deborah Gruenfeld, and Cameron Anderson, "Power, Approach, and Inhibition," Research Paper no. 1669, University of California, Berkeley, CA, 2000.

Deborah Kolb, *Everyday Negotiation: Navigating the Hidden Agenda of Bargaining* (New York: Jossey-Bass, 2003).

Diane Lewis, "Management Consultants Decry Trump's Ways," *Boston Sunday Globe*, October 3, 2004, p. G7.

Jeffrey Pfeffer, *The Human Factor: Building Profits by Putting People First* (Boston: Harvard Business School Press, 1998).

Robert Simons, Henry Mintzberg, and Kunai Basa, "Memo to: CEOs," *Fast Company* 59 (May 2002): 117.

"US Workplace Bullying Survey," Workplace Bullying Institute and Zogby International, http://workplacebullying.org/research/WBI-Zogby2007Survey.html.

Mike Wilson, *The Difference between God and Larry Ellison: God Doesn't Think He's Larry Ellison* (New York: Collins Business, 2003).

"You're Up: Andy Litinsky," *Boston Globe Sidekick*, September 19, 2005, p. 9.

CHAPTER 6: TEARS: HEAL THE HIDDEN WOUND

Stephen Ducat, *The Wimp Factor: Gender Gaps, Holy Wars, and the Politics of Anxious Masculinity* (Boston: Beacon Press, 2005), p. 6.

Warren Farrell, *The Myth of Male Power* (New York: Simon & Schuster, 1993), pp. 27, 80.

Lisa Fleisher, "Accord Reached in Maternity Suit," *Boston Globe*, July 26, 2005, http://www.boston.com/news/local/articles/2005/07/26/accord_reached.

Sarah Jane Gilbert, "Manly Men, Oil Platforms, and Breaking Stereotypes," *Working Knowledge* (April 2008): 3, 5, 7.

Carol Gilligan, *The Birth of Pleasure* (New York: Alfred Knopf, 2000), p. 16.

Richard Knowles, *The Leadership Dance: Pathways to Extraordinary Organizational Effectiveness* (New York: Center of Self-Organizing Leadership, 2002).

Doug Lang, "My View," *Metro*, June 3, 2005, p. 10.

Caitlin Matthews, *Sophia: Goddess of Wisdom* (Wheaton, IL: Quest Books, 2001), p. 43.

Wesley Morris, "Women Are Key in Eastwood's Growth from Macho to Mellow," *Boston Globe*, February 20, 2005, p. N11.

William Pollack, *Real Boy: Rescuing Our Sons from the Myths of Boyhood* (New York: Henry Holt, 1998), pp. 25, 28, 33.

Topher Sanders, "Becoming 'Real' Men at Last," *Newsweek*, May 30, 2005, p. 13.

Julie Scelfo, "Men & Depression: Facing Darkness," *Newsweek*, February 26, 2007, p. 43.

Henry David Thoreau, "Economy," in *Walden* (New York: Thomas Cromwell, 1910), p. 8.

Virginia Valiant, *Why So Slow? The Advancement of Women* (Cambridge, MA: MIT Press, 1999), p. 49.

Karen Zittleman, "Being a Girl and Being a Boy: Voices of Middle Schoolers," American University, paper presented at the Annual Education Research Association Conference, San Francisco, CA, April 8, 2006.

CHAPTER 7: SPLIT VISION:
DISPELLING GENDER DISTORTION

Ashleigh Banfield, "Embedded Journalism," Landon Lecture at Kansas State University, April 24, 2003.

ZsuZsanna Budapest, *The Holy Book of Women's Mysteries* (Oakland, CA: Wingbow Press, 1989).

Diane Clehane, "So What Do You Do, Ashleigh Banfield, Court TV Anchor?" *Medill Journalism*, November 28, 2007, http://www.mediabistro.com/articles/cache/a9968.asp.

Jennifer Cognard-Black, "Extreme Makeover: Feminist Edition: How the Pitch for Cosmetic Surgery Co-Opts Feminism," *Ms.*, Summer 2007, pp. 47–49.

Dalton Conley and Rebecca Glauber, "Gender, Body Mass and Economics," New York University, National Bureau of Economic Research (NBER) Working Paper no. W11343.

D. J. Conway, *Maiden, Mother, Crone: The Myth & Reality of the Triple Goddess* (St. Paul, MN: Llewellyn Publications, 1994).

Clarissa P. Estes, *Women Who Run with the Wolves* (New York: Ballantine Books, 1992), p. 212.

Carine Fabius, *Ceremonies for Real Life* (San Francisco: Wildcat Canyon Press, 2003).

"Framing Gender on the Campaign Trail: Women's Executive Leadership and the Press," White House Project, http://www.thewhitehouseproject.org/culture/researchandpolls/FramingGender.php.

Morwenna Ferrier, "The New Nip and Tuck: Nipple Surgery Soars as Women Keen for Posh Appearance Go Under Knife," *London Daily News*, June 22, 2009, http://www.dailymail.co.uk/femail/article-1194147/A-new-nip-tuck-Nipple-surgery-soars-women-keen-Victoria-Beckhams-pert-appearance-knife.html.

Marija Gimbutas, *The Language of the Goddess* (London: Thames & Hudson, 2001).

Ellen Goodman, "The Victims of Fashion Cultism," *Boston Globe*, December 11, 2003, p. A23.

Caroline Heldman, "Out-of-Body Image," *Ms.*, Spring 2008, pp. 52–55.

Ariel Levy, *Female Chauvinist Pigs: Women and the Rise of Raunch Culture* (New York: Free Press, 2006), p. 31.

Danny Schechter, "The Link between the Media, the War, and Our Right to Know," May 1, 2003, http://www.mediachannel.org/views/dissector/moveon.shtml.

Laura Schlessinger, *Ten Stupid Things Women Do to Mess Up Their Lives* (New York: Harper Perennial, 2002).

Barbara Walker, *The Woman's Encyclopedia of Myths and Secrets* (San Francisco, CA: Harper, 1983).

———, *Women's Spirituality & Ritual* (Gloucester, MA: Fair Winds Press, 1990).

Naomi Wolf, *The Beauty Myth: How Images of Beauty Are Used against Women* (New York: Harper Perennial, 2002).

Virginia Valiant, *Why So Slow? The Advancement of Women* (Cambridge, MA: MIT Press, 1999), p. 3.

Starhawk and Donna Read, Belili Productions, http://www.gimbutas.org.

CHAPTER 9: BODIES: LISTEN TO INNER WISDOM

Carol Gilligan, *The Birth of Pleasure* (New York: Alfred Knopf, 2000), p. 161.

Wayne Horowitz, *Mesopotamian Cosmic Geography* (Winona Lake, IN: Eisenbrauns, 1998).

Dana C. Jack, *Silencing the Self: Women and Depression* (New York: Harper Paperbacks, 1993), p. 138.

Diane Wolkstein and Samuel Noah Kramer, *Inanna, Queen of Heaven and Earth* (New York: Harper Perennial, 1983).

CHAPTER 10: DIVINITIES: FOLLOWING
THE SPIRITUAL LIGHT

Hannah Arendt, *The Human Condition* (Chicago: University of Chicago Press, 1958), p. 241.

St. Augustin, *St. Augustine on the Holy Trinity, Doctrinal Treatises and Moral Treatise* (Whitefish, MT: Kessinger Publishing, 2004), p. 159.

Susan Bridle, "Daughter of the Goddess: An Interview with Z. Budapest," http://www.enlightennext.org/magazine/j10/budapest.asp?pf+1, p. 4.

D. J. Conway, *Maiden, Mother, Crone: The Myth and Reality of the Triple Goddess* (St. Paul, MN: Llewellyn Publications, 2001).

Mary Daly, *Beyond God the Father: Toward a Philosophy of Women's Liberation* (Boston: Beacon Press, 1993), pp. xvii–xx, 19.

Elizabeth DeBold, "The Divine Feminine, Unveiled," *EnlightenNext*, http://www.enlightennext.org/magazine/j39/divine-feminine.asp?page+1.

———, "Spiritual but Not Religious," *EnlightenNext*, http://www.enlightennext .org/magazine/j31/spiritual-not-religious.asp.

Mahatma Gandhi and Krishna Kripalini, *All Men Are Brothers: Autobiographical Reflections* (London: Continuum, 2005).

Wilma Mankiller, *The Reader's Companion to U.S. Women's History* (New York: Houghton Mifflin, 1999), p. 556.

Shirley Nicholson, *The Goddess Re-Awakening* (London: Theosophical Publishing House, 1994).

Charlene Proctor, "Divine Woman," *Goddess Network Newsletter*, February 2005.

Adrienne Rich, *On Lies, Secrets, and Silence* (New York: Norton, 1979), p. 190.

———, "Prepatriachal Female/Goddess Images," in *The Politics of Women's Spirituality*, ed. Charlene Spretnak (New York: Anchor Books 1982), p. 32.

Barbara Walker, *Restoring the Goddess: Equal Rites for Modern Women* (Amherst, NY: Prometheus Books, 2000).

CHAPTER 11: TILT: ACCEPTING THE GIFT OF INJUSTICE

Aldous Huxley, *The Perennial Philosophy* (New York: Harper Perennial Modern Classics, 2004), p.163.

Susan Sharpe, *Restorative Justice: A Vision for Healing and Change* (Edmonton: AB: Edmonton Victim Offender Mediation Society, 1998).

CHAPTER 12: RELATIONSHIPS: LETTING THE HEART FALL OPEN

Antonio Damasio, *Descartes Error: Emotion, Reason and the Human Brain* (New York: Penguin, 2005).

Carol Gilligan, *In a Different Voice* (Cambridge, MA: Harvard University Press, 1982), p. 9.

Linda Hartling, "Relational Intelligence: A Key to Success in the New Economy," *WCW Research Report*, Spring/Summer 2001.

KISP (The Committee for International Questions of the Interchurch Council for the Norwegian Church—Sturla Stalsett, leader), *Vulnerability and Security: Current Geopolitical Security Challenges from an Ethical and Theological Perspective* (Den Norske Kirken, 2000).

Rod Lehman, "The Heart of Philanthropy," Center for Contemplative Mind in

Society, http://www.contemplativemind.org/programs/philanthropy/hofp
.html.

Jeffrey Pfeffer, *The Human Equation: Building Profits by Putting People First* (Boston: Harvard Business School Press, 2001).

Shelley Taylor, *The Tending Instinct* (New York: Henry Holt, 2002), pp. 24, 91.

CHAPTER 13: LEADERSHIP: CULTIVATING FEMININE PRESENCE

Beatrice Bruteau, "The Unknown Goddess," in *The Goddess Re-Awakening,* S. Nicholson (Wheaton, IL: Theosophical Publishing House, 1989), p. 68.

Phyllis Chesler, *Woman's Inhumanity to Women* (Emeryville, CA: Thunder's Mouth Press, 2001), p. 24.

Jim Collins, *Good to Great: Why Some Companies Make the Leap . . . And Others Don't* (New York: HarperBusiness, 2001).

Helen Fisher, *The First Sex: The Natural Talents of Women and How They Are Changing the World* (New York: Random House, 1999), p. 5.

Wangari Maathai, Nobel Women's Initiative, http://www.nobelwomensinitiative
.org/about-us/laureates/person/prof-wangari-maathai.

Jane Margolis and Allan Fisher, *Unlocking the Clubhouse: Women in Computing* (Cambridge, MA: MIT Press, 2001).

Michele Miller, *The Natural Advantages of Women* (Austin, TX: Wizard Academy Press, 2003).

Daniel Pink, *A Whole New Mind: Moving from the Information Age to the Conceptual Age* (New York: Riverhead Books, 2005), p. 2.

Deborah Rosado Shaw, *Dream Big! A Roadmap for Facing Life's Challenges and Creating the Life You Deserve* (New York: Free Press, 2002).

THE WOMEN PARTICIPANTS

Some Web Sites/Books by Iron Butterflies

The women around the world who shared their stories with me include:

Ada Aharoni, writer, professor, and founder of International Forum for the Literature and Culture of Peace (IFLAC), Israel.

Not in Vain: An Extraordinary Life. San Carlos, CA: Ladybug Publishing House, 1998.

Peace Poems, A Bi-lingual Edition. Haifa, Israel: Cairo University, 1997.

Waves of Peace: In the Memory of Yitzhak Rabin, Galim 8, eds. Ada Aharoni and Judith Zilbershtein. Hatichon: Shfaram, 1997.

Woman: Creating a World beyond War and Peace. Haifa, Israel: New Horizon, 2001.

You and I Can Change the World: Toward 2000. Haifa, Israel: Micha Lachman, 1999.

International Forum for the Literature and Culture of Peace, http://www.iflac.com

Ada Aharoni's Homepage: Culture and Literature of Peace, http://www.iflac.com/ada

Judith Baker, consultant.

Carolyn Bennett, MD, member of Parliament and head of the Women's Liberal Caucus, Toronto, Ontario.
   Kill or Cure: How Canadians Can Remake Their Health Care System. Toronto: HarperCollins, 2000.
   Carolyn Bennett, MP, http://www.CarolynBennett.ca

Susan Boland, consultant with Bolex Consulting, Montreal, Quebec.

Jean Shinoda Bolen, MD, Jungian analyst and author, California.
   Crossing to Avalon: A Woman's Midlife Pilgrimage. San Francisco, CA: HarperSanFrancisco, 1994.
   Goddesses in Everywoman. New York: Harper Paperbacks, 2004.
   Jean Shinoda Bolen, MD, www.jeanbolen.com

Ricky Burges, CEO of the Western Australian Local Government Association, Perth, Western Australia.
   "Tempting Eve," http://www.mantis.com.au/tempting%20Ricky%20 Burges.pdf.

Janie Burks, CFO of Volunteers of America, Louisville, Kentucky.

Kim Campbell, former prime minister of Canada, international speaker, and consultant.
   Time and Chance: The Political Memoirs of Canada's First Woman Prime Minister. Toronto, ON: Doubleday, 1996.
   The Right Honourable Kim Campbell, Canada's 19th Prime Minister, http://www.kimcampbell.com

Janice Cook, artist in London.

Donatella Cinelli Colombini and her friends and employees, namely, Maureen Ashley, Alexandra Fisher, Marie-Sylvie Haniez, Barbara Magnani, Antonella Maroni, and Daniela Scrobogna. Donatella is the owner of Fattoria del Colle, a vineyard run by women in Tuscany, and founder of the global event Wine Day.
   Donattella Cinelli Colombini, Agriturismo in Toscana, http://www .cinellicolombini.it

Andra Douglas, owner of the New York Sharks, women's football team, New York, New York.

New York Sharks Women's Tackle Football Team, www.nysharks football.com

Fins Up! Foundation for Female Athletics, www.finsupfoundation.org

Angela Farmer, yoga guru, Greece and Canada.

DVD: *Listening to Inner Voices, Breathe*

Transform Yourself with Angela & Victor, http://angela-victor.com

Carrol Fiorino, head nurse at Hunterdon Medical Center, Hunterdon, New Jersey.

Marsha Firestone, CEO of Women Presidents' Organization, New York, New York.

Women Presidents' Organization, www.womenpresidentsorg.com

Alison Godfrey, CEO of HeartWaves, alternative health and exercise program, Califon, New Jersey.

LifeWaves International, www.lifewaves.com

SuperWave Fusion, www.superwavefusion.com

Baroness Susan Greenfield, Oxford professor, director of the Royal Institution of Great Britain, and host of six-part BBC series on the brain and mind.

The Human Brain: A Guided Tour. New York: Basic Books, 1998.

ID: The Quest for Identity in the 21st Century. New York: Scepter Publishers, 2009.

Myra Hart, former executive vice president of growth and development of Staples and retired Harvard Business School professor, Boston, Massachusetts.

Azizah al-Hibri, professor at University of Richmond and founder of Karamah: Muslim Women Lawyers for Human Rights, Washington, DC.

Karamah: Muslim Women Lawyers for Human Rights, www .karamah.org

Eileen Hoffman, MD, author, advocate of women's health, and associate professor of medicine at NYU School of Medicine, New York, New York.

Our Health, Our Lives. New York: Pocket Books, 1995.

Eileen Hoffman, MD, www.dreileenhoffman.com

American College of Women's Health Physicians, www.acwhp.org

Swanee Hunt, former ambassador to Austria, founder of the Institute for Inclusive Security that includes Women Waging Peace network, and founding director of the Women and Public Policy Program at Harvard, Cambridge, Massachusetts.

> *Half-Life of a Zealot*. Durham, NC: Duke University Press, 2006.
>
> *This Was Not Our War: Bosnian Women Reclaiming Peace*. Durham, NC: Duke University Press, 2005.
>
> Swanee Hunt, www.Swaneehunt.com
>
> Hunt Alternatives Fund: The Institute for Inclusive Security, www .inclusivesecurity.org
>
> Hunt Alternatives Fund, www.hunt alternatives.org
>
> Harvard Kennedy School Women and Public Policy, http://www.hks .harvard.edu/wappp

Carol Jamison, director of customer service in software company, Concord, Massachusetts.

Eddie Bernice Johnson, US congresswoman from Texas.

> Congresswoman Eddie Bernice Johnson, Representing the 30th District of Texas, www.ebjohnson.house.gov/index.html

Paula Josa-Jones, choreographer, Connecticut.

> *Buddha's Beasts and the Isle of Delights*, children's book collaboration with artist Pam White.
>
> *Pony Dances*, book of dance and equine photography in collaboration with photographer Jeff Anderson, 2010.
>
> *Dive* and *Branch*, dance films created in collaboration with video artist Ellen Sebring.
>
> *In the Woods*, a dance film work in progress with video artist Ellen Sebring.
>
> *Ride*, a documentary of the creation of RIDE, a collaboration with video artist Ellen Sebring.
>
> *Tilt*, a dance film collaboration with video artist Ellen Sebring.

Barbara Kingsolver, Pulitzer Prize finalist, novelist, essayist, and environmentalist.

> Kingsolver, www.kingsolver.com

Merle Lefkoff, cofounder of the Madrona Institute, applying complexity to diplomacy and peacemaking.

> The Madrona Institute, www.madrona.org

Laura Liswood, secretary general of the Council of Women World Leaders.

The Loudest Duck: Moving beyond Diversity While Embracing Difference to Achieve Success at Work. New York: Wiley, 2009.

Women World Leaders: Great Politicians Tell Their Stories. Washington, DC: Council Press, 2007.

Laura Liswood: Secretary General, Council of Women World Leaders; Senior Advisor, Goldman Sachs, http://lauraliswood.org

The Aspen Instititute, Council of Women World Leaders, www.cwwl .org

Maria Lopez, visiting scholar at the Women's Research Center at Brandeis University, former federal judge, and former TV judge, Boston, Massachusetts.

Linda Lundström, Canadian clothes designer and creative director of Lundström brand, Toronto, Ontario.

Lundström, www.lundstrom.ca

Janice Mirikitani, poet laureate for San Francisco and executive director of Glide, a nonprofit for eliminating poverty, San Francisco, California.

Love Works. San Francisco: City Lights Foundation, 2001.

Shedding Silence. Berkeley, CA: Celestial Arts Publishers, 1995.

Glide, www.glide.org

Pat Mitchell, executive director of Paley Center for Media and former CEO of PBS.

The Paley Center for Media, www.paleycenter.org

Candice Carpenter Olson, founder of iVillage and CEO of Transformation Foundation, New York, New York.

Chapters. New York: McGraw-Hill, 2002.

Mary Lou Quinlan, CEO of Just Ask a Woman advertising company, New York, New York.

Just Ask a Woman: Cracking the Code of What Women Want and How They Buy. Hoboken, NJ: John Wiley & Sons, 2003.

Time Out for Good Behavior: How Hard-Working Women Can Take a Break and Change Their Lives. New York: Broadway, 2005.

What She's Not Telling You: Why Women Hide the Truth and What Marketers Can Do about It. New York: Just Ask a Woman Media, 2009.

Just Ask a Woman, www.justaskawoman.com

Kim Polese, CEO of SpikeSource, Inc., and former CEO and chairperson of Marimba, Silicon Valley, California.
SpikeSource, www.spikesource.com

Katherine Ragsdale, Episcopal priest and director of the Episcopal Divinity School, Arlington, Massachusetts.
Sermons by Katherine Ragsdale, www.ragsdalesermons.blogspot.com

Linda Rusch, former vice president of Patient Care Services at Hunterdon Medical Center, Hunterdon, New Jersey.

Kathe Schaaf, family therapist, cofounder of Gather the Women Congress, a global women's network for peace, and cofounder of Women's Spiritual Coalition, Los Angeles, California.
Reclaiming Grace: One Woman's Journey of Remembering Her Spiritual Power, forthcoming.

Nancy Schwoyer, cofounder and president emerita at Wellspring House, Inc., a shelter helping families move out of poverty, Gloucester, Massachusetts; visiting fellow, Center for Social Policy, University of Massachusetts, Boston.
Wellspring, www.wellspringhouse.org

Deborah Rosado Shaw, former CEO of Umbrellas Plus and founder of Dream Big.
Dream Big! New York: Simon & Schuster, 2002.

Paula Slovenkai-Driscoll, artist and mother, Concord, Massachusetts.

Patricia Smith Melton, founder of Peace x Peace, playwright, photographer, and filmmaker, McLean, Virginia.
Sixty Years, Sixty Voices: Israeli and Palestinian Women. Venice, VA: Peace x Peace, 2008.
Film: *Peace by Peace: Women on the Frontlines*
Sixty Years, Sixty Voices, www.60voices.org
Peace x Peace, Connecting Women for Peace, www.peacexpeace.com

Justina Trott, MD, FACP, director of Women's Health Services at the Sante Fe National Community Center of Excellence in Women's Health, Robert Wood Johnson Health Policy, Fellow 2008–2009 and chair of the New Mexico Governor's Women's Health Advisory Council, Santa Fe, New Mexico.

Women's Health Services, www.womenshealthsantafe.org

Robert Wood Johnson Foundation, Health Policy Fellows, http://www .healthpolicyfellows.org/home.php

New Mexico Governor's Women's Health Office, http://nmwellwoman .com/ home/about us/council members/

Cynthia Trudell, senior vice president and chief of personnel at PepsiCo, and former CEO of Saturn division of General Motors.

Diana Twyman, president of Cornucopia Innovation Consulting, Chicago, Illinois.

Violet, aboriginal elder and land advisor to the government, Perth, Western Australia.

Janiece Webb, senior vice president at Motorola, Chicago, Illinois.

Nikki Watkins, independent consultant, London.

Janet Whitla, former CEO of EDC, an education research organization, Watertown, Massachusetts.

Christine Todd Whitman, president of the Whitman Strategy group and former governor of New Jersey and EPA administrator.

It's My Party Too. New York: Penguin Books, 2006.

The Whitman Strategy Group, www.whitmanstrategygroup.com

Republican Leadership Council, www.republican-leadership.com

Jody Williams, 1997 Nobel Peace Prize laureate, founding coordinator of the International campaign to ban landmines, and cofounder of Nobel Women's Initiative, Fredericksburg, Virginia.

Nobel Women's Initiative, www.nobelwomeninitiative.org